AUDITS OF 401(K) PLANS

BY DELOITTE & TOUCHE, LLP

T0338241

Notice to readers

Audits of 401(k) Plans is intended solely for use in continuing professional education and not as a reference. It does not represent an official position of the American Institute of Certified Public Accountants, and it is distributed with the understanding that the author and publisher are not rendering legal, accounting, or other professional services in the publication. This course is intended to be an overview of the topics discussed within, and the author has made every attempt to verify the completeness and accuracy of the information herein. However, neither the author nor publisher can guarantee the applicability of the information found herein. If legal advice or other expert assistance is required, the services of a competent professional should be sought.

> **You can qualify to earn free CPE through our pilot testing program.**
> **If interested, please visit https://aicpacompliance.polldaddy.com/s/pilot-testing-survey.**

ISBN 978-1-119-72203-8 (Paper)
ISBN 978-1-119-61502-6 (ePDF)
ISBN 978-1-119-66596-0 (ePub)
ISBN 978-1-119-72220-5 (oBook)

Course Code: 733853
AFKP GS-0418-0B
Revised: **October 2019**

V10018720_052120

Table of Contents

Chapter 1	1-1
Introduction and Background	1-1
Background information	1-3
Operation and administration	1-6
Accounting records	1-8
Reporting standards	1-10
Governmental regulations	1-11
Audit requirements	1-12
Reporting and disclosure requirements under ERISA	1-16
SEC Form 11-K filing requirements	1-17
ERISA limited-scope audits	1-19

Chapter 2	2-1
Planning	2-1
Pre-engagement activities	2-3
Audit planning	2-6
Communication and coordination	2-10
Understanding the plan and its environment, including its internal control	2-11
Audit documentation	2-13
Preliminary analytical review procedures	2-14
Audit risk factors	2-15
Internal control structure	2-21
Consideration of fraud	2-22
Plan's use of third-party service organizations	2-29
Party in interest transactions	2-30
Plan's use of voice response or internet recordkeeping system	2-32
Accounting estimates	2-33
Going concern considerations	2-34

Chapter 3	3-1
Internal Control Structure	3-1
Understanding internal control	3-4
The components of internal control	3-6
Acquiring knowledge of the controls	3-9

Assessing control risk   3-10

Plan's use of third-party service organizations   3-11

Plan's use of voice response and internet-based recordkeeping systems   3-16

Documentation   3-17

Communicating control deficiencies   3-18

Chapter 4   4-1

Auditing the Statement of Net Assets Available for Benefits   4-1

Accounting guidance   4-3

Listing of investments   4-4

Valuation of investments   4-5

Investment options   4-6

Audit objectives   4-8

Audit procedures   4-9

Investments in master trusts and similar vehicles   4-11

Investments in registered investment companies (mutual funds) and common or commingled trust funds   4-13

Investments with insurance companies   4-15

Direct filing entities (DFE)   4-20

Other investments   4-21

ERISA limited-scope auditing procedures   4-24

Contributions receivable   4-26

Notes receivable from participants receivable   4-27

Cash balances   4-29

Other assets   4-30

Accrued liabilities   4-31

Chapter 5   5-1

Auditing the Statement of Changes in Net Assets Available for Benefits   5-1

Investment income   5-3

ERISA limited-scope audit   5-7

Investment expenses   5-8

Contributions from employers   5-9

Individual participant accounts   5-12

Participant eligibility   5-17

Contributions from other identified sources   5-18

Withdrawals   5-19

Loans   5-20

Administrative expenses   5-22

Chapter 6   6-1

Other Auditing Considerations   6-1

Plan tax status   6-2
Testing for discrimination   6-7
Consequences of violations   6-8
Failure to pass nondiscrimination tests   6-9
Commitments and contingencies   6-10
Subsequent events   6-12
Representations from plan management   6-14
Illustrative attachment to management representation letter   6-18
Form 5500 and supplemental schedules   6-21
Information for supplemental schedules from trustee or custodian   6-28
Terminating plans   6-32
Plan mergers   6-35
Party in interest transactions   6-36
Initial audit of the 401(k) plan   6-41
Form 11-K: The Sarbanes-Oxley Act of 2002   6-44
Communication with those charged with governance   6-47

Chapter 7   7-1

The Auditor's Report and Financial Statement Disclosures   7-1

The auditor's report   7-4
Standard report   7-7
Additional communications: Emphasis-of-matter and other-matter paragraphs 7-10
Modified reports   7-12
Non-GAAP basis financial statements   7-14
Reports filed pursuant to the SEC Form 11-K   7-16
ERISA limited-scope reports   7-21
Financial statement disclosures   7-24

Appendix A   A-1

ERISA and Related Regulations   A-1

Appendix A   A-3

Glossary   Glossary 1

Index   Index 1

Solutions

	Solutions 1
Chapter 1	Solutions 1
Chapter 2	Solutions 4
Chapter 3	Solutions 6
Chapter 4	Solutions 8
Chapter 5	Solutions 10
Chapter 6	Solutions 12
Chapter 7	Solutions 17

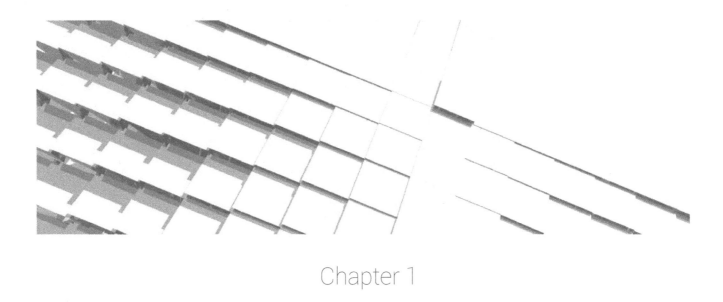

Chapter 1

Introduction and Background

Learning objectives

After completing this chapter, you should be able to do the following:

- Recognize the basic features of 401(k) plans.

- Identify the general features of 401(k) plan operation and administration.

- Identify the general reporting requirements for 401(k) plans.

Introduction

This course has been prepared to assist the independent qualified public accountant in accounting, auditing, and reporting on financial statements of 401(k) defined contribution retirement plans. This course will help them identify the uniqueness of these types of audits.

Generally accepted auditing standards and generally accepted accounting principles apply in general to employee benefit plans. This course assumes that the user is generally knowledgeable in the field of accounting and auditing. Rather than discussing the broad application of those standards and principles, the course focuses primarily on the special issues involved in accounting, auditing, and reporting on financial statements of 401(k) employee benefit plans. The course does not discuss the application of all generally accepted accounting principles and auditing standards as they pertain to the auditing of general financial statements.

This course focuses on *single-employer* sponsored 401(k) plans. However, multiemployer sponsored 401(k) plans would be treated as single-employer plans for purposes of reporting to the regulatory agencies described in the following text.

Background information

A 401(k) plan may be incorporated into a profit-sharing, stock bonus, thrift, or savings plan. A 401(k) plan gives participants the option of receiving a cash payment immediately (salary) from the employer (taxable) or having the cash contributed to the plan as contributions on the participant's behalf (tax-deferred). Government and not-for-profit entities have 403(b) or 457(b) plans that are similar in nature to the 401(k) plans. Although this course does not specifically address governmental plans, certain auditing procedures discussed herein might be helpful to the auditor of governmental plans. Certain 403(b) plans (primarily those with 100 or more participants) have an audit requirement.

> **Multiemployer plan considerations:**
>
> A 401(k) plan may be sponsored by a single employer, multiple employers, or under a multiemployer arrangement. The majority of 401(k) plans are single-employer plans; however, you should be aware of the existence of multiemployer plans. The most basic distinction between single and multiemployer plans is how they are administered. Single-employer plans are generally established and operated by the management of one employer or a controlled group of corporations, called the *plan sponsor*. In contrast, multiemployer plans are typically established through collective bargaining agreements negotiated between a group of employers (such as construction) and the union representing the employees. These plans are managed by a joint employer or union board of trustees.

The various types of defined contribution plans that 401(k) plans are typically part of are briefly described in the text that follows. Such plans can permit employee contributions. The distinguishing characteristic of the plans is often how the sponsor contribution is derived or treated.

- A profit-sharing plan is a defined contribution plan that is not a pension plan (as defined in the Internal Revenue Code) or a stock bonus plan. It is a plan in which the sponsor contributes money to participants' accounts either on a discretionary basis (that is, not mandatory) or as a percentage of profits, compensation, or other factors. A profit-sharing plan must be designated as such in the plan document.
- A stock bonus plan is a defined contribution plan in which employer contributions to the plan are normally made in the stock of the employer. If stated in the plan document, the participant may request to be paid in cash instead of employer stock.
- A thrift or savings plan is a profit-sharing or stock bonus plan whereby participants make contributions to the plan from after-tax dollars. Employee contributions are often matched by the sponsor, either in whole or in part.
- A money purchase pension plan is a defined contribution pension plan whereby employer contributions are based off of a predetermined formula that is not related to profits and the plan is designated as a pension plan by the plan sponsor.

When participants elect to contribute to a 401(k) plan, they agree to have a portion of their wages before income taxes contributed to specific investments. These contributions are taken out of their wages and invested in the investment option(s) offered by the plan and selected by the participant. Plans also may provide for after-tax contributions, or may offer a Roth 401(k) feature, in which contributions are made on an after-tax basis.

The pre-tax deductions that the participant makes are called deferrals and are generally calculated as a percentage of total compensation. In other words, for each payroll cycle, the stated percentage amount is deducted from the participant's gross income before taxes are withheld and this money is then invested in the 401(k) plan. The employee can change the deferral rates periodically as permitted by the plan document. Many plans now have automatic enrollment or the ability for participants to change their contribution percentage via an online system.

Defined contribution plans require that a separate account be maintained for each participant. This provides the participant with information as to total dollars in his or her account and the allocation of those dollars among the various investment options. Each individual participant account is maintained within the plan. In a 401(k) plan, generally, participants direct the selection of investments in their account and bear the investment risk of their individual account. The value of a participant's account fluctuates according to (a) amounts contributed to the account by the sponsor or participant (or both), (b) investment experience on such amounts, (c) participant-initiated withdrawals, (d) expenses, and (e) any forfeitures allocated to the account. Many plans permit a participant to withdraw a portion of his or her account in the form of a loan from the plan. Loans by participants are treated as receivable of the plan. (See chapter 4 for further information.) Withdrawals from the plan can be made according to the plan provisions when an employee terminates employment, retires, or is eligible for a hardship withdrawal.

Under a defined contribution plan, the sponsor contribution rate is generally determined periodically at the discretion of the sponsor or by contractual agreement, or both. When a participant retires or withdraws from the plan, the amount allocated to the participant's account, the vested amount, represents the participant's accumulated benefits. Participants are always fully vested in the amount of their employee contributions. The vested amounts of a participant's account balance may be paid to the participant or used to purchase a retirement annuity. (Vesting will be discussed in more detail in chapter 5.)

Multiemployer plan considerations:

A multiemployer plan is a pension or postretirement benefit plan (to which more than one employer is required to contribute) that is maintained pursuant to one or more collective bargaining agreements between one or more employee organizations and more than one employer. A multiemployer plan is usually administered by a board of trustees composed of management and labor representatives and may also be referred to as a joint trust or union plan. Multiple employer plans are plans that are maintained by more than one employer but not treated as a multiemployer plan. Multiple employer plans are generally not collectively bargained and are intended to allow participating employers to pool their assets for investment purposes and to reduce the costs of plan administration. A multiple employer plan maintains separate accounts for each employer so that contributions provide benefits only for employees of that contributing employer. Generally, many employers participate in a multiemployer or multiple employer plan, and an employer may participate in more than one plan. The employers participating in multiemployer plans usually have a common industry bond—but for some plans, the employers are in different industries and the labor union may be their only common bond. Multiple employer plans do not involve a union. For example, local chapters of a not-for-profit entity may participate in a plan established by the related national organization. Although this course does not specifically address multiemployer or multiple employer plans, certain auditing procedures herein address multiemployer or multiple employer plans and might be helpful to the auditor of multiemployer or multiple employer plans. For a resource reference, see the publication "Payroll Auditing—A Guide for Multiemployer Plans" by Beebe and Vivirito, published by the International Foundation of Employee Benefit Plans.

A 403(b) plan is a retirement savings arrangement sponsored by certain not-for-profit organizations (such as hospitals and private colleges) and public schools. The 403(b) plans are defined contribution plans with individual salary deferral limits that are similar, but not identical, to 401(k) programs. Contributions to a 403(b) plan typically include employee salary deferrals. Not-for-profit organizations often times establish a 401(a) plan that funds employer-matching contributions to a 403(b) plan. Auditors should obtain an understanding of the deferrals made under the 403(b) plan in order to determine if the employer match under the 401(a) plan is properly determined. Investments for funding these 403(b) arrangements are restricted by law to annuity contracts (403[b][1] arrangements) or custodial accounts holding the shares of regulated investment company stock (for example, mutual funds) (403[b][7] arrangements). All 403(b) plans are subject to the same Form 5500 reporting and audit requirements that currently exist for Section 401(k) plans. For large 403(b) plans, as defined by the Employee Retirement Income Security Act (ERISA), reporting requirements include not only the completion of the entire Form 5500 but also the engagement of an independent qualified public accountant to conduct an independent audit of the plan. Although this course does not specifically address 403(b) plans, certain auditing procedures herein might be helpful to the auditor of 403(b) plans. There is a separate AICPA course offered for 403(b) plans, *Audits of 403(b) Plans*.

Operation and administration

A 401(k) plan is contributory, with contributions from both employers and participants or from participants only. Contributions from employers may be discretionary or may be required.

A defined contribution plan is established by the plan document and relevant plan provisions are detailed in the plan document. These provisions are established and maintained by the plan sponsor. They define such matters as age and service requirements, which must be satisfied to allow an employee to participate in the plan, vesting, and loans. They also identify the plan's fiduciary(ies), fiduciary responsibilities (those relating to maintaining control and management of the plan), and the delegation of fiduciary responsibilities in connection with the administration of the plan. A plan subject to the Employee Retirement Income Security Act of 1974 (ERISA) must be in writing. Sponsoring organizations, such as banks, insurance companies, or stock brokers, prepare and update standard plans called master or prototype plans that are available to a plan sponsor to enable the plan sponsor to establish a qualified plan by customizing a standard plan to meet the plan sponsor's needs. These standardized plans generally have IRS approval.

The named fiduciary is responsible for the general operation and administration of the plan in addition to identifying a plan administrator. The plan administrator of a single employer plan is usually an officer or other employee of the plan sponsor, whereas the plan administrator for a multiemployer plan generally is a board of trustees. The plan administrator reports directly to those charged with governance of the plan, which may be an oversight committee or the plan sponsor's board of directors or other management group. The fiduciary has responsibility to make sure that the plan is operating in accordance with the terms of the plan document, trust instrument, if any, and all applicable government rules and regulations. Generally, the fiduciary makes policy decisions concerning such matters as interpretation of the plan provisions, determination of the rights of the participants under the plan, how investments are to be managed, and the performance or the delegation of responsibilities for operating and administering the plan.

The ultimate responsibility for the oversight of the plan rests with the fiduciary. However, the plan's day-to-day administration (for example, collecting contributions, paying benefits, managing cash and investments, loan administration, maintaining records, and the preparation of reports) is often assigned to various entities such as (*a*) the plan sponsor; (*b*) a trustee, such as a trust department of a bank or insurance company; (*c*) an investment advisor; (*d*) a third-party administrator or recordkeeper; or (*e*) a person or persons designated as the plan administrator.

A plan usually has a trust instrument or agreement that details the authority and responsibilities of the trustee(s) and any investment advisors or managers. This document should include or be consistent with the plan's investment policy and therefore may restrict the investment options permitted by the plan. In addition, the trust agreement should describe the fees to be paid to the trustees, investment advisors, and managers for services provided to the plan. It also will describe who is responsible for payment of these services—that is, the participants or the plan sponsor.

The U.S. Department of Labor (DOL) has launched a campaign to educate plan sponsors regarding their fiduciary responsibilities under ERISA. As part of this campaign, the DOL has published several publications, including one entitled *Meeting Your Fiduciary Responsibilities*.

Knowledge check

1. The named fiduciary is not responsible for

    a. The identification of the plan administrator.
    b. The operation of the plan in accordance with the plan instrument.
    c. Day-to-day administration of the plan.
    d. Certifying investments.

Accounting records

Accounting records for a defined contribution plan should be maintained in a reliable manner so as to permit effective management and operation of the plan. Accounting records must be in a format that will make sure reliable financial reporting of the plan. The complexity of the plan will determine the nature of the accounting records and will vary with such factors as the frequency of sponsor contributions, the number of investment options available for participants to select, rules regarding the administration of loans, the variety of options available to terminated participants, and the delegation of administrative duties.

The various accounting and plan records of a 401(k) plan are often maintained at several locations. Depending on the nature of the plan, how fiduciary responsibilities are allocated, and who is responsible for various administrative duties, plan records may be maintained by various trustees, insurance companies, recordkeepers, the plan administrator, and the plan sponsor—including the payroll and human resources departments.

The records of the plans normally should include the following:

- *General accounting records*—Plans are required to maintain records of their receipts and disbursements; however, in many cases, they are prepared by the trustee, insurance company, or recordkeeper. Many times, general ledgers are not maintained by the plan sponsor:
  - Trust or custodian statements are maintained by the trust or custodian system and represent the books and records of the plan. These statements detail all receipts and disbursements, including investment transactions, during the period. The trustee or custodian system records contributions, earnings and losses, plan investments, expenses, and distributions.
  - Recordkeeper statements are maintained by the recordkeeping system and represent both the activity posted to each participant's account during the period, as well as a plan-level consolidation of all such activity. The recordkeeping system helps track and properly allocate contributions, earnings and losses, plan investments, expenses, and distributions in a participant's account.
- *Investment asset records*—ERISA requires detailed reporting of investment assets in addition to the supplemental schedules. The supplemental schedules include schedules of (*a*) assets (held at end-of-year); (*b*) assets (acquired and disposed of within year); (*c*) loans or fixed income obligations in default (*d*) leases in default or classified as uncollectible; (*e*) reportable (5 percent) transactions; and (*f*) nonexempt transactions. See chapter 6 for additional information on the contents of the supplemental schedules. These records are generally maintained by the trustee or custodian or plan sponsor (or a combination of these entities).
- *Participants' records*—Records should be maintained to determine each employee's eligibility to participate in the plan. Many plans have age and service requirements that the employee must satisfy before he or she is eligible to participate in the plan. Eligibility also can be affected by breaks in service (leaving the employment of the plan sponsor and then returning or taking long-term disability, for example). These records are generally maintained by the human resources and payroll departments at the plan sponsor or the administrative office of a third-party administrator for a multiemployer plan.
- *Contribution records*—Separate contribution records should be maintained for employee and sponsor contributions. The plan sponsor generally retains payroll records detailing employee contributions. Sponsor contributions should be accounted for separately to make sure that the contributions are

being made in accordance with the plan document. As with participant contributions, the plan sponsor maintains records of sponsor contributions.

You should be aware that many plans accept contributions into a Roth IRA account. Contributions into a Roth IRA are made post-tax (after all federal and state taxes are withheld as opposed to a 401(k) contribution that is made pre-tax). However, subsequent distributions from a Roth IRA are not taxable to the participant (401(k) contributions are usually subject to tax upon distribution). Because of these differences, it is imperative that contributions to a Roth IRA and the related earnings on those contributions be maintained in a separate account so that the proper tax treatment can be made by the participant when those monies are distributed.

- *Distribution records* — Records of all distributions to participants (for persons who have left employment at the plan sponsor, retired, elected to cease contributing to the plan, and so on), including loans, should be maintained. These records will detail distribution amounts, payment schedule (lump sum or over a period of several years), payment commencement date, forfeitures (if any), and information to determine the tax consequences of the distribution to the participant.

As mentioned earlier, separate records must be maintained if contributions to a Roth IRA were permitted. This will enable management to identify for the participant which distributions are taxable upon withdrawal and which are exempt from taxation.

- *Individual participant's account information* — For each employee who participates in the 401(k) plan, a separate participant statement that identifies the participant's share of the total net assets of the plan must be maintained. The plan instrument will describe how changes in the value of net assets are to be allocated to the participant's accounts. The individual participant account records must be reconciled with the plan sponsor's records to determine that the total of all individual participants' accounts equals the total of all allocated plan assets. Revenue Ruling 70-125 of the Internal Revenue Code requires that these totals be in agreement.
- *Administrative expenses* — Invoices, contracts, agreements, or other written evidence will normally be provided to verify these expenses. These expenses may include fees for the recordkeeper, trustee fees, attorney's fees (for example, to write a plan amendment), independent auditor fees (for example, performance of the audit), and so on.
- *Reconciliations* — The plan administrators ordinarily reconcile the company's records for the plan to data obtained from third-party administrators and the information provided by the trustee; plan administrators also investigate any discrepancies in the information provided.

Reporting standards

ERISA sets forth the requirements for annual reporting of employee benefit plans, including 401(k) plans. Annually, the sponsor must provide certain information to various federal governmental agencies including the DOL and the IRS. The DOL currently requires the following financial statements and supplemental schedules, if applicable:

- Statement of Net Assets Available for Benefits (comparative) and Statement of Changes in Net Assets Available for Benefits
- Schedule of Delinquent Participant Contributions; Schedule of Assets (Held at End-of-Year) and Schedule of Assets (Acquired and Disposed of Within Year)
- Schedule of Reportable Transactions; Schedule of Loans or Fixed-Income Obligations in Default or Classified as Uncollectible
- Schedule of Leases in Default or Classified as Uncollectible

Nonexempt transactions

For most plans, the information is currently reported on Form 5500, *Annual Return/Report of Employee Benefit Plan*, which is filed with the Department of Labor. Form 5500 generally includes financial statements prepared in conformity with accounting principles generally accepted in the United States (GAAP). If the financial statements are not in compliance with GAAP in any significant way, that departure must be identified in the footnotes to the financial statements. ERISA also requires plans to furnish to each plan participant, at least annually, a statement of the participant's total vested and nonvested accrued benefits and a summary annual report (SAR). (See appendix A of the AICPA Audit and Accounting Guide *Employee Benefit Plans* for a further description of ERISA and related regulations.)

The previously mentioned Form 5500 filing and audit requirement is also required for 403(b) plans that have 100 or more participants.

Some 401(k) defined contribution plans are required to register and file a report with the SEC under the requirements of the Securities Exchange Act of 1933 (1933 Act). These requirements mandate registration, typically using Form S-8 for employer securities offered to the plan. This then requires the plan to file a Form 11-K under the Securities Exchange Act of 1934. The 1933 Act provides exemptions for registration requirements for plans that do not involve the purchase of employer securities with employee contributions. All other plans are subject to the 1933 Act provided they are both voluntary and contributory. You should consult with the plan's legal counsel to determine whether the plan is subject to such reporting requirements. For additional information, see the section *SEC Form 11-K Filing Requirements later* in this chapter. Instead of requiring plans to file under Regulations S-X, Article 6A, the SEC has amended its rules for Form 11-K to permit plans subject to ERISA to elect to file financial statements in accordance with ERISA guidelines.

Governmental regulations

The IRC has many provisions that affect employee benefit plans including 401(k) plans. If the plan qualifies under Section 401(a) of the IRC, certain tax benefits are available. These include (*a*) current tax deductions by plan sponsors for contributions, subject to certain limitations; (*b*) deferment of income to participants until the benefits are distributed; (*c*) exemption of the plan's trust from income taxes, other than tax on unrelated business income; and (*d*) favorable tax treatment of certain benefit distributions to participants or their estates.

Administrators of a 401(k) plan subject to ERISA must file an annual report for each plan every year. Under the "80-120 rule," if a plan has between 80 and 120 participants (inclusive) at the beginning of the plan year, the plan may elect to file a "small" or "large" plan Form 5500 for the plan year based on the annual return or report form that was filed for the previous year.

Plans with 100 or more participants at the beginning of the plan year that file Form 5500 are required to have an annual audit of their financial statements. Plans with fewer than 100 participants at the beginning of the plan year that filed as a small plan in the previous year are exempt from the audit requirement. Plans with fewer than 100 participants that do not meet certain DOL requirements regarding "qualifying plan assets" are not eligible for the small pension plan audit waiver and are required to have an annual audit of their financial statements. Also, plans with fewer than 100 participants that elect to file as a large plan under the 80-120 rule, rather than as a small plan filer in the previous year, are also required to engage an independent qualified public accountant to audit the plan.

(Note that these same requirements are in effect for 403(b) plans.)

Knowledge check

2. The following 401(k) plan does not require an audit:

    a. A plan with 121 participants at the beginning of the plan year.
    b. A plan with 90 participants at the beginning of the plan year that files Form 5500 Schedule I.
    c. A plan with 80 participants at the beginning of the plan year that files Form 5500 Schedule H.
    d. A plan with 500 participants at the beginning of the plan year.

Audit requirements

ERISA also requires an annual audit of plan financial statements by an independent qualified public accountant. Most plans with 100 or more participants in the plan at the beginning of the year satisfy this requirement. See previous discussion for more information on determining when an audit is required. The independent auditor's objectives and responsibility are established under generally accepted auditing standards (GAAS), which state that the auditor is to express an opinion on whether the financial statements are fairly presented in conformity with generally accepted accounting principles. The auditor also should state that the related supplemental information is presented fairly, in all material respects, when considered in conjunction with the financial statements taken as a whole. The opinion should identify the country of origin of the accounting principles that were used to prepare the financial statements. In addition, the auditing standards that you followed in performing the audit should be stated. The audit requirement is an important tool used by ERISA to protect plan participants. However, an audit performed under generally accepted auditing standards is not designed to make sure that all the requirements of ERISA, the DOL, and the IRS are satisfied. However, the annual report and the financial statements prepared by the plan administrator and the independent auditor's report assist these regulatory agencies in their monitoring and oversight functions. The audit is one of the important components of the financial information reported by the plan administrator, although the audit does not make sure compliance with all legislative and regulatory requirements.

As mentioned earlier, 403(b) plans with 100 or more participants as of the beginning of the plan year are also subject to the audit requirements stated earlier.

The decision tree in the following material reflects the previously mentioned requirement.

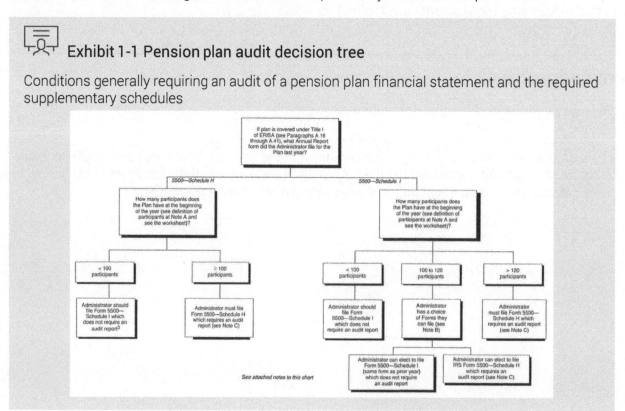

Exhibit 1-1 Pension plan audit decision tree

Conditions generally requiring an audit of a pension plan financial statement and the required supplementary schedules

Note A—Participants are defined by the DOL as follows:

Active participants

- Any individuals who are currently in employment covered by a plan and who are earning or retaining credited service under a plan
- Any individuals who are currently below the integration level in a plan that is integrated with social security, or eligible to have the employer make payments to a 401(k) or section 125 arrangements. (Participants only have to be eligible for the plan, not necessarily participating in a 401(k) or Section 125 arrangement.)
- Any nonvested individuals who are earning or retaining credited service under a plan

The term *active participant* does not refer to nonvested former employees who have incurred the break-in-service period specified in the plan.

Inactive participants

Any individuals who are retired or separated from employment covered by a plan and who are receiving or entitled to receive benefits.

The term *inactive participant* does not refer to any individual to whom an insurance company has made an irrevocable commitment to pay all the benefits to which the individual is entitled under the plan.

Deceased participants include the following:

- Any deceased individuals who have beneficiaries who are receiving or are entitled to receive benefits under the plan

The term *deceased participant* does not refer to any individual to whom an insurance company has made an irrevocable commitment to pay all the benefits to which the beneficiaries of the individual are entitled under the plan.

Note B—*80–120 Rule* (Does not apply in the initial year of the plan)

Under 29 CFR 2520.103-1d, if a plan has between 80 and 120 participants (inclusive) as of the beginning of a plan year, it may elect to file the same category of form it filed in the prior year (for example, Form 5500, Schedule I "Financial Information—Small Plans") and avoid the audit requirement. This means that plans with between 80 and 120 participants at the beginning of the plan year that filed a Form 5500, Schedule I, "Financial Information—Small Plans," in the prior year may elect in the current year to complete Form 5500 following the requirements for a small plan. There is no limit to the number of years this election can be made. DOL officials have indicated that health and welfare plans with 100 or more participants that involve employee contributions generally are required to have an audit unless employee contributions are used to purchase insurance from a third-party insurer or forwarded to a health maintenance organization within prescribed timeframes, even if the plan sponsor does not maintain a trust and considers the assets to be subject to the rights of general creditors (29 CFR 2520.104-44). In these circumstances, careful consideration is given as to whether an audit is required.

If Form 5500 is filed, an audit of the plan's financial statements may be required except that (1) plans that have a short plan year of seven months or less may elect to defer (but not eliminate) the audit requirement, and (2) plans whose sole assets are insurance contracts that fully guarantee benefit payments are not required to be audited.

Exhibit 1-2 Small pension plan audit waiver (SPPAW) summary

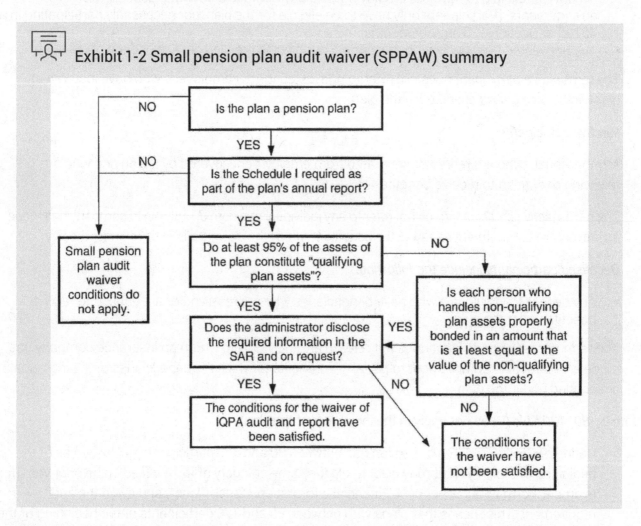

In determining whether a 401(k) plan has 100 "participants," each employee who is eligible to make a contribution, (that is, has satisfied the eligibility requirements of the plan such as age and service), is counted as a participant regardless of whether or not that employee elects to contribute or has an account under the plan.

The plan administrator must file the annual report by the last day of the seventh month after the end of the plan year, including a short plan year (any plan year less than 12 months). For a plan that is terminating, the plan's final Form 5500 is due within seven months following the date the plan's assets were completely distributed. A one-time extension of time up to two and one-half months may be granted for filing the annual report if Form 5558, *Application for Extension of Time to File Certain Employee Plan*

Returns, is filed with the IRS before the normal due date of the report. The plan administrator must file a copy of the extension with the annual report. In addition, if the plan sponsor's corporate tax return has been extended, then the plan will automatically receive an extension for one and one-half months. Again, a copy of the extension must be filed with the annual report.

Knowledge check

3. The plan sponsor has the following active employees at the beginning of the plan year:

    Vested employees 77

    Nonvested employees earning service 12

    Nonvested employees not eligible because of the plan's age and service requirements 14

    Nonvested employees eligible for the plan electing not to participate 22

    What is the total number of participants at the beginning of the plan year?

    a. 77.
    b. 89.
    c. 103.
    d. 111.
    e. 125.

Reporting and disclosure requirements under ERISA

ERISA imposes various rules regarding the operation and reporting practices for employee benefit plans. It establishes minimum standards of vesting for defined contribution plans sponsored by private entities in addition to establishing extensive reporting requirements as described previously. ERISA gives the IRS and DOL authority to issue reporting and disclosure requirements and certain administrative responsibilities.

ERISA also sets standards of fiduciary conduct and imposes specific restrictions and responsibilities on fiduciaries. These responsibilities include managing and operating the plan in the best interests of the plan participants. The fiduciary is prohibited from permitting the plan to engage in prohibited (nonexempt) party in interest transactions. (See chapter 3, "Internal Control Structure," and chapter 6, "Other Auditing Considerations.")

In addition, ERISA gives the DOL authority to reject reports of plans that do not meet the reporting and disclosure requirements. Working papers that support audits of employee benefit plans must be maintained for a period of six years. Section 502(c)(5) of ERISA describes penalties that the DOL can assess up to $1,000 a day for failure or refusal to file a report.

FASB ASC 962, *Plan Accounting—Defined Contribution Pension Plans*, addresses the accounting and reporting specifically for defined contribution pension plans. Accounting principles generally accepted in the United States of America are also effectively established through the AICPA Audit and Accounting Guide *Employee Benefit Plans*. In addition, FASB ASC 815, *Derivatives and Hedging*, and FASB ASC 820, *Fair Value Measurement*, have been reflected throughout this course where applicable.

Knowledge check

4. Working papers that support audits of employee benefit plans that do not file form 11-K with the SEC must be maintained for a period of

    a. Five years.
    b. Six years.
    c. Seven years.
    d. Indefinitely.

SEC Form 11-K filing requirements

As noted previously, certain plans and related entities may be subject to the requirements of the Securities and Exchange Act of 1933 (1933 Act). These requirements mandate registration, usually on Form S-8 for plan securities, and require annual reporting on Form 11-K under the Securities and Exchange Act of 1934 (1934 Act). Section 3(a)(2) of the 1933 Act permits an exemption from this reporting requirement for defined contribution plans that do not offer, as an investment option, the purchase of employer securities with employee contributions. All other 401(k) plans that offer an employer stock investment option to participants on a voluntary and contributory basis are subject to the 1933 Act. The plan administration should consult with legal counsel to determine if an 11-K filing is required for the plan.

For a plan to be both voluntary and contributory, the employees must be given the option to contribute their own funds to the plan and, in doing so, the participants must know that these contributions could be used, at any point, to acquire employer securities.

As an option, the 1934 Act permits plans subject to ERISA filings to elect to file plan financial statements and schedules prepared in accordance with the financial reporting requirements of ERISA rather than follow the requirements of the 1934 Act as contained in Article 6A of Regulation S-X. Plans subject to the SEC Form 11-K filing requirements generally must be audited by an independent public accountant. However, the SEC will not accept an ERISA limited-scope audit report filed in connection with an 11-K filing even if the plan has elected to file its financial statements in accordance with the financial reporting requirements of ERISA, rather than Article 6A of Regulation S-X. Plans that file reports on Form 11-K in connection with the 1934 Act must do so within 90 days after the end of the plan's fiscal year. A plan that files under the ERISA guidelines must file the Form 11-K within 180 days after the plan's fiscal year-end. See chapter 7, "The Auditor's Report and Financial Statement Disclosures," for additional information.

Note that many of the provisions of the Sarbanes-Oxley Act of 2002 apply to the audits of employee benefit plans that file on Form 11-K. Audit reports issued for public entities subject to the requirements under Sarbanes-Oxley Act of 2002 must reference the standards issued by the PCAOB. These standards have been adopted by the PCAOB and approved by the Securities and Exchange Commission:

- AS 1215: *Audit Documentation*
- AS 6115: *Reporting on Whether a Previously Reported Material Weakness Continues to Exist*
- AS 2201: *An Audit of Internal Control Over Financial Reporting That Is Integrated with An Audit of Financial Statements*
- AS 2820: *Evaluating Consistency of Financial Statements*
- AS 1220: *Engagement Quality Review*
- AS 1101: *Audit Risk*
- AS 2101: *Audit Planning*
- AS 1201: *Supervision of the Audit Engagement*
- AS 2105: *Consideration of Materiality in Planning and Performing an Audit*
- AS 2110: *Identifying and Assessing Risks of Material Misstatement*
- AS 2301: *The Auditor's Responses to the Risks of Material Misstatement*
- AS 2810: *Evaluating Audit Results*

- AS 1105: *Audit Evidence*
- AS 1301: *Communications with Audit Committees*
- AS 2701: *Auditing Supplemental Information Accompanying Audited Financial Statements*
- AS 2410: *Related Parties*

See chapter 6, "Other Auditing Considerations," for additional information.

ERISA limited-scope audits

As permitted by 29 CFR 2520.103-8 of the DOL's Rules and Regulations for Reporting and Disclosure under ERISA, the plan administrator is permitted to instruct you not to perform any auditing procedures with respect to information prepared and certified by a bank or similar institution or by an insurance carrier that is regulated, supervised, and subject to periodic examination by a state or federal agency and that acts as trustee or custodian for the plan's assets. The ERISA limited-scope audit is available, however, only if the trustee or custodian certifies both as to accuracy and completeness of the information submitted. Certifications that address only accuracy or completeness, but not both, do not comply with the DOL's regulations, and, therefore, are not adequate to allow plan administrators to limit the scope of the audit.

This ERISA limited-scope audit provision does not apply to information regarding investments held by a broker-dealer or some investment companies, that is, those that are not chartered and regulated by a federal or state agency. The ERISA limited-scope audit applies only to a bank, an insurance carrier, or a similar institution that is federally or state chartered and is regulated, supervised, and subject to periodic examination by a state or federal agency. The ERISA limited-scope audit applies only to investment information (including investments, investment income, and related expenses, as well as notes receivable from participants), and does not extend to withdrawals, contributions, or other information, whether or not it is certified by the trustee or custodian. Note that whereas notes receivable from participants are not characterized as "investments" for financial statement reporting purposes, loans by participants are treated as a receivable of the plan (see chapter 4 for further information). Notes receivable from participants are reported on Form 5500 as investments, and if held and certified by the trustee, would not be subject to audit.

Thus, except for the investment-related activity certified by the trustee or custodian (or both), an auditor conducting an ERISA limited-scope audit would need to include in the scope of the audit all other functions performed by the plan sponsor or other third-party service organizations. The nature and scope of testing will depend on a variety of factors, including the nature of the functions being performed by the third-party service organization and whether a SOC 1® report that addresses areas other than investments is available, if deemed necessary. If a SOC 1® report is available, the nature and scope of testing will depend on the type of SOC 1® report and the related results. (See chapter 3 for further information on SOC 1® reports.) The ERISA limited-scope audit does not relieve the plan from the requirement to have an audit.

AU-C section 402, *Audit Considerations Relating to an Entity Using a Service Organization* (AICPA, *Professional Standards*), addresses the user auditor's responsibility for obtaining sufficient appropriate audit evidence in an audit of the financial statements of an entity that uses one or more service organizations.

AT-C section 320, *Reporting on an Examination of Controls at a Services Organization Relevant to User Entities' Internal Control Over Financial Reporting* (AICPA, *Professional Standards*), contains performance and reporting requirements and application guidance for a service auditor examining controls at organizations that provide services to user entities when those controls are likely to be relevant to user entities' internal control over financial reporting. The AICPA Guide *Reporting on an Examination of Controls at a Service Organization Relevant to User Entities' Internal Control Over Financial Reporting (SOC 1®)* contains guidance to assist service auditors in performing and reporting on these engagements.

Plan investments not held by a qualifying institution should be subjected to appropriate audit procedures. Plans may hold investment assets, only a portion of which is covered by a certification by a qualifying institution. In that case, the balance of the investments is not eligible for the ERISA limited-scope audit and should be subjected to auditing procedures by the plan auditor. In these circumstances, the ERISA limited-scope audit report would be required if the plan's assets that are not audited (that is, those assets covered by the trustee's or custodian's certification) are material to the plan's financial statements taken as a whole. See chapter 7 for a sample of the auditor's report in this situation.

When you are engaged to perform an ERISA limited-scope audit and consequently disclaims an opinion on the financial statements as a whole, you are not permitted to issue an opinion on the supplemental schedules. However, because the DOL requires supplemental schedules to be presented with the financial statements, you are required to follow the guidance in AU-C section 720, *Other Information in Documents Containing Audited Financial Statements* (AICPA, *Professional Standards*). See chapter 7 for further discussion when reporting on supplemental schedules when performing an ERISA limited-scope audit.

Knowledge check

5. Which of the following is an example of a certification that would be acceptable for an ERISA limited-scope audit?

    a. ABC Bank certifies the attached statements are complete and accurate.
    b. XYZ Insurance Company certifies the attached information is accurate.
    c. DEF Recordkeeper certifies that the attached information is complete and accurate.
    d. RST Brokerage Company certifies that they hold the following investments and the information is complete and accurate.

6. The 401(k) plan for ABC Corp. holds investments in two separate institutions. One is a regulated bank (holds 95 percent of the investments); the other is a broker-dealer (holds the remaining 5 percent of the investments). Provided all other requirements regarding limited-scope are met, the auditors may limit their testing of investments

    a. Only for the investments held by the bank.
    b. Only for the investments held by the broker-dealer.
    c. On all investments held by both the bank and the investment company.
    d. On none of the investments because some of the investments are held by a company that does not qualify for the ERISA limited-scope audit.

7. What type of audit report should be issued for ABC Corp. in question 6, assuming no errors or irregularities were noted during the audit?

    a. Unqualified audit report.
    b. ERISA limited-scope audit report.
    c. Disclaimer due to omitted information.
    d. Adverse opinion because a majority of the investment information was not audited.

8. An ERISA limited-scope audit under the DOL regulations limits the scope in relation to

    a. Investment allocation testing for participant accounts.
    b. Contributions.
    c. Expenses.
    d. Investments and investment activity.

Chapter 2

Planning

Learning objectives

After completing this chapter, you should be able to do the following:

- Identify the requirements for an ERISA limited-scope audit.

- Identify the key parties involved with 401(k) plans.

- Recognize prohibited transactions.

- Identify the kinds of information to gather.

- Distinguish the risk factors and internal control considerations of 401(k) plan audits.

- Identify the requirements of the risk assessment standards in planning the audit of a 401(k) plan.

- Recall the requirements of AU-C section 260 to communicate the timing and planned scope of the audit of a 401(k) plan to those charged with governance.

Introduction

Like any financial statement audit, planning must occur for the 401(k) plan audit to be in accordance with generally accepted auditing standards (GAAS) (all plans) or the PCAOB standards (for a plan subject to the Sarbanes-Oxley Act of 2002). An overall strategy must be developed for the expected scope and conduct of the audit. The planning process includes gaining an understanding of the 401(k) plan being

---

audited and its environment—including internal control, assessing risk, developing an audit strategy, and communicating with those charged with governance.

Considerations for public entity audits (plans that file Form 11-K) that are performed in accordance with the PCAOB standards are covered in chapter 6. Although there is currently a slight divergence between generally accepted accounting standards (GAAS) and PCAOB standards, both sets of auditing standards must be complied with for audits of employee benefit plans that are public entities and are also subject to Employee Retirement Income Security Act (ERISA).

The following AU-C sections (AICPA, *Professional Standards*) provide guidance on how to apply the audit risk model in planning and performing an audit of nonissuers and provide guidance on planning an audit in accordance with GAAS:

- AU-C section 200, *Overall Objectives of the Independent Auditor and the Conduct of an Audit in Accordance With Generally Accepted Auditing Standards*
- AU-C section 300, *Planning an Audit*
- AU-C section 315, *Understanding the Entity and Its Environment and Assessing the Risks of Material Misstatement*
- AU-C section 320, *Materiality in Planning and Performing an Audit*
- AU-C section 330, *Performing Audit Procedures in Response to Assessed Risks and Evaluating the Audit Evidence Obtained*
- AU-C section 402, *Audit Considerations Relating to an Entity Using a Service Organization*
- AU-C section 450, *Evaluation of Misstatements Identified During the Audit*
- AU-C section 500, *Audit Evidence*
- AU-C section 520, *Analytical Procedures*
- AU-C section 530, *Audit Sampling*

The auditor of an employee benefit plan should also have sufficient knowledge of the rules and regulations affecting employee benefit plans, including those issued by ERISA, and related Department of Labor (DOL) and IRS regulations. (See appendix A, "ERISA and Related Regulations," of the AICPA Audit and Accounting Guide *Employee Benefit Plans*.)

Pre-engagement activities

Audit scope

When deciding on the nature, timing, and extent of auditing procedures to perform, you should first obtain a clear understanding of the scope of the audit to be performed (including whether the audit is an initial audit, a merged plan, or a final audit) and your reporting responsibilities for any supplemental schedules that will accompany the financial statements. You should also understand the nature of the trust arrangement and the types of investments in which the plan invests. You should also determine the role of third-party service organizations in the plan.

You should not accept an audit unless you will be able to meet the responsibilities and requirements related to the engagement. Factors you should consider include expertise in the benefit plan area, ability to meet the engagement's time requirements and deadlines, and ability to meet ERISA audit requirements. If you are considering a benefit plan audit engagement, you should also take into account section 1.200 of the AICPA Code of Professional Conduct, which requires independence in the performance of professional services. You should consider whether certain relationships or activities impair independence with respect to a potential client.

The plan administrator will elect either a full or limited audit scope, which must be clearly defined before you begin any procedures. This is often accomplished by the use of an engagement letter, which is required by AU-C section 210, *Terms of Engagement* (AICPA, *Professional Standards*).

Engagement letter

The engagement letter is used to document the auditor's understanding with the client regarding the objectives and scope of the audit (full or ERISA limited-scope), the form of the report(s), and the extent of the auditor's responsibilities for these areas:

- If the engagement is to be an ERISA limited-scope audit, the plan administrator's responsibilities as they relate to the completeness and accuracy of the trustee certification (see 29 CFR 2520.103-5).
- Whether there are any other scope limitations imposed by management.
- Management's responsibility for establishing an accounting and financial reporting process for determining fair value measurements.
- Management's agreement that it acknowledges and understands its responsibility for the preparation of the supplemental schedules in accordance with the applicable criteria and that management will include the auditor's report on the supplemental schedules in any document that contains the supplemental schedules and that indicates that the auditor has reported on such supplemental schedules, and to present the supplemental schedules with the audited financial statements or, if the supplemental schedules will not be presented with the audited financial statements, to make the audited financial statements readily available to the intended users of the supplemental schedules no later than the date of issuance by the entity of the supplemental schedules and the auditor's report therein.

- The auditor's responsibility with respect to supplemental schedules that accompany the financial statements.
- The auditor's responsibility with respect to consideration of the plan's qualification for tax-exempt status, with sufficient specificity to make it clear that the audit does not contemplate an opinion on plan tax qualification.
- The auditor's responsibility with respect to information in Form 5500.
- The auditor's responsibility with respect to reporting matters that come to your attention regarding lack of compliance with ERISA requirements. Though you do review the plan's tax-exempt status, you do not render an opinion on the plan's tax qualification. Also, the audit is not intended to search for lack of compliance with ERISA requirements—only to report it if noncompliance is noted. The engagement letter helps to minimize the risk that the plan sponsor may inappropriately rely on you to protect the sponsor against certain risks or to perform certain functions that are the plan's responsibility.
- Whether due to complex or subjective nature of the subject matter, the audit may require the special skills and knowledge of a specialist (for example, use of actuaries for defined benefit pension plans and health and welfare plans; or a valuation professional for investments for whose valuations are subjective—such as derivative financial instruments, nonpublicly held stock, and real estate).
- If applicable, the auditor's responsibilities with respect to electronic filings (such as Form 5500 or SEC Form 11-K).
- The effects of other regulations or laws, such as Sarbanes-Oxley Act of 2002 and the Health Insurance Portability and Accountability Act of 1996 (HIPAA) and the use of protected personal information.
- If applicable, the involvement of third-party service organizations or affiliates of the public accounting firm (such as the use of staff from a foreign office or location).
- The auditor's responsibilities under GAAS in accordance with AU-C section 260, *The Auditor's Communication With Those Charged With Governance* (AICPA, *Professional Standards*).
- The agreement of management to make available to the auditor draft financial statements and any accompanying other information in time to allow the auditor to complete the audit in accordance with the proposed timetable. This could also include information from service organizations, such as the trustee and recordkeeper. The auditor may assist in drafting the financial statements, in whole or part, based on information provided to the auditor by management during the performance of the audit. However, the concept of an independent audit requires that the auditor's role does not involve assuming management's responsibility for the preparation and fair presentation of the financial statements or assuming responsibility for the entity's related internal control and that the auditor has a reasonable expectation of obtaining the information necessary for the audit insofar as management is able to provide or procure it. Accordingly, the premise is fundamental to the conduct of an independent audit. To avoid misunderstanding, agreement is reached with management that it acknowledges and understands that it has such responsibilities as part of agreeing and documenting the terms of the audit engagement. When the auditor or a third party has assisted with drafting the financial statements, it may be useful to remind management that the preparation and fair presentation of the financial statements in accordance with the applicable financial reporting framework remains management's responsibility.
- The agreement of management to inform the auditor of events occurring or facts discovered subsequent to the date of the financial statements, of which management may become aware, that may affect the financial statements.
- Arrangements concerning the involvement of internal auditors and other staff of the entity.
- Arrangements made with the predecessor auditor, if any, in the case of an initial audit for the successor firm.

Full-scope versus ERISA limited-scope audit

The plan administrator must choose to have either a full-scope audit performed or, if the plan qualifies, an ERISA limited-scope audit. A full-scope audit of a 401(k) plan is performed in accordance with generally accepted auditing standards (GAAS) and you should subject all of the accounts to testing. If the plan administrator instructs you to perform an ERISA limited-scope audit, you need not perform any auditing procedures with respect to investment information prepared and certified by a qualifying institution—for example, a bank; trust; or insurance company, but not a broker-dealer or investment company. To be qualified, a bank or insurance carrier must (1) act as trustee or custodian for the plan; (2) be state or federally chartered; and (3) be regulated, supervised, and subject to periodic examination by a state or federal agency. In addition, the qualifying institution must certify as to the completeness and accuracy of the investment information. The ERISA limited-scope audit option is not available for assets held by a broker-dealer or an investment company. Certifications from the plan's recordkeeper are not acceptable unless the recordkeeper meets the qualifications—for example, is a bank, trust, or an insurance company. Also, you may limit your testing only with respect to investments and investment-related information certified by that trustee. You should audit all other accounts in the 401(k) plan—such as contributions, benefit payments, and administrative expenses.

Communication with those charged with governance

Generally accepted auditing standards now require the auditor to communicate with those charged with governance, even if the plan does not have an audit committee. Communications are required both at the beginning and end of the audit, for both full- and ERISA limited-scope audits.

AU-C section 260 requires the auditor to communicate with those charged with governance an overview of the planned scope and timing of the audit.

Those charged with governance is defined as the person(s) with responsibility for overseeing the strategic direction of the plan and obligations related to the accountability of the plan.

In accordance with paragraphs .19 and .28 of AU-C section 610, *Using the Work of Internal Auditors* (AICPA, *Professional Standards*), in communicating an overview of the planned scope and timing of the audit to those charged with governance in accordance with AU-C section 260, the external auditor should communicate how the external auditor plans to use internal auditors in obtaining audit evidence and to provide direct assistance. In addition, paragraph .30 of AU-C section 610 states that prior to using internal auditors to provide direct assistance, the external auditor should obtain written acknowledgment from management or those charged with governance, as appropriate, that internal auditors providing direct assistance to the external auditor will be allowed to follow the external auditor's instructions, and that the entity will not intervene in the work the internal auditor performs for the external auditor.

This communication may be included within the engagement letter (or other suitable form of written agreement of the terms of engagement) or could be included in a separate document prepared by the external auditor and acknowledged in writing by management or those charged with governance, as appropriate.

You should coordinate with the client to identify the appropriate person(s) within the plan's governance structure with whom to communicate. For a single-employer employee benefit plan, the individual charged with governance may include the named fiduciary, which is often the plan sponsor; an officer thereof; the plan's oversight committee; or the sponsor's board of directors. **Multiemployer plan considerations:** For a multiemployer plan, those charged with governance, for example, might be a board of trustees.

You should also consider communicating planning matters early in an audit engagement, and for an initial engagement, as part of the terms of the engagement. You should communicate with those charged with governance the auditor's responsibilities under GAAS and an overview of the planned scope and timing of the audit. This may include how you propose to address the significant risks of material misstatement, the approach to internal control, the concept of materiality, and the use of internal audit.

The auditor's assessment of risk

Audit procedures performed to obtain an understanding of the plan and its environment, including its internal control, to assess the risks of material misstatement at the financial statement and relevant assertion levels are referred to as *risk assessment procedures*. GAAS requires that the auditor perform risk assessment procedures to provide a basis for the assessment of risks at the financial statement and relevant assertion levels.

You should plan the audit to obtain reasonable assurance that the financial statements are not materially misstated. The planning process requires you to develop an overall strategy that you will follow during the course of the audit that is responsive to the assessment of the risks of material misstatement based on your understanding of the plan and its environment, including its internal control. The nature, timing, and extent of audit procedures to be performed will vary according to the size and complexity of the plan's operations, and any restrictions placed on the audit. You should prepare a written audit program for every audit that is performed. (See chapter 6 for a discussion of first-year audits of new and existing plans.)

Identification of significant risks

As part of the assessment of the risks of material misstatement, you should determine which of the risks identified are, in your judgment, risks that require special audit consideration (such risks are defined as "significant risks"). One or more significant risks normally arise on most audits. In exercising this judgment, you should consider inherent risk to determine whether the nature of the risk, the likely magnitude of the potential misstatement including the possibility that the risk may give rise to multiple misstatements, and the likelihood of the risk occurring are such that they require special audit consideration. Significant risks common to defined contribution plan audits include the risk that

- Significant transactions are processed by an outside service organization and no SOC 1® (SOC 1®) report is available.
- Significant transactions are processed by an outside service organization and the SOC 1® report has qualifications, exceptions, or carve-outs.
- Substantial doubt about the plan's ability to continue as a going concern as a result of the plan sponsor's risk of ability to continue as a going concern.
- The plan holds hard to value investments that could result in participant purchases and sales at inappropriate valuations.
- The integrity of the individual account balances is not maintained when the recordkeeper has changed or where there is a transfer of assets received from another plan.
- In a private company leveraged employee stock ownership plan (ESOP), company stock is not valued at fair value in accordance with GAAP.
- The following are examples of identified risks of what can go wrong at the relevant assertion level for participant accounts and allocations:
  - Participant investment options or salary deferral amounts may not be in accordance with their stated elections, causing the participant's account to be overstated or understated.
  - Allocations of income or expenses may be inaccurate, causing the participant's account to be overstated or understated.
  - Lack of reconciliations or improperly prepared reconciliations by management could result in missing contributions or improper allocations.

- For self-directed brokerage accounts, a lack of reconciliations between the trustee, the recordkeeper, and the brokerage firm could result in incomplete or inaccurate reporting.
- For self-directed brokerage accounts, fees being charged for recordkeeping are not applied correctly.
- Delinquent loans or loans in default are not properly identified on a timely basis and are not accounted for in accordance with GAAP.

In addition to the audit risks noted previously, you should be aware of the risk that errors and irregularities may cause the financial statements to contain a material misstatement. Although you are not required to search for errors or irregularities, you should design the audit to provide reasonable assurance that errors and irregularities that are material to the financial statements will be detected. AU-C section 240, *Consideration of Fraud in a Financial Statement Audit* (AICPA, *Professional Standards*), describes the auditor's responsibilities to plan and perform the audit to obtain reasonable assurance as to whether the financial statements are free of material misstatement, whether caused by error or fraud. (See "Consideration of Fraud" later in this chapter.)

Considering whether testing in the plan sponsor audit can be used in the 401(k) plan audit

If, as the auditor for the 401(k) plan, you also audit the plan sponsor's financial statements, you will often find it efficient to coordinate some of the testing during the audit of the sponsor's financial statements. This is especially true for the testing of payroll data, employee contributions, employer contributions, and participant eligibility testing. You need to determine the scope of the testing that was performed during the corporate audit as it may not satisfy specific testing required for the 401(k) audit. For example, payroll testing may have been performed as a high-level analytical test while the 401(k) audit requires much more detailed testing to be performed.

The actual level of testing that you perform depends on your professional judgment as to the level of risk and on your decision whether to rely on controls, the risk of error associated with the account to be tested, and the expected effectiveness of audit tests to be performed. Included in these considerations are the materiality of the items being tested, the type and quality of evidential matter available, and the nature of the audit objective to be achieved. The results of your substantive tests and your assessment of the level of inherent risk and control risk should provide a reasonable basis for your opinion.

Knowledge check

1. Which of the following factors is not required to be communicated to those charged with governance?

    a. The timing of the audit.
    b. An overview of planned audit scope.
    c. A detailed listing of all procedures that the audit plans to perform.
    d. The auditor's assessment of risk and identification of significant risks.

2. Auditors use their professional judgment to determine the actual level of testing to be performed on the basis of all of the following, except:

    a. The risk of error associated with a particular account.
    b. Decision to rely on controls.
    c. Expected effectiveness of the audit tests to be performed.
    d. Input from the audit committee of the plan.

3. Factors that may increase the level of audit risk associated with an employee benefit plan include which of the following?

    a. Investment by the plan in marketable securities.
    b. Merger of a plan into the plan during the year.
    c. An audit committee for the plan with responsibility for the financial oversight of the plan.
    d. Use of a third-party bank as a trustee.

Communication and coordination

Two important aspects of planning and performing any 401(k) plan audit are communication and coordination with the many parties who are involved in the administration of the plan. These parties may include the following:

- The plan sponsor (plan document, any amendments to the plan, plan mergers, and the like, minutes applicable to the plan, IRS determination letter)
- Payroll department (payroll records)
- Human resource department (to test participant eligibility), management information systems group (processing of plan information)
- Treasury (timely deposit of employee monies, employer contributions, if any)
- Administrators (determine scope)
- Recordkeeper (records of plan activity)
- Investment trustees or custodians (certified trust statements)
- Investment managers (other investment information)
- Insurance companies (investments) and attorney (existence of claims against the plan)
- ERISA legal counsel

During the planning phase, it is important for you to identify these parties and coordinate with them to receive the information necessary to perform the audit.

Understanding the plan and its environment, including its internal control

AU-C section 315 sets standards and provides guidance about how you obtain an understanding of the plan and its environment, including its internal control, for the purpose of assessing the risk of material misstatement.

Information gathering

As we have just noted, you should communicate with various parties (such as the plan sponsor, the payroll department, and the human resources department) to obtain the necessary information to adequately plan the audit. More specifically, you should consider performing the following steps:

1. Make inquiries of plan management about the basis of accounting that will be used to issue the plan's financial statements (for example, accounting principles generally accepted in the United States of America or another basis of accounting permitted by ERISA and DOL regulations, such as the modified cash basis of accounting).
2. Make inquiries of plan management as to whether the plan has either an audit committee or a group equivalent to an audit committee that has been formally designated with responsibility for oversight of the financial reporting process.
3. Make inquiries of plan management about whether it has knowledge of fraud or suspected fraud affecting the plan involving (a) management, (b) employees who have significant roles in internal control, or (c) others where fraud could have a material effect on the financial statements. In addition, inquire as to whether management has received communication of fraud or suspected fraud affecting the plan from employees, former employees, participants, trustees or custodians, regulators, beneficiaries, service organizations, third-party administrators, or others.
4. Make inquiries of plan management regarding its acknowledgement of its responsibilities for the design and implementation of programs and controls to prevent and detect fraud.
5. Make inquiries of plan management about who maintains the plan's accounting records and participant data, whether the plan keeps a list of identified parties in interest, whether a control is in place to identify nonexempt or prohibited party in interest transactions (to enable the plan sponsor to become aware if such a transaction occurs), and whether the sponsor intends to terminate the plan (as this will affect the audit report). Review accounting records for large, unusual, or nonrecurring transactions or balances, paying particular attention to transactions recorded at or near the end of the plan year. In response to inquiries made, additional inquiries should be made to determine whether other risk assessment procedures are necessary.
6. Review the minutes of the retirement committee, board of trustees of the plan, or any other executive meetings for information about transactions approved or discussed at these meetings. Review conflict-of-interest statements, if any, obtained from plan officials.
7. Obtain and read the following items:
   a. The plan document, including amendments, to gain a full understanding of the plan's operations
   b. The agreements with the trustee(s) (for example, to determine what fee arrangements have been contracted for)
   c. The prior-year Form 5500 filing and prior-year audit report (to identify if significant changes have occurred in the current year)

d. The IRS determination letter (to verify the plan has appropriate tax-exempt status)

e. Reports from service auditors (to evaluate controls at third-party service organizations), and internal auditors (to review testing they have performed on the plan)

f. Minutes of trustee, benefits committee, or board of directors meetings applicable to the plan

8. Consider whether transactions are occurring but are not being accounted for in the plan records—for example, receiving or providing services at no charge or whether the plan sponsor is paying plan expenses.

9. Coordinate with the plan administrator to determine the location of investments and how those assets are safeguarded, whether there are any amendments to the plan, and whether any compliance issues (that is, prohibited transactions) affect the plan. You should also determine the nature and type of investments held by the plan and if any of the investments are unusual or hard to value.

10. Obtain a list of all known parties in interest and inquire whether there were any transactions with them during the plan year.

11. Obtain a trustee report as of the end of the plan year. This report also should list benefit withdrawals and loans made to employees during the plan year. Review the extent and nature of business transacted with the plan's major investees, suppliers, borrowers, lessees, and lenders for indications of previously undisclosed relationships.

12. If an insurance company acts as trustee, perform procedures similar to those outlined in the previous paragraph.

13. Obtain and review any service auditor reports (SOC 1®) applying to parties involved in the operation of the plan, and reports of internal auditors on the operations of the plan. (See chapter 3, "Internal Control Structure.")

14. Contact legal counsel for the plan and determine whether any litigation or claims exist with respect to the plan. Review invoices from law firms that have performed regular or special services for the plan for indications of parties in interest or nonexempt party in interest transactions. If legal counsel was consulted, send an inquiry letter to the legal counsel. The matters described in a–f should be addressed in the attorney's letter.

a. Breach of fiduciary responsibilities

b. Prohibited party in interest transactions

c. Loans or leases in default reportable to the DOL

d. Events that may jeopardize the plan's qualified tax status

e. Legal actions brought against the plan on behalf of plan participants

f. Review or inquiry by the DOL, IRS, or other regulatory agencies of the plan's activities or filings

15. Review correspondence from, and forms filed with, the DOL and other regulatory agencies for information about transactions with parties in interest.

16. Provide members of the engagement team with the names of known parties in interest, so that during the audit, they may become aware of transactions with those parties.

17. Inquire if there is an intention to terminate the plan, or merge or transfer into or out of the plan.

Audit documentation

AU-C section 230, *Audit Documentation* (AICPA, *Professional Standards*), addresses the auditor's responsibility to prepare audit documentation for an audit of financial statements. Audit documentation that meets the requirements of AU-C section 230 and the specific documentation requirements of other relevant AU-C sections provides

- evidence of the auditor's basis for a conclusion about the achievement of the overall objectives of the auditor; and
- evidence that the audit was planned and performed in accordance with GAAS and applicable legal and regulatory requirements.

In addition, the auditor would be required to assemble the audit documentation to form the final audit engagement file within 60 days of the issuance of the audit report. The engagement file must be retained for a period no shorter than 5 years. Audit firms are required to establish policies and procedures for the retention of engagement documentation. Statutes, regulations, or the audit firm's quality control policies may specify a retention period longer than 5 years.

You should prepare and maintain audit documentation, the form and content of which should be designed to meet the circumstances of the particular audit engagement. Audit documentation is the principal record of auditing procedures applied, evidence obtained, and conclusions you reach in the engagement. The quantity, type, and content of audit documentation are matters of your professional judgment.

Audit documentation serves mainly to

- provide the principal support for your auditor's report, including the representation regarding observance of the standards of fieldwork, which is implicit in the reference in the report to generally accepted auditing standards; and
- provide assistance to you in the conduct and supervision of the audit.

Examples of audit documentation are audit programs, analyses, memoranda, letters of confirmation and representation, abstracts or copies of entity documents, and schedules or commentaries you prepare or obtain. Audit documentation may be in paper form, electronic form, or other media.

Audit documentation should be sufficient to (*a*) enable members of the engagement team with supervision and review responsibilities to understand the nature, timing, extent, and results of auditing procedures performed, and the evidence obtained; (*b*) indicate the engagement team member(s) who performed and reviewed the work; and (*c*) show that the accounting records agree or reconcile with the financial statements or other information being reported on.

In addition to the previously mentioned requirements, AU-C section 230 provides further requirements about the content, ownership, and confidentiality of audit documentation.

Preliminary analytical review procedures

AU-C section 520 provides guidance on the use of analytical procedures and requires you to use preliminary and overall analytical review procedures in all audits. You should perform preliminary analytical procedures in planning the audit to assist in understanding the plan and its environment and to identify areas that may represent specific risks relevant to the audit.

Preliminary analytical procedures usually focus on account balances aggregated at the financial statement level and on the relationships between account balances. These procedures highlight transactions that occurred since the prior-year audit and identify fluctuations that may indicate a significant risk associated with that particular account.

If you identify significant fluctuations, you should perform further analysis and inquiry and identify plausible explanations for the differences. It is also important for you to talk to the plan administrator about any significant changes in the plan terms (for example, contribution rate) or in the number of participants (layoffs or a new group added to the plan, and so on).

Some examples of preliminary analytical review procedures that you may perform include

- comparing investment balances and rates of return with the prior year and with published rates for similar securities;
- analyzing the changes in the employer contribution ratio. Divide the total sponsor contributions to the plan by the number of active participants. Compare this average to the average obtained in prior years; and
- reviewing fluctuations of various account balances for reasonableness.

Knowledge check

4. All of the following are correct regarding preliminary analytical review procedures, except
    a. They should be performed near the completion of the audit.
    b. They are generally performed on account balances aggregated at the financial statement level.
    c. They are generally performed to identify fluctuations that have occurred that may indicate a specific risk associated with that account.
    d. They serve to highlight transactions that have occurred since the prior-year audit.

Audit risk factors

In obtaining an understanding of the plan and its environment and assessing the risks of material misstatement, GAAS requires a discussion among the members of the audit team, including the auditor with final responsibility for the audit, to discuss the susceptibility of the plan's financial statements to material misstatement, including fraud. This discussion could be held concurrently with the discussion among the audit team that is specified by AU-C section 315 to discuss the susceptibility of the plan's financial statements to fraud.

Risk assessment should be considered at the overall financial statement level and also for relevant assertions for classes of transactions, account balances and disclosures, as shown in the following table. The results of the risk assessment are then used to develop a detailed audit plan for the nature, timing, and extent of further audit procedures.

In representing that the financial statements are fairly presented in accordance with GAAP, management implicitly or explicitly makes assertions regarding the recognition, measurement, and disclosure of information in the financial statements and related disclosures. Assertions fall into the following categories:

	Classes of transactions and events during the period	Account balances at the end of the period	Presentation and disclosure
Occurrence or Existence	Transactions and events that have been recorded in the statements of changes in net assets available for benefits and changes in the actuarial present value of accumulated plan benefits have actually occurred during the period covered by the financial statements and are in accordance with the plan document. *Example: All investment transactions are recorded during the period covered by the financial statements and are in accordance with the plan document.* *Example: Participants earning benefits during the year were eligible under the terms of the plan.* *Example: Contributions and benefits paid are properly recorded during the period covered by the financial statements and are in accordance with the plan document.*	Assets and liabilities included in the statement of net assets available for benefits and that accumulated benefit obligations actually exist as of the end of the period covered by the financial statements. *Example: Investments exist as of the end of the period covered by the financial statements.* *Example: The actuarial present value of accumulated plan benefits exists as of the end of the period covered by the financial statements.* *Example: Notes receivable from participants, contributions receivable, and accrued expenses exist as of the end of the period covered by the financial statements.*	Disclosed events and transactions in the notes to the financial statements have occurred during the period covered by the financial statements. *Example: Information about investments is properly presented and disclosed.* *Example: Information about benefit obligations is properly presented and disclosed.* *Example: Information about notes receivable from participants is properly presented and disclosed.*

	Classes of transactions and events during the period	*Account balances at the end of the period*	*Presentation and disclosure*
Rights and Obligations	—	The plan holds or controls the rights to recorded asset balances and accrued expenses, and accumulated plan benefits are actually obligations of the plan as of the period covered by the financial statements. **Example:** *Investments are owned by the plan and free of liens, pledges, and other security interests or, if not, the security interests are identified.* **Example:** *Claims incurred but not reported are obligations of the plan that arose during the period covered by the plan's financial statements.* **Example:** *Actuarial present value of accumulated plan benefits are obligations of the plan.*	Disclosed events and transactions in the notes to the financial statements have occurred during the period covered by the financial statements and are in accordance with the plan document. **Example:** *Information about investments is properly presented and disclosed.* **Example:** *Information about benefit obligations is properly presented and disclosed.* **Example:** *Information about notes receivable from participants is properly presented and disclosed.*
Completeness	All transactions and events that should have been recorded in the financial statements have been properly recorded in the financial statements. **Example:** *All participant contributions that should have been recorded under the terms of the plan have been recorded in the plan financial statements, and participant data is complete and accurate.* **Example:** *Benefits for all eligible participants that should have earned benefits under the terms of the plan have been recorded.* **Example:** *All administrative expenses that should have been recorded under the terms of the plan have been recorded.*	All assets, accrued liabilities, and benefit obligations that should have been recorded have been recorded. **Example:** *All assets relating to participant contributions that should have been recorded under the terms of the plan have been recorded.* **Example:** *Benefit obligations due under the plan relating to eligible participants have been recorded.*	All disclosures that should have been included in the financial statements have been included. **Example:** *All disclosures relating to participant contributions that should have been included in the financial statements have been included.* **Example:** *All disclosures relating to benefit obligations under the plan have been included.*

	Classes of transactions and events during the period	*Account balances at the end of the period*	*Presentation and disclosure*
Accuracy or Valuation and Allocation	Amounts and other data relating to recorded transactions and events have been recorded appropriately. **Example:** *Investment principal and income transactions are properly recorded, and investment transactions are properly valued in accordance with accounting principles generally accepted in the United States of America as promulgated by the FASB (U.S. GAAP.)* **Example:** *Participant contributions have been calculated in accordance with the plan document and in accordance with the participant's request.* **Example:** *Benefit payments have been calculated in accordance with the plan document and the participant's request.*	Assets, accrued liabilities, and accumulated benefit obligations are included in the financial statements at appropriate amounts, and any resulting valuation or allocation adjustments are recorded appropriately. **Example:** *Investments are valued at period-end in accordance with U.S. GAAP.* **Example:** *Accrued liabilities are included in the financial statements at appropriate amounts.* **Example:** *The present value of accumulated benefit obligations is included in the financial statements at appropriate amounts, based on appropriate assumptions.*	Financial and other information is disclosed fairly and at appropriate amounts. **Example:** *Investment information is properly disclosed and in the appropriate amount.* **Example:** *Disclosures relating to participant contributions are properly disclosed and in the appropriate amount.* **Example:** *Plan benefit obligations are properly disclosed and at appropriate amounts.*
Cut-off	Transactions and events have been recorded in the correct accounting period. **Example:** *Employer contributions receivable have been properly recorded.* **Example:** *Claims payable and claims incurred but not reported have been properly recorded*	—	—
Classification and Understandability	Transactions and events have been recorded in the proper accounts. **Example:** *Benefit payments to participants have been properly classified.* **Example:** *Insurance premiums paid have been properly classified as benefits.* **Example:** *Administrative expenses have been properly classified.*	—	Financial information is appropriately presented and described, and information in disclosures is expressed clearly. **Example:** *Plan benefit obligation information (for example, vested and nonvested participants) is appropriately presented.* **Example:** *Fully benefit-responsive investment contracts are appropriately presented in accordance with the appropriate financial reporting framework.* **Example:** *Notes receivable from participants are appropriately presented as a receivable, not included as an investment.*

When planning and performing an audit of a 401(k) plan, you need to be aware that certain aspects of these plans may be subject to a greater level of audit risk. Some account balances and transactions have a higher level of risk associated with them than others. Amounts that are determined by use of estimates carry a higher level of risk than amounts that can be confirmed with an outside party. Other areas that may present an audit risk when auditing 401(k) plans are (*a*) the fair value of investments with no readily ascertainable market value, (*b*) new types of investments, and (*c*) expenses paid from plan assets.

Audit risk at the account balance or transaction level consists of inherent risk, control risk, and detection risk. Inherent risk is that which is considered normal with respect to the particular account or activity. Control risk is directly related to the reliability of the data being tested. The risk of material misstatement is a combination of inherent risk and control risk. The auditor should assess these two risks and then design audit procedures to reduce detection risk to an appropriately low level.

Your determination as to the level of risk on the audit or for selected audit areas may affect your decisions as to the desired experience level and expertise of professionals assigned to the engagement and the level of professional skepticism to exercise in performing the audit. If you determine that there is a higher level of risk for this audit, a professional with more experience in 401(k) plans should participate in the audit and a higher level of skepticism should be exercised during the course of the audit.

When determining the level of audit risk, you should be especially alert with respect to the following factors.

Plan management characteristics and integrity

- Plan management has been involved with previous prohibited (or nonexempt) transactions, other alleged incidents of illegal activity, distortions of financial statements, or enforcement actions of regulatory agencies.
- Plan management has frequently changed trustees, attorneys, auditors, or other third-party service organizations.
- Plan management has failed to engage reputable professional third parties appropriate to the plan's needs (for example, attorneys, trustees, or auditors).
- Plan management appears willing to accept unusually high levels of risk in making significant decisions (for example, investments in real estate or other investments not readily marketable).
- Important or unexpected changes in plan management have recently occurred or are likely to occur.
- Plan management ignores DOL or IRS inquiries.
- Plan management ignores the auditor's management letter comments.

Overall commitment to accurate financial reporting

- You are aware of transactions without substantial economic justification in the past or in the current period (such as, soft dollars, churning).
- The financial statements are not prepared in accordance with GAAP, when required.
- The plan has received reporting deficiency letters from the DOL relating to previously submitted Form 5500 filings.
- Plan management has not corrected previous reporting deficiencies pointed out in DOL letters and has failed to implement procedures for monitoring new or revised DOL reporting requirements.

Control environment

- Plan management appears unconcerned about deficiencies in the accounting systems and control procedures or fails to correct these deficiencies brought to its attention.
- The plan's policies on matters such as compliance with ERISA and DOL reporting regulations, acceptable business practices, conflicts of interests, and codes of business conduct are not established or not adequately communicated.
- Plan management does not obtain and read the SOC 1® Service Auditor Reports for its outside service providers, such as the recordkeeper.
- The plan has failed to establish procedures to prevent prohibited transactions and other illegal acts, to identify the use of derivatives, and you have not been able to obtain satisfactory representations from plan management at appropriate levels of authority concerning compliance with laws and regulations.
- Previous audits have resulted in significant audit adjustments.
- The general state of the plan records has been poor.
- The plan often fails to meet closing schedules, report deadlines, and so on.

Management structure

- Supervision and monitoring appear inappropriate to the size and nature of the plan.
- There is inadequate supervision and monitoring of (a) decentralized activities such as plan investment decision making; (b) geographically dispersed plans or plan records and input data; (c) data processing operations, especially decentralized data processing operations; and (d) third-party service organizations.
- There is inadequate communication of the scope of authority and responsibility to data processing and accounting personnel, and third-party organizations responsible for providing plan services.
- The plan does not have an audit committee or other group with responsibility for the oversight of the plan's financial reporting process.

Impact of information technology

- The nature and extent of use of information technology is inappropriate in relation to the size and nature of the plan.
- There is an absence of appropriate resource commitments (such as, an inadequate number of staff to develop, operate, and maintain necessary systems).

Audit committee

- The entity does not have an audit committee or other group responsible for overseeing of the plan's financial reporting process.
- The audit committee (or other group) has not established a schedule of regular meetings to set policies and objectives and has not reviewed the plan's investment performance and taken appropriate action, and minutes of such meetings are not prepared and signed on a timely basis.
- The audit committee (or other group) has less than an appropriate level of knowledge of the plan's operation to carry out oversight responsibilities.

Nature of the plan

- Plan management lacks experience in dealing with employee benefit matters.
- Significant accounting estimates that involve greater-than-normal subjectivity, complexity, or uncertainty are required.

External influences that might affect the plan

- The plan has received an unfavorable determination letter from the IRS.
- The plan's investment performance has been significantly better or worse than that of investment portfolios with similar investment objectives.
- Tax law changes or new revenue rulings could adversely affect the plan's qualified tax status.

Financial results

- Plan management places undue emphasis on investment earnings (for example, too many investments in high-risk securities).
- The investment policy is either overly aggressive or highly conservative or does not exist.
- A significant portion of investment advisor compensation is based on financial results.
- Plan management has changed investment strategies significantly or frequently.

Nature of the audit engagement

- This is a first-time engagement.
- Plan management is placing unreasonable constraints on the auditor's time or fees.
- The plan engages in unique, highly complex, and material transactions that pose difficult "form-over-substance" questions.
- Special problems exist relating to accounting estimates or measurements that are of unusual significance because of the nature of the plan or the relative importance in the financial statements.
- There are significant nonmonetary transactions (for example, soft dollars).

Business relationships and related parties

- The auditor may not have a clear understanding of the nature of significant transactions and business relationships between the plan and other entities, particularly if the other entities are presented as third parties, when in fact they are related parties. This also could affect the auditor's conclusions about management integrity.

Engagement history and client relationships

- Plan management has not given auditors full cooperation in the past.
- This is a first-time engagement.
- Plan management is placing unreasonable constraints on fees.
- There is a history of significant parties in interest or nonexempt transactions.

Internal control structure

AU-C section 315 requires the auditor to obtain an understanding of the five components of internal control sufficient to assess the risks of material misstatement of the financial statements whether due to error or fraud, and to design the nature, timing, and extent of further audit procedures. AU-C section 315 describes the components of internal control, explains how you should consider controls in assessing the risks of material misstatement, and provides guidance about how the entity's use of information technology affects your understanding of internal control. In obtaining this understanding, you may obtain an understanding surrounding the internal controls in place at the plan administrator (such as participant data, payroll, oversight of outside service organizations, and so on) as well as the controls in place at outside service organizations (for example, payroll, investments, recordkeeping, and the like).

The following lists examples of controls to consider. Assess whether each of the following has occurred:

- The plan's management has controls in place to maintain compliance with applicable rules and regulations (for example, DOL, IRS, or PCAOB) and provisions of the plan document.
- Controls at outside service organizations (for example, recordkeeper and payroll) are appropriate, and whether the user controls specified in the SOC 1® report are in place.
- The plan has a system for paying and denying benefit distributions and making loans.
- All investment transactions and investment income have been received and recorded appropriately.
- The participant data and payroll information provided to the recordkeeper is accurate.
- Payroll withholdings are reconciled periodically to amounts received by the trust.
- Plan personnel have the capability to prepare the plan's financial statements.
- Employer and employee contributions are complete and accurate.
- The plan administrator has procedures to monitor the activities of the outside service organizations.

Internal control is defined as the structure of the client's methods and procedures to verify that controls operate effectively and continuously. Controls are defined as activities, including control procedures and monitoring activities, performed or directed by management that (*a*) prevent or detect misstatements in the financial statements that are deemed material and (*b*) safeguard the assets of the plan.

Once controls are identified, you should

- test the design and implementation of the controls identified, typically by performing a walkthrough (in all audits), as a basis for assessing risk; and
- perform tests to confirm that the controls have been operating effectively and consistently throughout the period, (if a control reliance strategy is adopted).

Tests of controls are normally based on inquiry, which is then supplemented by observation, examination of documentary evidence, or re-performance. Chapter 3 discusses internal controls of 401(k) plans more fully.

Consideration of fraud

AU-C section 240 describes the auditor's responsibilities to plan and perform the audit to obtain reasonable assurance as to whether the financial statements are free of material misstatement, whether caused by either error or fraud. Changes effected by AU-C section 240 include the following:

- A required brainstorming session among the audit team members to discuss potential for material misstatement due to fraud
- An increased emphasis on inquiry as an audit procedure that increases the likelihood of fraud detection
- Expanded use of analytical procedures to gather information used to identify risks of material misstatement due to fraud
- The consideration of other information, such as client acceptance and continuance procedures, during the information gathering phase
- Expanded guidance on evaluating information obtained and identifying the risks that may result in material misstatement due to fraud
- The presumption that improper revenue recognition is a fraud risk for all entities. For employee benefit plans, this risk is primarily related to investment income resulting from inappropriate investment valuation. **Multiemployer plan considerations:** For multiemployer plans, the auditor should consider whether employers are motivated to understate the employer contributions due.
- Mandate of certain audit responses on every audit engagement. These responses are designed to specifically address the risk of management override over internal controls.
- Requirements for the auditor to take into account an evaluation of the entity's programs and controls that address the identified fraud risks

AU-C section 240 also provides guidance in fulfilling those responsibilities, as they relate to fraud, in an audit conducted in accordance with generally accepted auditing standards. The auditor's primary concern arises when fraudulent acts and errors result in a material misstatement of the financial statements. Fraud is differentiated from error according to whether the underlying act that caused the misstatement was intentional or unintentional. Two types of misstatements are relevant to the auditor's consideration of fraud in a 401(k) audit—*misstatements arising from fraudulent financial reporting* and *misstatements arising from misappropriation of assets.*

Following are examples of risk factors that relate to the two types of fraud relevant to the auditor's consideration—that is, fraudulent financial reporting and misappropriation of assets. Risk factors are further classified based on the three conditions generally present when fraud exists:

1. *Incentive* or *pressure* to perpetrate fraud
2. *Opportunity* to carry out the fraud
3. *Attitude* or *rationalization* to justify the fraudulent action

Although the risk factors cover a broad range of situations, they are only examples and, accordingly, the engagement team may wish to consider additional or different risk factors. Not all of these examples are relevant in all circumstances, and some may be of greater or lesser significance in entities of different size or with different ownership characteristics or circumstances. Also, the order of the examples of risk factors provided is not intended to reflect their relative importance or frequency of occurrence.

Suggested responses from the auditor are listed after the risk factors.

Fraudulent financial reporting

Fraudulent financial reporting may result from several practices: alteration of accounting records or supporting documents that are used to prepare financial statements; misrepresentation or intentional omission of significant information from the financial statements; or intentional misapplication of accounting principles relating to amounts, classification, manner of presentation, or disclosure.

Risk factors relating to misstatements arising from fraudulent financial reporting

Incentives or pressures

Financial stability or profitability of the plan is threatened by economic, industry, or entity operating conditions, such as (or as indicated by) the following:

- Significant declines in customer demand and increasing business failures exist in either the industry or the economy in which the entity operates.
- The plan sponsor is in an industry that is declining in stability, which could lead to difficulties in meeting financial commitments to the plan, including contributions or debt repayments, or both.
- The plan holds employer securities and the employer is in an industry in which the value of the securities is subject to significant volatility or is not readily determinable.
- Plan sponsor or plan restructuring (for example, layoffs, spin-offs, business combinations, and bankruptcy)
- Severely deteriorating financial condition or the threat of regulatory intervention of the plan
- The plan has limited investment options or has invested significantly in employer assets other than employer securities (for example, real estate).

Excessive pressure exists for management to meet the requirements or expectations of third parties due to the following:

- Senior management of the plan sponsor appoints itself trustee of the plan and uses that position to benefit the plan sponsor—for example, uses the plan's money to do speculative investing or to support the employer through buying employer assets or leasing assets at below market rates.

Opportunities

The nature of the industry or the plan's operations provides opportunities to engage in fraudulent financial reporting that can arise from the following:

- Significant related party transactions not in the ordinary course of business or with related plans not audited or audited by another firm
- Indications of significant or unusual party in interest transactions not in the ordinary course of operations
- Excessive or unusual transaction or prohibited party in interest transactions with the plan sponsor, plan management, or administrator

Internal control components are deficient as a result of the following:

- Inadequate monitoring of controls, including having automated controls and controls over interim financial reporting
- Failure by management to have adequate valuations performed, including actuarial valuations and valuations of real estate partnerships and other hard-to-value assets
- The plan administrator lacks an understanding of the major regulations that govern the plans (that is, Employee Retirement Income Security Act of 1974 [ERISA] and the IRC).
- Unusually high levels of participant complaints and corrections to account balances or plan records
- Lack of qualified service organization or change in service organization
- Unusually high levels of manual processes or inadequate review of plan transactions

Attitudes or rationalizations

We may not be able to observe risk factors reflective of attitudes or rationalizations by board members, management, or employees that allow them to engage in or justify fraudulent financial reporting. Nevertheless, if we become aware of the existence of such information, we should consider it in identifying the risks of material misstatement arising from fraudulent financial reporting.

We may become aware of the following matters that may indicate a risk factor:

- Management displaying a significant disregard for regulatory authorities.
- Management displays a significant disregard toward compliance with ERISA and IRC and DOL regulations.
- The plan administrator or trustees have been investigated by the DOL or IRS for fiduciary violations in operating the plan.
- Lack of management candor in dealing with plan participants, claimants, outside service organizations, actuaries, and auditors regarding decisions that could affect plan assets, including restructuring or downsizing arrangements
- The plan has participated in a voluntary compliance program in conjunction with the IRS or DOL (such participation could be an indication of ineffective management of the plan or controls over the plan).
- Named fiduciary not actively involved in the plan's activities
- High level of plan participant complaints
- Over-reliance on third party service organizations, lack of monitoring of third-party service organizations, and lack of review of outsourced plan operations

Auditor responses

In a 401(k) plan audit engagement, you may want to consider these responses to the aforementioned situations:

- Obtain the requisite investment information directly from the plan trustee, assets custodian, or insurance company, and obtain the same information from the party named as having discretion to make investment decisions—such as the plan administrator, the plan's investment committee, or the plan's investment advisor (the directing party). Review and reconcile the directing party's reports (investment position and activity) with those of the trustee, asset custodian, or insurance company.
- Apply the following procedures to understand fully a party in interest transaction:
  - Confirm transaction amount and terms, including guarantees and other significant data, with the other party or parties to the transaction.

- Inspect contracts and evidence in possession of the other party or parties to the transaction.
- Confirm or discuss significant information with intermediaries—such as banks, guarantors, agents, or attorneys, to obtain a better understanding of the transaction.
- Refer to financial publications, trade journals, credit agencies, and other information sources when there is reason to believe that unfamiliar customers, suppliers, or other business enterprises with which material amounts of business have been transacted may lack substance.
- With respect to material uncollected balances, guarantees, and other obligations, obtain information about the financial capability of the other party or parties to the transaction. Such information may be obtained from audited financial statements, unaudited financial statements, income tax returns, and reports issued by regulatory agencies, taxing authorities, financial publications, or credit agencies. You should decide on the degree of assurance required and the extent to which available information provides such assurance.
- For single-employer plans, obtain the most recent financial statements of the plan sponsor and review them for indicators of financial difficulties.
- **Multiemployer plan considerations:** For multiemployer plans, obtain an understanding of the industry sponsoring the plan.

Misappropriation of assets

Misstatements arising from misappropriation of assets involve the theft of an entity's assets where that theft causes the financial statements not to be presented in conformity with generally accepted accounting principles. This can occur through embezzlement of receipts, stealing assets, or improper payment of benefits or expenses.

Risk factors relating to misstatements arising from misappropriation of assets

Some of the risk factors related to misstatements arising from fraudulent financial reporting also may be present when misstatements arising from misappropriation of assets occur (for example, ineffective monitoring of management and weaknesses in internal control may be present when misstatements due to either fraudulent financial reporting or misappropriation of assets exists).

Incentives or pressures

Personal financial obligations may create pressure on management or employees with access to cash or other assets susceptible to theft to misappropriate those assets. (Access to assets, such as access to participant data communicated to the trustee, may be indirect.)

- Known personal financial pressures affecting employees with access to plan assets

Adverse relationships between the plan sponsor or plan administration and employees with access to cash or other assets susceptible to theft may motivate those employees to misappropriate those assets. For example, adverse relationships may be created by the following:

- Known or anticipated future employee layoffs
- Recent or anticipated changes to employee compensation or benefit plans
- Promotions, compensation, or other rewards inconsistent with expectations
- Individuals involved in plan administration known to be dissatisfied

Opportunities

Certain characteristics or circumstances may increase the susceptibility of assets to misappropriation. For example, opportunities to misappropriate assets increase when there are the following:

- A company sponsoring multiple defined benefit pension plans—some underfunded, some overfunded
- Lack of qualified outside service organization to serve as trustee or custodian of plan assets
- Non-readily marketable, specialized, or unique investments and management's lack of understanding of such investments (for example, nonregulated investments such as hedge funds and "alternative investments," derivative products, securities lending arrangements, junk bonds, real estate, securities traded in non-U.S. markets, limited partnerships, and real property)

Inadequate internal control over assets may increase the susceptibility of misappropriation of those assets. For example, misappropriation of assets may occur because there are any of the following:

- Lack of appropriate management oversight
- Lack of review of plan investment transactions including accounting for investment income (for example, by the trustee, sponsor, or the plan's investment committee)
- Lack of segregation of duties or independent checks
- Lack of independent preparation and review of reconciliations of trust assets to participant accounts or accounting records of the plan
- Lack of segregation of duties related to benefit payments, contributions, deferral changes, payment of administrative expenses, investment transactions, and loans or independent checks
- Plan administrator does not maintain independent records and periodically check information provided to the plan's trustee, asset custodian, or insurance company
- Lack of appropriate system of authorization and approval of transactions
- Lack of complete and timely reconciliations of assets
- Lack of approval of transactions with parties in interest that could lead to prohibited transactions
- Lack of timely and appropriate documentation for transactions (for example, plan amendments or returned checks)
- Trustee does not prepare required supplemental information (for example, historical cost records not maintained)
- Lack of controls over benefit payments, including the termination of payments in accordance with plan provisions
- Lack of appropriate segregation of plan assets from the sponsor's assets or inappropriate access to plan assets by plan sponsor
- SOC 1® report indicating a lack of adequate controls at an outside service organization
- Use of a service organization that does not provide a SOC 1® report
- Unreconciled differences between net assets available for benefits per the trustee, asset custodian, or insurance company records and the recorded participant accounts for a defined contribution plan (unallocated assets or liabilities)
- Inadequate management understanding of information technology, which enables information technology employees to perpetrate a misappropriation
- Inadequate access controls over automated records, including controls over and review of computer systems event logs

Attitudes or rationalizations

We may not be able to observe risk factors reflective of employee attitudes or rationalizations that allow employees to justify misappropriations of assets. Nevertheless, if we become aware of the existence of such information, we should consider it in identifying the risks of material misstatement arising from misappropriation of assets.

If we have observed the following attitudes or behavior of employees who have access to assets susceptible to misappropriation, then there may be increased risk:

- Disregard for the need for monitoring or reducing risks related to misappropriations of assets
- Disregard for internal control over misappropriation of assets by overriding existing controls or by failing to correct known internal control deficiencies
- Behavior indicating displeasure or dissatisfaction with the plan or plan sponsor or the plan sponsor's treatment of the employee
- Changes in behavior or lifestyle that may indicate assets have been misappropriated

Auditor responses

In a 401(k) plan engagement, you may want to consider the following responses:

- Review reconciliations of the assets held by the trust with participant records throughout the year. Review any reconciling adjustments for propriety.
- Review the account activity for participants who have access to plan assets and assist in administering the plan.
- Consider the possible risk of material misstatement where there is no qualified outside service organization acting as a trustee or custodian (or both) for plan assets. In these instances, you should physically inspect assets and examine other evidence relating to ownership. In addition, you should test the fair value of investments by reference to market quotations or other evidence of fair value in accordance with AU-C section 540, *Auditing Accounting Estimates* (AICPA, *Professional Standards*).
- Recognize that a risk of material misstatement exists with regard to unreconciled differences between net assets available for benefits per the trustee, custodian, or insurance company records and the recordkeeping amounts. If the totals according to the records of the trustee or custodian (or both) are higher than the recordkeeping totals, (excluding accrual adjustments), an unallocated asset exists that should be allocated to participant accounts. If the totals in records of the trustee or custodian (or both) are lower than the recordkeeping totals (excluding accrual totals in adjustments), plan assets may have been misappropriated, requiring further investigation by you (for example, reconciliation of monthly trustee or custodian activity to the recordkeeper).
- Consider that a risk of material misstatement may exist with regard to remittance of employee contributions for a defined contribution plan with a sponsor experiencing cash flow problems. In these instances, you may perform a reconciliation of total employee contributions per the payroll register to the recordkeeping report for the year. In addition, the auditor may select certain pay periods to test for the timely remittance of employee contributions in accordance with regulations.
- Review the timeliness of contributions from the plan sponsor throughout the year.
- Compare canceled checks to disbursement records. Where withdrawals are paid by check disbursements, compare the signature on the canceled check to participant signatures on other employee documents.
- Confirm withdrawals with participants or beneficiaries.
- Review plan expenses to verify that the plan is not paying for expenses that the employer should be paying for.

Knowledge check

5. All of the following conditions should heighten the auditor's concern for fraudulent financial reporting, except

   a. Plan sponsor is in a declining industry, with increasing business failures and large decreases in customer demand.
   b. A significant portion of the plan investments are invested in stock of the employer.
   c. Significant or unusual parties in interest transactions not in the ordinary course of plan operations.
   d. An outside bank or insurance company serves as trustee or custodian of the plan.

Plan's use of third-party service organizations

Many 401(k) plans use outside service organizations to perform certain administrative procedures for the operation of the plan. Some use a third-party administrator to perform recordkeeping functions or to review, process, and pay withdrawals for participants. In auditing such a plan, you should consider AT-C section 320, *Reporting on an Examination of Controls at a Service Organization Relevant to User Entities' Internal Control Over Financial Reporting* (AICPA, *Professional Standards,* AT-C sec. 320), provides guidance on factors that you should be familiar with when third-party service organizations perform significant operations.

AU-C section 402, *Audit Considerations Relating to an Entity Using a Service Organization* (AICPA, *Professional Standards*), provides guidance for the user auditors who audit a plan that uses a service organization to process transactions (for example, trustee of investments, recordkeeper of plan, or payroll processor). A SOC 1® report provides you with an understanding of the controls in effect at the service organization and may help you assess the risks of material misstatement and to design further audit procedures to respond to significant risks. The use of SOC 1® reports for transactions processed by outside service organizations will be covered again in chapter 3, "Internal Control Structure."

Party in interest transactions

Throughout the entire audit process, you should consider the possible existence of party in interest transactions. Plan fiduciaries are prohibited from causing a plan to engage in certain party in interest transactions due to the potential risk of abuse. Parties in interest for a 401(k) plan include, but are not limited to, the following:

- Fiduciaries or employees of the plan or plan sponsor
- Service organizations for the plan
- An employer whose employees are covered by the plan
- An employee organization (union) whose members are covered by the plan
- A person who owns 50 percent or more of the previously stated employer or employee organization
- Relatives of the aforementioned persons

Certain plan transactions with these parties in interest are considered to be prohibited transactions. As required under ERISA, any prohibited transaction, *regardless of materiality*, must be disclosed in the plan's annual report filed with the DOL. Here are examples of a transaction between a 401(k) plan and a party in interest that are usually considered prohibited:

- Direct or indirect sale, exchange, or lease of property
- Lending of money or other extension of credit (this includes sponsors failing to deposit monies withheld from participants pay checks [salary deferrals] on a timely basis as well as repayments of notes receivable from participants)
- Furnishing of goods, services, or facilities
- Transfer of plan assets to a party in interest for the use or benefit of a party in interest
- An acquisition of employer securities or real property in violation of the 10-percent limitation

Certain transactions with parties in interest do not result in prohibited or nonexempt transactions. Payments to parties in interest for reasonable compensation for services provided to the plan (such as legal, accounting, trustee) and payments for office space and other services necessary for the plan to operate are permitted. In addition, payments to beneficiaries are not considered prohibited transactions, if made in accordance with the policy set forth in the plan document and applied similarly to all participants and beneficiaries.

Prohibited transactions may affect both the plan financial statements and the party in interest involved in the transaction. A plan fiduciary is responsible for reimbursing the plan for any losses incurred resulting from breach of fiduciary responsibility and for reimbursing the plan for any profits that the fiduciary received through use of the plan's assets. It is possible that a plan receivable resulting from such a prohibited transaction could be significant. In accordance with FASB ASC 450, *Contingencies*, the potential effects on the plan of any contingencies resulting from the prohibited transaction may need to be disclosed in the plan's financial statements. In addition, an excise tax may be assessed against the party in interest involved in this transaction up to the full dollar value of the prohibited transaction. Also, the fiduciary must ordinarily reverse the transaction, compensate the plan for any losses incurred as a result of the prohibited transaction, and return any profits made as a result of using plan assets.

An audit conducted in accordance with generally accepted auditing standards is not designed, nor is it expected, to provide assurance that all party in interest transactions are identified. However, you should be aware that these transactions may exist and be aware of the requirement to disclose them if you discover them. That is, you are not responsible to search for party in interest transactions, only to report them if they are identified in connection with performing standard audit procedures.

Suggested audit procedures are described in chapter 6, "Other Auditing Considerations."

If you identify prohibited transactions during the course of the audit, you should challenge other aspects of the audit, especially the reliability of other representations made by management. The implications of particular prohibited transactions will depend on the relationship of those who engaged in the transactions (and their concealment, if any), to specific control procedures and the level of management or employees involved. You should consult plan counsel if you suspect or identify prohibited transactions.

The DOL's Rules and Regulations state that required supplemental schedules—including the schedule of nonexempt transactions—be submitted along with the basic financial statements in the annual report filed with the DOL. The DOL requires that all nonexempt party in interest transactions be disclosed in the supplementary schedules without regard to materiality. See chapter 7, "The Auditor's Report and Financial Statement Disclosures," for sample auditor reports.

Knowledge check

6. All of the following are considered to be parties in interest for a 401(k) plan, except

    a. An employee of the plan sponsor.
    b. The independent auditor for the 401(k) plan.
    c. A union whose members are covered by the plan.
    d. The father of an employee of a bank (the bank is the trustee of the plan assets).

Plan's use of voice response or internet recordkeeping system

Many 401(k) plans permit the participants to enroll in the plan, change their investment options, change their contribution percentage, obtain withdrawals or loans, or make other changes through the use of a voice response recordkeeping system or Internet-based system. Typically, the participant is notified that he or she may call a toll free phone number or log onto a website, enter in his or her preselected employee identification code number, and make the changes or requests desired. The service organization that receives these requests generally processes the change(s), sends the participant a confirmation letter that includes the updated information, then discards the information (or holds it for a short time). The use of voice response and Internet recordkeeping is a valuable, time-saving, and simple way for participants to modify their benefit options easily. However, the system presents some challenging obstacles to you in verifying the accuracy of the individual participant account balances.

In planning the audit, you should find out from the plan administrator whether the plan utilizes a voice response or Internet recordkeeping system. If it does, you should also determine if a paper trail is maintained of the changes requested by participants. (Will the records be available to you during the course of the audit?) If the paper trail is maintained, you can use this to check the accuracy of the individual account balances. You should request that the paper trail be maintained. If no trail is maintained, you will have to perform alternate procedures.

One such procedure that may be performed is for you to send a confirmation letter to the participants selected for testing. The letter should include a copy of the participant's account summary as of the end of the plan year detailing the balance in each investment account. If you work with the plan administrator to send out the confirmations soon after they are originally sent to the participants, there may be a higher response rate than if they are sent out several months after the plan year-end.

Chapter 3 contains more information on voice response and Internet recordkeeping systems as they relate to the internal control structure.

Accounting estimates

Certain areas of 401(k) plans, especially the fair value of non-readily marketable securities, require accounting estimates that may be material in the preparation of the plan's financial statements. AU-C section 540 provides guidance on obtaining and evaluating sufficient competent evidential matter to support significant accounting estimates. Although plan management is responsible for developing the estimates, you are responsible for evaluating the reasonableness of the estimates. This is accomplished by applying appropriate procedures and planning in performing the audit. You should consider both subjective and objective factors, such as whether appraisals are obtained, the age of the appraisals, and procedures used to estimate fair value, including application of a discount rate.

Going concern considerations

AU-C section 570A, *The Auditor's Consideration of an Entity's Ability to Continue as a Going Concern* (AICPA, *Professional Standards*), provides guidance to evaluate whether there is substantial doubt about the entity's ability to continue as a going concern. For financial reporting purposes, continuation of a plan as a going concern is assumed in the absence of significant evidence to the contrary. Evidence that would suggest doubt as to the entity's ability to continue as a going concern generally relates to its ability to continue to meet its obligations as they become due (for example, without an extraordinary contribution by the plan sponsor or substantial disposition of assets outside the ordinary course of business).

During the audit, you may become aware of information that raises doubt about the plan sponsor's ability to continue as a going concern. Employee benefit plans, particularly 401(k) plans, are not automatically and necessarily affected by the plan sponsor's financial difficulties. However, you should determine whether these difficulties pose any imminent danger to the plan itself and should consider the sponsor's plans for resolving the difficulty.

AU-C section 570A states that the auditor is responsible for evaluating whether there is substantial doubt about the plan's ability to continue as a going concern for a reasonable period of time. In August 2014, FASB issued ASU No. 2014-15, *Presentation of Financial Statements—Going Concern (Subtopic 205-40): Disclosure of Uncertainties about an Entity's Ability to Continue as a Going Concern*. The ASU requires an evaluation for a period of one year after the date that the financial statements are issued (or available to be issued). If substantial doubt exists, then disclosure should be made of the following in the footnotes:

- Pertinent conditions and events giving rise to the assessment of substantial doubt about the plan's ability to continue as a going concern for a reasonable period of time
- The possible effects of such conditions and events
- Plan management's evaluation of the significance of those conditions and events and any mitigating factors
- Possible termination of the plan
- Plan management's intentions to address the current financial situation
- Information about the recoverability or classification of recorded asset amounts or the amounts or classification of liabilities

A going-concern uncertainty explanatory paragraph is required regardless of your assessment of asset recoverability and amount and classification of liabilities. If you conclude that the disclosures are inadequate, then a departure from generally accepted accounting principles exists, which would result in you issuing a qualified opinion on the plan's financial statements.

Note that in the event that, as a result of going concern, the entity decides to terminate the plan, the liquidation basis of accounting may be necessary. See chapter 6 for more information on the liquidation basis of accounting for plans.

The AICPA Auditing Standards Board issued four auditing interpretations to address some of the effects related to FASB ASC 205-40. These auditing interpretations to AU-C section 570 address the following topics:

- The definition of *substantial doubt* about an entity's ability to continue as a going concern
- The definition of *reasonable period of time*
- Interim financial information
- Consideration of financial statement effects

See Interpretation Nos. 1–4 in AU-C section 9570A, *The Auditor's Consideration of an Entity's Ability to Continue as a Going Concern: Auditing Interpretations of Section 570A* (AICPA, *Professional Standards*), and www.aicpa.org to view these interpretations. (www.aicpa.org/Research/Standards/AuditAttest/Pages/RecentAAInterpretations.aspx.)

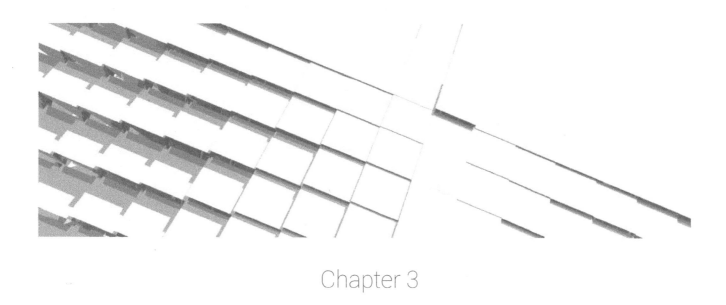

Chapter 3

Internal Control Structure

Learning objectives

After completing this chapter, you should be able to do the following:

- Identify the components of internal control.

- Identify the areas in which to focus on controls including the use of service organizations.

Introduction

AU-C section 315, *Understanding the Entity and Its Environment and Assessing the Risks of Material Misstatement* (AICPA, *Professional Standards*), addresses the auditor's responsibility to obtain a sufficient understanding of the entity and its environment, including its internal control, to assess the risks of material misstatement of the financial statements whether due to error or fraud; and to design the nature, timing, and extent of further audit procedures.

AU-C section 315 requires the auditor to obtain an understanding of the five components of internal control sufficient to assess the risks of material misstatement of the financial statements whether due to error or fraud, and to design the nature, timing, and extent of further audit procedures. This understanding may encompass controls placed in operation by the plan and by the service organization whose services are part of the plan's information system.

You should obtain a sufficient understanding by performing risk assessment procedures to

- evaluate the design of controls relevant to an audit of financial statements.
- determine whether they have been implemented.

This is not to be confused with AS 2201, *An Audit of Internal Control Over Financial Reporting That Is Integrated With An Audit of Financial Statements* (AICPA, *PCAOB Standards and Related Rules*). Form 11-K does not require a 302 certification and therefore, a Form 11-K does not require an opinion on internal controls.

In obtaining this understanding, consider how an entity's use of information technology (IT) and manual procedures may affect controls relevant to the audit. Use the understanding to do the following:

- Identify types of potential misstatements.
- Consider factors that affect the risks of material misstatement.
- Design tests of controls, when applicable, and substantive procedures.

In an employee benefit plan audit, you may decide to test whether

- the client's IT system is being properly utilized to determine participant data (for example, payroll and employee information) and pension and health benefit payments.
- a database system is being properly utilized to check for duplicate payments, improper utilization, and other payments made in the health care payment system.
- pension credits earned are being properly accounted for and utilized in calculating the payment of benefits.
- passwords are utilized by the plan and appropriate restrictions exist to prevent or detect fraud.
- the IT system is accurately allocating shared expenses between plans that share facilities and other expenses.

Obtaining an understanding of internal controls is distinct from testing the operating effectiveness of controls. The objective of obtaining an understanding of controls is to evaluate the design of controls and determine whether they have been implemented for the purpose of assessing the risks of material misstatement. In contrast, the objective of testing the operating effectiveness of controls is to determine whether the controls, as designed, prevent or detect and correct a material misstatement.

Paragraph .41 of AU-C section 315 defines internal control as "a process—effected by those charged with governance, management, and other personnel—designed to provide reasonable assurance about the achievement of the entity's objectives with regard to the reliability of financial reporting, effectiveness and efficiency of operations, and compliance with applicable laws and regulations." Internal control consists of five interrelated components:

- Control environment
- The entity's risk assessment process
- The information system, including the related business processes relevant to financial reporting and communication
- Control activities relevant to the audit
- Monitoring of controls

Knowledge check

1. Internal control consists of five interrelated components. Which of the following is NOT included in these five components?

    a. The control environment.
    b. Risk assessment.
    c. Information and communication systems.
    d. Control activities.
    e. Scope of the audit.

Understanding internal control

In obtaining an understanding of the control environment, you should obtain sufficient knowledge of the control environment to understand the attitudes, awareness, and actions of those charged with governance (for example, the plan administrator, the administrative committee or board of trustees, and others) concerning the plan's internal control and its importance in achieving reliable financial reporting. In this connection, you should consider management's philosophy and operating style, the plan's organizational structure, methods of assigning authority and responsibility, management's integrity and ethical values, management's commitment to competence, and other factors related to the control environment. This understanding would also include consideration of the plan administrator's and others' attitudes, awareness, and actions related to the Employee Retirement Income Security Act (ERISA) or other compliance matters (for example, ERISA's prohibited transaction rules) that might affect the plan's financial statements and schedules. The control environment is normally enhanced by the existence of an audit committee; however, many employee benefit plans do not have audit committees and, therefore, it is important for you to consider whether the plan's investment or administrative committee has been formally designated with responsibility for oversight of the financial reporting process.

Obtaining an understanding of the control environment applies to all audits of employee benefit plans regardless of the scope of the audit, the size of the plan being audited, or the control reliance strategy adopted. In other words, you should be obtaining an understanding of the internal control environment and documenting your understanding if you perform either a full-scope or ERISA limited-scope audit (except with respect to investments and investment income for an ERISA limited-scope audit). Typical areas of focus for the controls in a 401(k) plan include the following:

- Plan administration including participant enrollments, eligibility, and so on
- Investments and related income (for a full-scope audit only)
- Contributions
- Withdrawals
- Transfers
- Loans
- Rollover of employee contributions from one plan to another
- Employer matching contributions
- Forfeitures of employer-matching contributions
- Recordkeeping system
- Compliance with rules and regulations affecting the plan

According to AU-C section 315, internal control is a process—effected by those charged with governance, management, and other personnel—designed to provide reasonable assurance about the achievement of the entity's objectives with regard to reliability of financial reporting, effectiveness and efficiency of operations, and compliance with applicable laws and regulations. For an audit of a 401(k) plan, this would include ERISA, the IRC, and the Department of Labor's Rules and Regulations.

Knowledge check

2. If the plan administrator has engaged the auditor to perform an ERISA limited-scope audit with respect to investments, the auditor is not required to document which of the following internal controls?

    a. Internal controls as they relate to investments.
    b. Internal controls as they relate to contributions to the plan.
    c. Internal controls as they relate to financial reporting for the plan.
    d. Internal controls as they relate to benefit payments from the plan.

The components of internal control

Internal control consists of five distinct components that AU-C section 315 defines as follows:

- *Control environment* sets the tone of an organization influencing the control consciousness of its people—it is the foundation for all other components of internal control, providing discipline and structure.
- *The entity's risk assessment process* is the entity's identification and analysis of relevant risks to the achievement of its objectives, and forms a basis for determining how such risks should be managed.
- *The information system, including the related business processes relevant to financial reporting and communication,* is the identification, capture, and exchange of information in a form and time frame that enable people to carry out their responsibilities.
- *Control activities relevant to the audit* are the policies and procedures that help make sure that management directives are carried out.
- *Monitoring of controls* is the process that assesses the quality of internal control performance over time.

The five components of internal control apply to the audits of all 401(k) plans (except with respect to investments for an ERISA limited-scope audit). You should consider them in obtaining your understanding of a plan's internal control to enable you to plan the audit and to determine the controls in place by the plan and the extent to which the controls are operating as intended. You should use this knowledge to identify the types of potential misstatements, consider the factors that can affect the risk of material misstatement, and design the substantive tests for the audit. For additional information regarding the types of controls that may exist for employee benefit plans, refer to chapter 4 of the AICPA Audit and Accounting Guide *Employee Benefit Plans*.

Control environment

In obtaining an understanding of the plan's control environment, you learn about the attitude, awareness, and actions of plan management and those charged with governance concerning the significance of the control environment and its importance to the plan operations. Specifically, you should consider the effect on the control environment of various control environment factors: management's philosophy and operating style, the plan's organizational structure, plan management's integrity and ethical values, the participation by board of directors or trustees in the plan's operations, the assignment of authority and responsibility, plan management's commitment to competence, and other similar control environment factors.

The entity's risk assessment process

The plan's risk assessment for financial reporting purposes is its identification, analysis, and management of risks relevant to the preparation of financial statements. The financial statements must be fairly presented in conformity with generally accepted accounting principles and in accordance with the DOL's rules and regulations for reporting and disclosure. The risks relevant to financial reporting include both internal and external factors that may adversely affect the plan's ability to record, process, summarize, and report financial data. You should obtain sufficient knowledge about the plan's risk assessment process to understand how management considers risks relevant to financial reporting and how it addresses such risks.

Control activities relevant to the audit

Control activities are the policies and procedures that make sure that plan management directives are followed. The control activities that may be relevant to an audit of a 401(k) plan might be those governing information processing, physical controls over assets, and segregation of duties. You should obtain an understanding of the specific control activities relevant to planning the audit. However, this does not require you to understand the control activities related to each account balance, transaction class, and footnote disclosure in the plan's financial statements.

The information system, including the related business processes relevant to financial reporting and communication

The information system consists of the methods established to record, process, summarize, and report plan transactions and to maintain accountability for the plan's net assets. Communication involves providing an understanding of individual roles and responsibilities pertaining to internal control over financial reporting. Specifically, you should obtain sufficient knowledge about the plan's information system to understand the following:

- The classes of transactions that are significant to the plan's operations and to the plan's financial statements.
- The accounting records, supporting information, and specific accounts in the plan's financial statements involved in the processing and reporting of transactions.
- How the plan's information system captures other events and conditions that are significant to the financial statements.
- The processing of accounting information involved from the initiation of a transaction (for example, enrollment of a plan participant, payment of distributions, and the like) to its recording in the plan's financial statements (including the plan's use of computers).
- The financial reporting process used to prepare the plan's financial statements, including significant accounting estimates (such as for determining the fair value of investment contracts in accordance with FASB ASC 962, *Plan Accounting—Defined Contribution Pension Plans*) and disclosures.

Monitoring of controls

Finally, the last component of a plan's control environment is monitoring—the process that assesses the quality of internal control performance over time. Essentially, it involves gauging the effectiveness and efficiency of controls in place and taking the corrective action necessary to correct deficiencies in the internal control structure. In examining this aspect of the plan's control environment, you should obtain sufficient knowledge of the major types of resources employed by plan management to monitor internal control over the plan's financial reporting and operations. In the cases of entities with large and complex 401(k) plans, the plan sponsors often use their internal audit function to monitor the effectiveness of controls in place over the plan's operations. You may be able to enhance the efficiency of your audits by reviewing the results of audits performed by internal audit departments. See AU-C section 610, *The Auditor's Consideration of the Internal Audit Function in an Audit of Financial Statements* (AICPA, *Professional Standards*), for additional guidance in this area and for a discussion of your responsibilities when relying on the work of internal auditors.

Acquiring knowledge of the controls

As indicated previously, you are required to obtain and document an understanding of the plan's internal control structure regardless of the type of audit performed. The nature and extent of the audit work to be performed in this area will vary according to the size and complexity of the plan. In obtaining an understanding of the controls relevant to the planning phase of the audit engagement, you should perform procedures sufficient to demonstrate knowledge of the design of the controls relating to each of the five internal control components. In most circumstances, you acquire this knowledge through (1) discussions with plan management, including the plan administrator and the individuals responsible for the day-to-day plan administration; (2) inspection of plan documents, evidence of transactions (for example, enrollment forms, investment election forms, loan requests, and so on); and (3) observation of the plan's activities. Also, you should consider the extent of services provided by the third parties.

An auditor often audits the plan sponsor in addition to the sponsor's employee benefit plans—generally, the plan sponsor is audited several months before the plan audits. In such case, you may be able to maximize the efficiency of your 401(k) audit by relying on the testing or documentation (or both) of controls over the sponsor's payroll system performed as part of the audit of the plan sponsor when performing procedures in the internal control area for the plan. In many cases, in the audit of a 401(k) plan, the plan sponsor's payroll system is an integral system with respect to the plan because the employee contributions to the plan are calculated by the payroll system. In these situations, you may need to modify the testing performed of the payroll system for purposes of the sponsor audit to include certain attributes relevant to the plan—such as deductions for employee contributions, repayment of loans, and eligibility.

Knowledge check

3. The tests of controls that you may perform include all of the following, except for

    a. Inquiries of plan management.
    b. Examination of supporting records and documents.
    c. Observation of the processing of transactions.
    d. Confirmation of investments held with the recordkeeper.

Assessing control risk

After obtaining the understanding of the internal control structure, you assess control risk—the risk that a material misstatement of the plan's financial statements would not be prevented or detected on a timely basis by the plan's internal control. You should assess control risk in terms of the five financial statement assertions: existence or occurrence, completeness, rights and obligations, valuation or allocation, and presentation and disclosure. You may assess control risk at the maximum level (the greatest probability that a material misstatement would not be prevented or detected on a timely basis by an entity's internal control) because you believe that controls are unlikely to pertain to an assertion, or are likely to be ineffective or because evaluating their effectiveness would not be efficient in performing the audit. Alternatively, you could assess control risk at a lower level, depending on the degree of evidential matter obtained about the effectiveness of the design and operation of controls. You may obtain the evidential matter from tests of controls performed in connection with the procedures you performed to understand the plan's internal control structure. The tests of controls that you may perform include inquiries of plan management and personnel involved with plan administration, examination of supporting records and documents, and observation of the processing of transactions.

Plan's use of third-party service organizations

The requirement to obtain an understanding of the internal control environment extends not only to the plan sponsor's control environment, but often to the control environment in place at the various third parties. These include trustees or custodians (or both) and recordkeepers who provide services to the plan. In most plans, the plan administrators have contracted with third parties to perform various services to the plan. Among such services are investing plan assets; processing all recordkeeping transactions for the plan, which can include enrolling eligible participants in the plan; recording contributions, plan transfers, loans, and withdrawals; and allocating income to the individual participant accounts. Often, third parties are also responsible for performing the plan's required anti-discrimination tests and preparing required DOL filings. The extent to which you should consider the internal control components under the direction of a third-party service organization depends on the level of services provided by the third party, and for trustees or custodians of plan assets, the degree of discretionary authority that the trustee or custodian has over plan assets.

A service organization's services are part of a plan's information system if they affect any of the following:

- The classes of transactions in the plan's operations that are significant to the plan's financial statements.
- The procedures (both manual and automated) by which the plan's transactions are initiated, authorized, recorded, processed, and reported from their occurrence to their inclusion in the financial statements.
- The related accounting records (whether electronic or manual) supporting information, and specific accounts in the plan's financial statements involved in initiating, authorizing, recording, processing, and reporting the plan's transactions.
- How the plan's information system captures other events and conditions that are significant to the financial statements.
- The financial reporting process used to prepare the plan's financial statement's including significant accounting estimates and disclosures.
- Controls surrounding journal entries—including nonstandard journal entries used to record nonrecurring, unusual transactions, or adjustments, whether they reside with the plan or the recordkeeper, or both.

Service auditor reports

In addition to the previously mentioned details, you should consider other available information about the service organization's policies and procedures usually disclosed in a service auditor report. The service auditor report may be obtained from either the plan sponsor or directly from the third-party service organization. AU-C section 402, *Audit Considerations Relating to an Entity Using a Service Organization* (AICPA, *Professional Standards*), provides guidance relating to a user auditor's responsibility for obtaining sufficient appropriate audit evidence in an audit of the financial statements of a user entity that uses one or more service organizations. AT-C section 320, *Reporting on an Examination of Controls at a Service Organization Relevant to User Entities' Internal Control Over Financial Reporting* (AICPA, *Professional Standards*), contains performance and reporting requirements and application guidance for a service auditor examining controls at organizations that provide services to user entities when those controls are likely to be relevant to user entities' internal control over financial reporting (for example, bank trust departments, plan recordkeepers, and payroll processing service organizations). Reports issued under AT-C section 320 will hereinafter be referred to as SOC 1® reports.

Two types of SOC 1® reports may be issued by a service auditor:

- A *type 1 SOC 1® report* is a report on the fairness of the presentation of management's description of the service organization's system and the suitability of the design of the controls to achieve the related control objectives included in the description as of a specified date. Type 1 SOC 1® reports are designed to provide information about the flow of transactions within, and controls over, relevant applications at the service organization and whether such controls were suitably designed and had been placed in operation. Such a report, either alone or in conjunction with controls at the user entity, does not provide any evidence of the operating effectiveness of the relevant controls.
- A *type 2 SOC 1® report* is a report that also includes the service auditor's opinion on the operating effectiveness of the controls and a detailed description of the service auditor's tests of the operating effectiveness of the controls and the results of those tests throughout a specified period. Type 2 SOC 1® reports provide additional information about the nature, timing, extent, and results of the service auditor's tests of specified controls at the service organization that may be useful if the user auditor intends to place reliance on controls at the service organization to reduce the extent of his or her substantive procedures.

Although a type 2 report may be used to reduce substantive procedures, neither a type 1 nor a type 2 report is designed to provide a basis for assessing control risk sufficiently low to eliminate the need for performing any substantive tests for all of the assertions relevant to significant account balances or transaction classes.

As service auditor reports are prepared to satisfy multiple users, you should decide whether the specific tests of controls and results in the service auditor's report are relevant to assertions significant to the plan's financial statements. In addition, you should determine that the tests of controls included as part of the service auditor report represent the relevant controls that will support your assessed level of control risk for the plan audit. For example, in certain cases the plan may utilize a third party to serve as both trustee of plan assets and recordkeeper for the plan's individual account records. In this case, you should verify that the service auditor report covers all services that the third party is providing to the plan.

In this process, you should consider the professional reputation of the service auditor to determine that the service auditor is adequately qualified to prepare the service auditor report.

The AICPA EBP Audit Quality Center provides a tool for auditors. This nonauthoritative tool, "Documentation of Use of a Type 2 Service Auditor's Report in an Audit of an Employee Benefit Plan's Financial Statements," is intended to assist auditors in auditing the financial statements of employee benefit plans that use one or more service organizations (user auditors). It is designed to assist user auditors in documenting their procedures and findings related to controls at a service organization that are likely to be relevant to the employee benefit plan's internal control over financial reporting.

ERISA limited-scope audits

For an ERISA limited-scope audit, you have no responsibility to obtain an understanding of the controls maintained by the certifying institution over assets held and investment transactions executed by the institution. Therefore, in an ERISA limited-scope engagement, to the extent that the service organization is providing only investment transaction services, no SOC 1® report is required. However, if the service organization is also providing services such as the processing of participant-level transactions, a SOC 1® report may be obtained, if it is available and covers these activities.

User controls

A service provided by a service organization may be designed with the assumption that certain controls will be implemented by the user organization (the plan). For example, the service may be designed with the assumption that the plan administrator has controls in place that provide reasonable assurance that employees are eligible, authorized, and valid participants before submitting employee application forms to the recordkeeper or enrolling employees through online access.

Typically, a SOC 1® report will have a section describing the assumed user controls that are in place at the plan sponsor. You should read and determine whether the complementary user controls are required and whether they are relevant to the service provided to the plan. If they are relevant to the plan, you should consider such information in assessing the risks of material misstatement and test the relevant user controls if relying on controls.

Different service auditor reports on different operations

In some cases, the larger service organizations commonly engage their auditors to issue multiple service auditor reports to cover different parts of their operations. In these situations, you should obtain the various service auditor reports (for example, trust investment services, recordkeeping services, and so on) covering the services provided to the plan by the third-party organization. Similarly, a plan may hold investments of the less traditional type such as real estate or non-readily marketable securities. In these cases, you should determine that the service auditor report for the trustee or custodian of plan assets includes a description and test of controls related to how those types of investments are valued. Generally, if a type 2 report is available, you will most likely not need to visit the third-party administrator to document and test controls because the required information should be in the service auditor report. Your use of a type 2 service auditor report can add to the efficiency of the audit process.

Importance of period covered by service auditor report

In any case, whether a type 1 or type 2 report is available, it should cover at least 6 months of the plan's year in order for you to use it in documenting your understanding of the controls in place at the service organization. To the extent that you obtain a service auditor report for a third-party organization covering a period of less than 12 months of the plan's year (but more than 6 months), you may still utilize the service auditor report. However, you should perform additional procedures to determine if there have been significant changes in the organization's internal controls (both in design and operation) during the period of the plan's year under audit to which the service auditor report does not extend.

For example, if a service auditor report on a trustee covers only the first six months of the plan's year, you should perform procedures to determine if there have been any significant changes in the internal control of the trustee during the last six months of the plan year that could affect your assessment of the plan's overall control environment and the design of substantive tests for the audit of the plan. Additional procedures that you may consider include making inquiries of plan management or the third-party organization (or both), visiting the third-party organization to perform tests of controls, or reviewing the results of any reviews performed by the third party's internal auditors.

Effect of exceptions

It is not uncommon for a type 2 SOC 1® report to have exceptions in tests of operating effectiveness. Those exceptions may result in a qualification of the report. It is important to consider the following when a SOC 1® report contains exceptions to determine if an expansion of the scope of detailed testing is necessary.

In such circumstances, you should consider the effect of such exceptions on the assertions, which is significant to the plan's financial statements, and to determine if the exceptions may prevent you from assessing control risk below the maximum or may otherwise affect the plan audit. In these circumstances, you may be able to identify mitigating controls at the plan sponsor level related to the exceptions, which you should consider in planning the audit. You should bring exceptions identified at the service organization to the attention of plan management so that management is aware of such matters in assessing any effect on the plan or the plan sponsor's relationship with the service organization. Finally, many service auditor reports will describe some types of controls that should be in place at the plan sponsor level and that will contribute to the complete and accurate processing of plan transactions. You should consider the effect on the risk assessment and audit plan of suggested controls that are not in place at the plan sponsor.

Unavailability of service auditor report

In certain situations, a service auditor report may not be available if the service organization did not engage auditors to issue such a report on its internal controls. Service auditor reports are generally available for most banks, insurance companies, and trust entities. However, many recordkeepers still do not engage their auditors to conduct AT-C section 320 reviews for them, particularly since having a service auditor report prepared is not mandatory. In these cases, you are still required to document your understanding of the control environment at the service organization. You may accomplish this through information that the plan sponsor may have regarding such controls at the service organization or through directly contacting the service organization or its auditor. To the extent you cannot obtain sufficient information about the controls at the service organization to sufficiently plan the audit, you should qualify your audit opinion or disclaim an opinion on the plan's financial statements because of a scope limitation.

Knowledge check

4. Which of the following can a type 1 SOC 1® report provide an auditor?

    a. An opinion on the effectiveness of user controls at the plan sponsor.
    b. Information and results so the auditor can eliminate testing.
    c. An opinion on the effectiveness of controls.
    d. A description of the controls at the service organization.

5. All of the following are considerations in using a service auditor's report (SOC 1® report) to understand controls at the service organization, except for

    a. Does the SOC 1® report cover the entity the plan is utilizing?
    b. Is the SOC 1® report a type 1 or type 2 report?
    c. Are there any exceptions to any controls?
    d. Is the service auditor's report obtained directly from the service auditor?

Plan's use of voice response and internet-based recordkeeping systems

It is a prevalent practice for 401(k) plans to use recordkeepers that prepare daily valuations of individual account records by means of voice-activated response or Internet-based systems to process participant-initiated transactions. In these cases, neither the plan sponsor nor the recordkeeper retain paper copies of those transactions. For example, in many cases, the plan sponsors no longer have records of transactions initiated by participants to transfer funds from one investment option to another—whereas in the past, the participants would have been required to complete paper forms to serve as supporting documentation. In addition, the IRS has stated that signatures on loan requests are no longer required from participants. Instead, participants may be able to call the recordkeeper or log onto the website to initiate a loan just as they can call to initiate transfers of funds between the various investment options.

In these cases, you will probably be unable to obtain a sufficient understanding of the control environment at the service organization without either obtaining a service auditor report or visiting the service organization to perform tests of controls or substantive testing procedures (or both). Moreover, the absence of a "paper trail" for the participant-initiated transactions will require alternative procedures for testing transactions such as confirming specific distributions (loans or enrollment information) directly with the participant. You might consider requiring copies of the files that record the participant-directed transactions. However, this may often require giving advance notice to the service organization, as the files are normally maintained only for a short period of time.

Documentation

As already noted, you are required to document your understanding of internal control and the assessment of control risk. You should document the key elements of the understanding of the five components of the plan's internal control obtained to assess the risks of material misstatement; the sources of information from which the understanding was obtained; and the risk assessment procedures. In addition, you should document the assessment of the risks of material misstatement both at the financial statement level and at the relevant assertion level. For financial statement assertions for which control risk is at the maximum level, you should also document the basis for the conclusion reached that the effectiveness of the design and operation of controls supports that assessed level. The nature and extent of your documentation depends on the nature and complexity of the plan's control environment, the extent to which the plan utilizes service organizations and other factors. You should also document any exceptions noted in internal control testing, if applicable, including exceptions identified within service auditor reports and the disposition of those exceptions. Your documentation does not have to be in any prescribed format, but may include flow charts; narratives; programs; and so on.

> **Help desk:**
>
> You should be aware that throughout the peer review process, there have been recurring Matters for Further Considerations (MFCs) that have been identified related to understanding the entity and its environment and assessing risks of material misstatement, as well as performing audit procedures in response to assessed risks. Some of these include the following:
>
> - No risk assessment was performed at the assertion level.
> - Working papers lacked documentation that supported assessing inherent risk at less than high.
> - Insufficient or no consideration of internal control during the risk assessment process.
> - Failure to identify the risk associate with IT.
> - Control risk was assessed at less than high without appropriate tests of controls.
> - Procedures performed were not responsive to the assessed levels of risk.
> - The link between procedures performed and the assessed level of risk was not readily determinable.
>
> It should be noted that even when a small client has unsophisticated IT systems, an assessment of IT risk is still required. Also, it is important for the auditor to understand the steps that are necessary in order to justify a reduction of control and inherent risk below high. In addition, a connection between the assessed level of risk and the substantive procedures performed should be made.

Communicating control deficiencies

AU-C section 265, *Communicating Internal Control Related Matters Identified in an Audit* (AICPA, *Professional Standards*), provides guidance on communicating matters related to internal control over financial reporting identified in an audit of financial statements and communicating, in writing, to management and those charged with governance significant deficiencies and material weaknesses identified in an audit. The plan auditor should evaluate the severity of internal control deficiencies identified during the audit to determine whether those deficiencies, individually or in combination, are significant deficiencies or material weaknesses. A deficiency in internal control exists when the design or operation of a control does not allow management or employees, in the normal course of performing their assigned functions, to prevent or detect misstatements on a timely basis. A material weakness is a deficiency (or combination of deficiencies) in internal control, such that there is a reasonable possibility that a material misstatement of financial statements will not be prevented or detected and corrected on a timely basis. A significant deficiency is a deficiency, or a combination of deficiencies, in internal control that is less severe than a material weakness, yet important enough to merit attention by those charged with governance.

Deficiencies identified during the audit that upon evaluation are considered significant deficiencies or material weaknesses should be communicated, in writing, to management and those charged with governance as part of each audit, including significant deficiencies and material weaknesses that were communicated to management and those charged with governance in previous audits, and have not yet been remediated. This written communication is best made by the report release date, which is the date the auditor grants the plan permission to use the auditor's report in connection with the financial statements, but should be no later than 60 days following the report release date.

If the plan auditor, as a result of the assessment of the risks of material misstatement, has identified risks of material misstatement due to fraud that have continuing internal control implications (whether or not transactions or adjustments that could be the result of fraud have been detected), the plan auditor should consider whether these risks represent significant deficiencies or material weaknesses relating to the entity's internal control that should be communicated to management and those charged with governance. The plan auditor also should consider whether the absence of deficiencies in programs and internal controls to mitigate specific risks of fraud or to otherwise help prevent, deter, and detect fraud represent significant deficiencies or material weaknesses that should be communicated to management and those charged with governance.

When reading a type 1 or type 2 SOC 1® report, the plan auditor may become aware of situations at the service organization that constitute significant deficiencies or material weaknesses for the user entity. Such situations may relate to the design or the operating effectiveness of the service organization's controls and it is important such deficiencies or material weaknesses be communicated to management and those charged with governance, as appropriate.

For a single-employer plan that does not have an audit committee, the individual with the level of authority and responsibility equivalent to an audit committee would normally be the named fiduciary, which is often the plan sponsor, an officer thereof, or the sponsor's board of directors. **Multiemployer plan**

considerations: For a multiemployer plan, authority and responsibility equivalent to that of an audit committee would ordinarily rest with the board of trustees.

The term *those charged with governance* is defined in AU-C section 230, *Audit Documentation* (AICPA, *Professional Standards*), as "the person(s) with responsibility for overseeing the strategic direction of the entity and obligations related to the accountability of the entity. This includes overseeing the financial reporting and disclosure process." This would generally include the plan's audit committee, the plan administrator, or other responsible party that would have the authority of an audit committee, for example, the investment committee or the board of directors. **Multiemployer plan considerations:** Multiemployers are beginning to sponsor more 401(k) plans; therefore, if you identify significant deficiencies and material weaknesses for a multiemployer-sponsored 401(k) plan, you should communicate them to the board of trustees. This is true whether the auditor is performing a full- or ERISA limited-scope audit.

Knowledge check

6. Deficiencies identified during the audit that upon evaluation are considered significant deficiencies or material weaknesses should be communicated, in writing, to management and those charged with governance as part of each audit, including significant deficiencies and material weaknesses that were communicated to management and those charged with governance in previous audits, and have not yet been remediated. This written communication is best made by the report release date, which is the date the auditor grants the plan permission to use the auditor's report in connection with the financial statements, but should be no later than 60 days following which date?

    a. Date the deficiencies were detected.
    b. Date the deficiencies were assessed.
    c. Plan year-end date.
    d. Report release date.

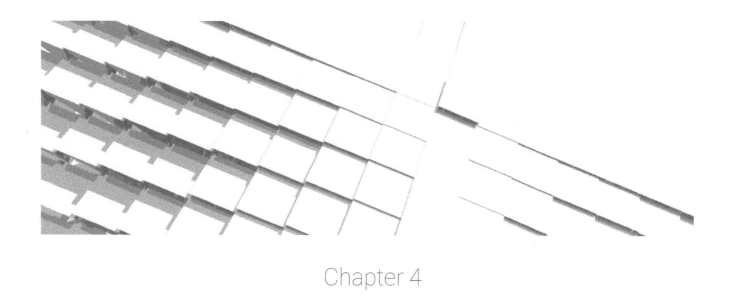

Chapter 4

Auditing the Statement of Net Assets Available for Benefits

Learning objectives

After completing this chapter, you should be able to do the following:

- Recognize the requirements of FASB ASC 820, *Fair Value Measurement*.

- Recognize the line items of the Statement of Net Assets Available for Benefits.

- Identify audit procedures and presentation requirements for plan investments and other plan assets.

- Recognize the requirements of FASB ASC 962-325.

Introduction

The Statement of Net Assets Available for Benefits details the assets and liabilities of the 401(k) plan. It is comparable to the balance sheet of most other entities' financial statements in that it presents the net assets available for benefits (assets minus liabilities) at a particular point in time (plan year-end). The net assets provide a basis to determine the plan's future ability to pay benefits when they are due. The statement of net assets available for benefits should be prepared using the accrual basis of accounting in order to be in compliance with accounting principles generally accepted in the United States of America. However, financial statements prepared on a special reporting framework are acceptable to the

DOL for purposes of Form 5500 filing. See chapter 7, "The Auditor's Report and Financial Statement Disclosures," for additional information.

Defined contribution plans provide benefits to participants based on the amounts contributed to or deducted from their individual accounts by the participants, contributions by the plan sponsor, forfeitures, investment earnings or losses, withdrawals, loans, and administrative expenses. Because the amount of benefit that a participant ultimately receives is directly related to the performance of the investment options selected by the participant, participants have a direct interest in understanding and monitoring the performance of their investments. The participants bear entirely the ultimate risk of how much is available to them at the time of their retirement.

Accounting guidance

FASB ASC 820 was issued in September 2006 and updated several times. It defines fair value, establishes a framework for measuring fair value, and expands disclosures about fair value measurements.

New Accounting Standards

> This course has been updated to include the following FASB Accounting Standards Update (ASU) whose provisions are not yet effective. The preparers of this course believe that many plans will want to adopt this new ASU early and therefore the provisions of this ASU have been reflected in the body of this course guide.

For those who are not early adopting this ASU, the AICPA is continuing to offer the 2018 edition of the AICPA Audit & Accounting Guide *Employee Benefit Plans* as a resource for requirements prior to the effective date of this ASU.

ASU No. 2017-06—In February 2017, FASB issued ASU No. 2017-06, *Plan Accounting: Defined Benefit Pension Plans (Topic 960), Defined Contribution Pension Plans (Topic 962), Health and Welfare Benefit Plans (Topic 965): Employee Benefit Plan Master Trust Reporting.*

The ASU relates primarily to the reporting by a plan for its interest in a master trust. The amendments clarify presentation requirements for a plan's interest in a master trust and require more detailed disclosures of the plan's interest in the master trust. The amendments also eliminate a redundancy relating to 401(h) account disclosures.

The amendments in FASB ASU 2017-06 are effective for fiscal years beginning after December 15, 2018, and early adoption is permitted. An entity should apply the amendments retrospectively to each period for which financial statements are presented.

This course has not been updated to include the following FASB ASU whose provisions are not yet effective.

> In August 2018, FASB issued ASU No. 2018-13, *Fair Value Measurement (Topic 820): Disclosure Framework—Changes to the Disclosure Requirements for Fair Value Measurement*, to modify the disclosure requirements on fair value measurements in FASB ASC 820, *Fair Value Measurement*. FASB ASU No. 2018-13 contains amendments that remove, modify or add disclosure requirements including those relating to transfers between levels of the fair value hierarchy, level 3 fair value measurements, and entities that calculate net asset value.
>
> The amendments in FASB ASU No. 2018-13 are effective for all entities for fiscal years beginning after December 15, 2019. Early adoption is permitted. Readers are encouraged to consult the full text of this ASU on FASB's website at www.fasb.org.

Listing of investments

Participant-directed investments may be listed on one line on the statement of net assets available for benefits. Original cost of investments is not required to be disclosed in the statement of net assets available for benefits, but may be required on the Schedule of Assets (Held at Year-End) for nonparticipant-directed investments.

Note that the agreements relating to investment accounts owned by plans can have various terms and provisions making it difficult to determine the nature of the entity. FASB ASC 946, *Financial Services— Investment Companies*, can provide helpful information in determining whether the plan holds (*a*) a "fund" or investment company which would be reported as a "fund" on the plan's financial statements or (*b*) an account with investments that are owned by the plan reported as individual investments on the plan's financial statements

As permitted by FASB ASC 962-325:

- If a 401(k) plan provides for participant-directed and nonparticipant-directed investment funds, the plan should disclose information in the financial statements or footnotes about the net assets and significant components of the changes in net assets related to the nonparticipant-directed investment funds.
- Participant-directed investments may be shown in the aggregate, as one-line item, in the statement of net assets available for benefits.
- The nonparticipant-directed investments should be presented in either the financial statements or footnotes by general type—such as mutual funds, government securities, or short-term securities.

Valuation of investments

The majority of investments in a 401(k) plan will be valued at fair value, that is, the amount that would be expected to be received in a current sale between a willing buyer and a willing seller. FASB ASC 820 defines the exchange price as the price in an orderly transaction between market participants to sell the asset or transfer the liability in the market in which the reporting entity would transact for the asset or liability, that is, the principal or most advantageous market for the asset or liability. The transaction to sell the asset or transfer the liability is a hypothetical transaction at the measurement date, considered from the perspective of a market participant that holds the asset or owes the liability. Therefore, the definition focuses on the price that would be received to sell the asset or paid to transfer the liability (an exit price), not the price that would be paid to acquire the asset or received to assume the liability (an entry price). According to FASB ASC 962-325-35-1, plan investments should generally be presented at their fair value at the reporting date. FASB ASC 962-325-35-1A states that if significant, the fair value of an investment should be reduced by brokerage commissions and other costs normally incurred in a sale (similar to fair value less cost to sell).

Certain contracts from insurance companies are presented at contract value. The term *investment contract* refers to (*a*) a traditional or separate account GIC contract, (*b*) a Bank Investment contract (BIC), (*c*) a synthetic GIC contract composed of a wrapper contract and the underlying wrapped portfolio of individual investments, or (*d*) a contract with similar characteristics. See the section titled "Investments with Insurance Companies" for further discussion on this topic.

Investment options

Many 401(k) plans offer a wide range of investment options. Some of these investments include marketable securities such as short-term investments, common or preferred stock, bonds and notes. Other types of investments include units of participation in a master trust, mortgages, real estate, leases, common or commingled trust funds maintained by a bank, trust company, or other financial institution; separate accounts maintained by an insurance company; and derivative investments. Because of the wide variety of investment options, your responsibility in understanding the different investment options available under a plan and determining an appropriate audit approach to test the investments may require significant planning.

Some of the most common types of investments that may be available to participants are described in the text that follows. More detailed descriptions are provided later in this chapter along with suggested audit procedures.

Units participation in a master trust

A master trust is a single trust that combines some or all of the assets of the employee benefit plans offered by one employer (or a group of corporations under common control). It is used when the assets of more than one related plan are pooled together for investment purposes. A unit of participation is an undivided interest in the assets of the master trust. See chapter 7 for reporting considerations.

Mutual funds

Maintained by registered investment companies, a mutual fund is a fund that receives monies from multiple employers, groups of corporations under common control, or individual investors. Monies are invested in specific investment vehicles often related to specific investment objectives (for example, high growth through investments in international equity funds). Earnings or appreciation in value for a 401(k) plan are reinvested back into the mutual fund.

Common or commingled trust funds

A common or commingled trust fund, maintained by a bank, trust company, or other financial institution, is a trust that receives monies from multiple employers or group of corporations under common control. Monies are invested in specified investment vehicles often related to specific investment objectives. Earnings or appreciation in value are reinvested back into the common or commingled trust fund.

Pooled separate accounts

A pooled separate account, maintained by an insurance company, is a pooled account established by an insurance company for the purpose of investing assets of one or more employee benefit plans of one or more sponsors. Monies invested in a pooled separate account are not commingled with other pooled separate accounts or with the general assets of the insurance company. Monies are invested in specified investment vehicles often related to specific investment objectives.

Self-directed accounts

In addition to specific investment vehicles previously described, participants also may have a self-directed account in which they may direct purchases of individual stocks and bonds, investments in real estate, limited partnerships, or other investment vehicles.

A self-directed account is one that allows participants to invest their account balances in any investment desired, sometimes with limitations that may be specified by the plan document. Under this type of account, a participant may authorize a purchase of an investment other than the common or commingled trust, pooled separate account, and so on, offered by the plan. The self-directed account is not a pooled investment; rather it is an account made up of all the individual investments owned by the plan that the participants have authorized to be purchased for them. Since the 2001 plan years, the DOL, through Form 5500 instructions, has allowed employee benefit plans to report investments made through participant-directed brokerage accounts as a single line item (other assets) on the Schedule H of Form 5500 rather than by type of asset on the appropriate line item for the asset category in parts I and II of Schedule H (for example, common stocks and mutual funds), provided the assets are not

- partnerships or joint-venture interests.
- real property.
- employer securities.
- investments that could result in a loss in excess of the account balance of the participant or beneficiary who directed the transaction.

Presently, this alternative reporting feature has not been made permanent. You should refer to Form 5500 instructions for the year you are auditing.

Knowledge check

1. A master trust

   a. Is a single trust that combines all of the employee benefit plans offered by one employer.
   b. Is a single trust that combines some or all of the employee benefit plans offered by one employer.
   c. Is a single trust that combines all of the employee benefit plans offered by two or more unrelated employers.
   d. Is a single trust that combines some or all of the employee benefit plans offered by two or more unrelated employers.

2. All of the following are correct regarding pooled separate accounts, except which?

   a. A pooled separate account is one in which only one plan participates.
   b. A pooled separate account is one in which two or more unrelated plans may participate.
   c. A pooled separate account's assets are combined with the general assets of the sponsoring insurance company.
   d. Because a pooled separate account is an unallocated contract, it should be recorded on the plan's financial statements as an investment.

Audit objectives

The audit objectives in auditing plan investments should enable you to determine whether the following are occurring:

- The investment transactions that are recorded are valid and are initiated in accordance with the established investment policies.
- Investments that are listed at year-end exist and are owned by the plan free of liens, pledges, and other security interests or, if not, whether the security interests are identified.
- Investments are valued in accordance with accounting principles generally accepted in the United States of America and income transactions are properly reflected.
- Investments and related income earned are fairly presented in the financial statements and all necessary reporting disclosures are made.

Audit procedures

The following are suggested procedures that you should consider when performing a full-scope audit of a 401(k) plan. (Procedures for an ERISA limited-scope audit are discussed later in this chapter.) The following are suggested audit procedures that may be performed for all investments in general. Additional procedures related to specific investments are covered after these procedures.

1. Confirm with the trustee (custodian) a report of all investment activity for the plan year. (Note that obtaining such information was recommended in chapter 2.) This report would normally include
   a. a Statement of Net Assets Available for Benefits at plan year-end and a Statement of Changes in Net Assets Available for Benefits for the period then ended;
   b. a listing of all investments held at year-end including a description of the investment, the number of shares of stock or units of each investment, par value, maturity date, interest rate, and the like;
   c. a listing of investments purchased during the plan year;
   d. a listing of investments sold during the plan year and realized gains or losses from the sale of those securities;
   e. interest, dividends, and other income earned on the investments during the plan year;
   f. unrealized appreciation or depreciation of plan investments held at plan year-end;
   g. investment information for the supplemental schedules required by the DOL for Form 5500 filing; and
   h. Listing of 5 percent transactions; listing of leases, loans, or fixed income obligations in default or restructured. (See chapter 6, "Other Auditing Considerations," for additional information.)
2. Reconcile the information confirmed by the trustee (custodian) to amounts included in the plan's financial statements.
3. Develop an understanding of the types of investments in the plan by reviewing the trustee report, reading the investment committee's minutes, obtaining the plan's investment strategy, and understanding the impact of that strategy on the plan's investment portfolio (that is, a more aggressive investment strategy increases the level of risk associated with those investments). Also, determine whether the types of investments held are consistent with the investment policy (for example, if the investment policy indicates no derivatives are to be held and interest rate swaps are held, risk may be increased regarding the trustee's understanding of the trust document).
4. Select investments from the ending fair value column of the trustee report. The number of selections should consider the results of the auditor's risk assessment procedures, review of the SOC 1® report, and so on. For the investments selected, determine whether the holding of these investments is permitted by the plan's investment policy. For the selected investments, test the ending fair value (and contract value, when applicable) by reference to market quotations or other evidence of fair value (in accordance with AU-C section 540, *Auditing Accounting Estimates*, [AICPA, *Professional Standards*]) at the plan year-end date. For investments that do not have a readily ascertainable fair value, determine whether the valuation methods used by the trustee or plan administrator appear reasonable, as explained earlier.
5. Make selections from the listing of investments purchased during the current plan year. For the investments selected, trace purchase price to an independent source on the trade date. The following list may be useful in providing independent sources for selected types of securities to verify a purchase price:
   a. Equity funds—Wall Street Journal, Standard & Poor's 500 Stock Index, Wilshire 5000 Stock Index, Dow Jones Industrial Index, and so on.
   b. Bonds—various Shearson Lehman Indexes (such as long-term, municipal, and so on).
   c. Mutual funds—various Lipper Indexes (growth fund, international, and so on).
   d. Money-market funds—Donoghue's 12-month yield, and so on.

Test the valuation of the investment by multiplying the purchase price times the number of shares or units purchased on that date.

6. Obtain information regarding the trustee's responsibility relative to the plan's investments and financial capability by performing the following procedures:
   a. Review the trust or custodial agreement provisions to determine the trustee's responsibilities.
   b. Determine whether the trustee has insurance covering the plan assets under its control.
   c. Read the most recent financial statements of the trustee.
7. Review the fair values of investments at year-end for unusual conditions (for example, unexpectedly large differences between cost and fair values, no fair value assigned, and so on).
8. If investment transactions are recorded on the settlement date rather than the trade date, determine whether the investments purchased or sold near the plan's year-end significantly affect the plan's year-end investment balances, and whether the fair value of these purchases and sales changed significantly from the trade date to year-end (to evaluate the effect on net appreciation for the year).
9. The auditor should obtain sufficient appropriate audit evidence to provide reasonable assurance that fair value measurements and disclosures in the financial statements are in conformity with GAAP. The guidance and disclosures contained in FASB ASC 820 are applicable. Examples of substantive procedures that the auditor may consider related to the valuation of investments include
   a. reviewing and evaluating the plan's methods and procedures for estimating the fair value of investments.
   b. determining whether the plan's methods and procedures for estimating fair value were followed.
   c. testing the underlying documentation supporting the estimates.
   d. determining whether the fair value of investments has been adequately tested if the investment manager's compensation is material and based on the fair value of the plan investments.
   e. inquiring if the plan's board of trustees, administrative committee, or other designated party has reviewed and approved estimates of the fair value of plan investments, and reading supporting minutes or other documentation.
   f. evaluating whether the entity has made adequate disclosures about fair value information.

Investments in master trusts and similar vehicles

When a company or a group of corporations under common control has more than one employee benefit plan, the company or group may invest some or all of the plans' assets into one combined account, a master trust. There is no requirement that the sponsor include all of the company's benefit plans into this master trust, nor do the benefit plans need to be of the same type (that is, defined contribution, defined benefit, health, and welfare). Often the sponsor sets up a master trust to consolidate the recordkeeping function and to reduce administrative expenses. Each plan within the master trust has an interest in the underlying assets of the master trust. Plan interests in master trusts may be divided interests, undivided interests, or a combination thereof. A plan has an undivided interest in a master trust when the plan holds a proportionate interest in the net assets of the master trust but no specific interest in any of the individual balances of the master trust. All other interests in a master trust are considered to be divided. It is not uncommon for DC plans to have a divided interest in a master trust because they include more participant-directed investments. The sum of the individual participant-directed investments in a master trust establishes the plan's divided interest in each general type of investment held by the master trust. In addition, master trust arrangements exist that have a combination of divided and undivided interests in certain investment pools. The master trust agreement will typically provide a description of the nature of the master trust. A bank often serves as trustee for a master trust, acts as custodian, and may or may not have discretionary control over how the monies are invested.

Under Employee Retirement Income Security Act (ERISA) guidelines, a master trust is not required to file audited financial statements with its Form 5500, although it does have special filing requirements under ERISA, as noted in the instructions for Form 5500. Under ERISA, the basic audit requirement is applied to each separate plan and not each separate trust. As a result, each plan that is part of a master trust must file a separate Form 5500 and satisfy the audit requirement, if applicable. However, in a full-scope audit, you should perform certain audit procedures on the master trust if a material amount of the plan's investments is part of a master trust. The audit procedures identified earlier to be performed for all general investments should provide support for the conclusion that investments in the master trust are fairly stated in all material respects. If you audit both the master trust and one or more of the plans that have monies invested in the master trust, it is often more efficient first to apply appropriate audit procedures to the master trust, then to verify that the method of allocating units of participation to the participating plans is reasonable.

If another independent auditor audits the master trust, you should obtain the master trust's financial statements from the other auditor and use the other auditor's report to determine whether the units of participation as stated for the plan under audit are reasonably stated. You should examine the method of calculating the units of participation and determine that it is consistent with the terms of the plan instrument. If you believe that the carrying amount of the units of participation may be impaired, you should consider reviewing interim financial statements of the master trust to determine whether a loss in value has occurred. The extent of these and additional procedures to be performed are based on your judgment and your assessment of risk. For example, a master trust that invests primarily in a discretionary master trust that invests in numerous non-readily marketable investments instead of mutual funds may require you to perform additional audit procedures, such as reviewing certain working papers of the master trust auditor.

If the master trust is not audited, you should perform procedures that enable you to obtain sufficient audit evidence to support assertions that are made in the plan's financial statements regarding plan investments. If that evidence is not obtained and the amount of investments held by the master trust is significant, you should qualify or disclaim an opinion on the plan's financial statements.

Investments in registered investment companies (mutual funds) and common or commingled trust funds

Registered investment company investments (mutual funds) and common or commingled trust funds are similar to master trusts in that monies invested in these funds come from more than one employee benefit plan or other entity. A quality that differentiates common or commingled trust funds and mutual funds from master trusts is that the benefit plans investing in the common or commingled trust funds and mutual funds do not have to be from the same company or group of corporations. A common or commingled trust fund is generally sponsored by a bank, trust company, or similar financial institution, while mutual funds are sponsored by registered investment companies.

As with the master trust, units of participation or shares indicate the interest each plan has in the underlying assets of the common or commingled trust or mutual fund. The purchase or redemption price is determined periodically by the trustee and is based on the current fair values of the underlying assets in the trust or mutual fund. Earnings or appreciation in value is generally reinvested back into the common or commingled trust fund and mutual fund. The financial statements of many common and commingled trust funds and mutual funds are examined and reported on by auditors engaged by the sponsoring bank, trust company, financial institution, or registered investment company.

Audit procedures where assets are invested in mutual funds

Audit procedures that you should perform if assets are invested in a registered invested company (mutual fund), in addition to the audit procedures previously performed for all investments in general, include the following:

1. Confirm directly with the trustee the number of units of participation held by the plan. (Note: A separate confirmation is not necessary if the mutual fund was included on the confirmation obtained previously when testing investments in general.)
2. Confirm contributions, transfers, withdrawals, or account balances (or a combination of these items) with individual participants.
3. Trace contributions and withdrawals from the plan records to the mutual fund's activity statements for the appropriate time period.
4. Obtain a copy of the audited financial statements of the mutual fund and perform the following procedures:
    a. Compare the unit information reported in the fund's financial statements to the unit information recorded by the participating plan. Such information would include fair value, purchases and sales values, and income earned and accrued. The fund's financial statements do not need to cover the exact period of time included in the plan's audit period; however, they should be recent enough to satisfy your objectives.
    b. Test the fair value of the investments in the mutual fund by comparing the per-unit fair value at year-end to market quotations in the fund's financial statements.
    c. Calculate the average rate of return realized by the plan and compare that to the rate stated in the financial statements.

d. Consider the effect that any reported matters (either in the auditor's report or in the notes to the financial statements) may have on the carrying amount of the units of participation held by the plan. If you believe that the carrying value may be negatively affected by matters noted in the audit report, you should consider reviewing interim financial statements of the mutual fund to determine whether a loss in value has occurred.

5. Evaluate the registered investment company's (mutual fund issuer or trustee) internal control procedures by obtaining and reading the service auditor's report (SOC 1® report) if available. That report may provide you with information regarding controls that affect the units of participation values and controls and enable you to determine that share transactions are operating effectively. See chapter 3, "Internal Control Structure," for additional information regarding service auditor reports.

The extent of testing necessary to obtain sufficient evidential matters is ultimately your decision. If you are unable to obtain sufficient evidential matter, it will be necessary for you to express a qualified opinion or disclaim an opinion because of the scope limitation.

Audit procedures where assets are invested in common or commingled trust funds

The following represent audit procedures that you should perform if assets are invested in a common or commingled trust fund, in addition to the procedures performed previously for all investments:

1. Confirm directly with the trustee the number of units of participation held by the plan. (Note: A separate confirmation is not necessary if the common or commingled trust fund or mutual fund was previously confirmed in testing investments in general.)
2. Obtain a copy of the audited financial statements, if available, of the common or commingled trust fund and perform these procedures:
   a. Compare the unit information reported in the fund's financial statements to the unit information recorded by the participating plan. Such information would include fair value, purchases and sales values, and income earned and accrued. The fund's financial statements do not need to cover the exact period of time included in the plan's audit period; however, they should be recent enough to satisfy your objectives.
   b. Consider the effect that any reported matters (either in the auditor's report or in the notes to the financial statements) may have on the carrying amount of the units of participation held by the plan. If you believe that the carrying value may be negatively affected by matters noted in the audit report, you should consider reviewing interim financial statements of the common or commingled trust fund to determine whether a loss in value has occurred.
   c. Determine if the fund owns any investment contracts. If the fund owns investment contracts, determine the plan's portion of fair value and the adjustment to contract value to be included on the plan's statement of net assets available for benefits.
3. Evaluate the internal control procedures of the common or commingled trust fund by obtaining and reading the service auditor's report (SOC 1® report) if available. That report may provide you with information regarding controls that affect the units of participation values and about controls to determine that share transactions are operating effectively. See chapter 3, "Internal Control Structure," for additional information when service auditor reports are not available.

The extent of testing necessary to obtain sufficient evidential matter is ultimately your decision.

If you are unable to obtain sufficient evidential matter, it may be necessary for you to express a qualified opinion or disclaim an opinion on the plan's financial statements because of the scope limitation.

Investments with insurance companies

Insurance companies offer many different types of investment options for employee benefit plans. The nature of the contract will determine the accounting and reporting requirements in the plan's financial statements.

Unallocated contracts are funding arrangements whereby monies are often held in the general account or pooled separate accounts of the insurance company until such time as a benefit payment comes due or it is necessary to purchase annuities for retirees or for participants who terminate employment. Unallocated contracts remain as assets of the plan, as responsibility for future benefit payments rests with the plan, not with the insurance company. Two popular types of unallocated contracts are the pooled separate accounts and guaranteed investment contract (GIC). A GIC is invested in the general assets of the insurance company and generally provides a stated (often referred to as "guaranteed") rate of return and has a set maturity date.

Contract value is the only required measure for fully benefit-responsive investment contracts. See the section, "Investment Contracts Reporting and Accounting Requirements," for further treatment of these concepts.

Fully benefit-responsive investment contracts as defined by the FASB ASC glossary, are limited to direct investments between the plan and the issuer. Plans may indirectly hold fully benefit-responsive investment contracts through beneficial ownership of common collective trusts (CCTs), which own investment contracts. Insurance company pooled separate accounts (PSAs) that hold investment contracts also have similar characteristics. Indirect investment in FBRICs through investment companies (for example, those included in the underlying investment of stable value CCTs) are not in the scope of part I of FASB ASU No. 2015-12. Accordingly, the plan's investment in the CCT or PSA is required to be reported at fair value. See chapter 7, The Auditor's Report and Financial Statement Disclosures, for required disclosures related to fair value measurements in accordance with FASB ASC 820, including the fair value measurement of investments in certain entities that calculate net asset value per share.

Pooled separate accounts

As described under the heading "Investment Options," a pooled separate account is established by an insurance company for the purpose of investing assets of one or more employee benefit plans of one or more sponsors. Monies contributed to a separate account are not commingled with assets of other plans, or with the general assets of the sponsoring insurance company. An individual separate account is a separate account in which only one plan participates, while a pooled separate account allows two or more unrelated plans to take part. As with the individual separate account, monies held by the insurance company in the pooled separate account are maintained separately from the assets of the insurance company. In a pooled separate account, like a common collective trust or mutual fund, units of participation or shares are used to distinguish each plan's share of assets.

Investment contracts reporting and accounting requirements

The majority of investments in a 401(k) plan will be valued at fair value. However, certain contracts should now be presented at contract value. FASB ASC 962-325 specifies the accounting for investment contracts issued by either an insurance company or other entity. Defined contribution plans should report fully *benefit-responsive* contracts at contract value on the statement of net assets available for benefits. Contract value is the amount a participant would receive if he or she were to initiate transactions (for example, make a withdrawal from the contract) under the current terms of the ongoing plan. Contract value is the accumulated contributions, plus accrued net investment income, less any withdrawals and administrative expenses. Non-benefit-responsive investment contracts should be presented at fair value on the statement of net assets available for benefits.

Benefit-responsiveness is defined as the extent to which an investment contract's terms permit and require withdrawals at contract value for benefit payments, loans, or transfers to other investment options offered to the participants of the plan. For a contract to be fully benefit-responsive, the plan must allow plan participants reasonable access to their funds—that is, withdrawals from the plan at contract value without a penalty assessed, and the freedom to switch investment options from this contract to another investment option offered by the plan. If a plan limits the number of times per year (such as, quarterly, semi-annually, and so on) that participants may access their funds or make changes in their investment options to control administrative costs, that limitation generally would not affect the benefit-responsiveness of the investment contracts held by the plan.

If a plan invests in multiple investment contracts, you should evaluate each contract separately to determine benefit-responsiveness. If a plan holds pooled funds that have investment contracts as the underlying securities, you should evaluate each contract in the pooled fund individually for benefit-responsiveness. If the pooled fund places any restrictions on the access to the funds for withdrawals, then none of the underlying investment contracts would be considered to be fully benefit-responsive.

Footnote disclosures for GICs

Disclosures for fully benefit-responsive contracts include the following:

- A description of the nature of those investment contracts (including how they operate) by the type of investment contract (for example, synthetic investment contracts or traditional investment contracts).
- A description of the events that limit the ability of the plan to transact at contract value with the issuer (for example, premature termination of the contracts by the plan, plant closings, layoffs, plan termination, bankruptcy, mergers, and early retirement incentives), including a statement that the occurrence of each of those events that would limit the plan's ability to transact at contract value with participants in the plan is not probable of occurring. [The term probable is used in this paragraph consistent with its use in FASB ASC 450-20-25.]
- A description of the events and circumstances that would allow issuers to terminate fully benefit-responsive investment contracts with the plan and settle at an amount different from contract value.
- The total contract value of each type of investment contract (for example, synthetic contracts or traditional investment contracts).

In addition, other types of investment contracts are covered in FASB ASC 962-325.

Synthetic GICs

Another form of a guaranteed investment contract is commonly referred to as a *synthetic GIC* because it simulates the performance attributes of an investment contract, but it does so through the purchase of financial instruments. The primary difference between a traditional GIC and the synthetic GIC is that in the synthetic GIC, the plan owns the underlying investments of the investment contract, whereas in the traditional GIC, the plan holds an interest in the investment contract, not directly in the underlying investments. The synthetic GIC, like other GICs, offers a guaranteed rate of return.

Typically, a bank or insurance company will offer the synthetic GIC, and then will contract with a third party to offer "the wrapper." To enable the plan to realize a guaranteed value for the assets if it needs to liquidate them to make benefit payments, a synthetic GIC utilizes a benefit-responsive wrapper contract issued by a third party that provides market and cash flow risk protection to the plan. The wrapper enables the plan to liquidate any or all of the securities that underlie the GIC to make benefit payments and still achieve the guaranteed rate of return. In essence, the wrapper absorbs the increases and decreases in the fair value of the underlying securities by offsetting any losses realized at the time of sale of the securities, or by absorbing the gains.

Similar to as discussed for GICs previously, synthetic GICs that are determined to be fully *benefit-responsive* should be now be presented at contract value on the statement of net assets available for benefits upon adoption of ASU 2015-12.

A key difference between traditional GICs and synthetic GICs is the report presentation in the plan's audited financial statements. Because plans that invest in synthetic GICs own the underlying assets, it is necessary to include on the Schedule H, Line 4i of Form 5500, Schedule of Assets (held at end of year), "each asset that comprises the synthetic GIC, including the wrapper." Each underlying asset, including the wrapper, will be reported at fair value. The underlying securities are valued at fair value and the wrapper will be separately fair-valued. Fair value for a GIC is generally calculated by discounting cash flows at current interest rates for similar investments. Other valuation methods may also be appropriate. The wrapper makes this type of GIC benefit-responsive because it permits participants easy access to their monies without concern of devaluation of their investment because the wrapper will absorb the market fluctuations in many, but not all, situations. The financial stability of both the issuer and the provider of the wrapper should be determined to assess whether an adjustment to contract value is needed.

Audit procedures for assets invested with insurance companies

As suggested in the AICPA Audit and Accounting Guide *Employee Benefit Plans*, you should consider the following additional audit procedures for assets invested with insurance companies:

1. Read the contract between the contract holder and the insurance company and evaluate whether they are investment or insurance contracts. (Note that insurance contracts require the concepts of mortality and morbidity and are unlikely to be found in a 401(k) plan.) If they are investment contracts, determine if they are fully benefit-responsive.

2. Confirm the following directly with the insurance company, as applicable (if the insurance company is benefit-responsive, perform procedures for benefit-responsive investment contracts):
   a. Contributions or premium payments made to the fund or account during the year. (This also may be available from the plan sponsor.)
   b. Interest, dividends, refunds, credits, and changes in value; and whether such amounts have been charged or credited during the year on an estimated or actual basis.
   c. The fair value of the funds in the general or separate account at the plan's year-end and the basis for determining such value.
   d. The amount of insurance company fee and other expenses chargeable during the year.
   e. Transfers from one investment option to another.
3. Determine that the issuing insurance company is a financially responsible party that should be able to satisfy the terms of the contract. To accomplish this, you may:
   a. Inquire of plan management how and why the issuing insurance company was selected.
   b. Examine financial statements of the insurance company to assess its solvency and financial stability. Consider whether any reported matters might have any effect on the recoverability of the plan's investment.
   c. Obtain a recent rating of the insurance company. Read the rating service's remarks to understand its concerns, if any, about the issuer.
   d. Determine if any fair value or penalty adjustments are included in the contract.
4. Decide whether the characteristics of the contract that restrict the use of assets require disclosure in the financial statements of the plan.

Audit procedures for assets invested with pooled separate accounts

For investments in pooled separate accounts, you are concerned with the plan's units of participation in the pooled separate account, and the plan auditor should examine documents that provide support for those transactions. To perform these procedures, the plan auditor should consider the following:

- Confirm directly with the insurance company the units of participation held by the plan.
- Examine documents approving and supporting selected investment transactions in units of participation—such as investment committee minutes; trust agreements; or investment guidelines, if applicable.
- Understand that if the pooled separate account's (PSA) financial statements have been audited by an independent auditor, you should obtain and read the PSA's financial statements and the auditor's report. The financial statements need not cover the exact period covered by the plan's financial statements; they should, however, be recent enough to satisfy you. You should consider the effect that any reported matters may have on the carrying amounts of the units of participation held by the plan, such as restrictions on redemption or subjectively determined values. If you believe the carrying amount may be impaired, you should consider applying analytical procedures to the interim financial information of the PSA from the date of the audited financial statements to determine whether such a loss in value has occurred.
- Understand that if the pooled separate account's financial statements have not been audited by an independent auditor, you should obtain a copy of a service auditor's report (SOC 1® report) relating to the PSA's activities, if such a report is available. The service auditor's report (if a type 2 report) may provide evidence as to the effectiveness of the insurance company's internal control regarding determining unit values and control over share transactions. If the service auditor's report is not available (or is a type 1 report), you should apply appropriate procedures, including obtaining an understanding of internal control and assessing control risk relating to the pooled separate account. In applying these procedures, you may use the work of the insurance company's independent internal auditor.

If you are unable to apply the auditing procedures previously described or not able to obtain satisfactory evidential matter, you should express a qualified opinion or disclaim an opinion on the plan's financial statements because of the scope limitation.

Audit procedures for assets invested in synthetic GICs

In addition to audit procedures listed in other areas, these procedures should be considered for synthetic GICs:

1. Confirm directly with the trustee or fund adviser, as appropriate, the units of participation held by the plan.
2. Examine documents approving and supporting selected investment transactions in units of participation—such as investment committee minutes, trust agreements, or investment guidelines, if applicable.
3. Obtain fair value and contract value for each contract or each investment such as common collective trusts (CCT) that invest in investment contracts.
   a. Obtain the detail of the underlying securities of the CCT to determine the type of underlying investments and to verify that they are valued appropriately.
   b. Determine if the investment contract is fully benefit-responsive.
4. Obtain information required for disclosure through reading the investment contract or confirmation with the issuer of the contract (or both).
5. Review the calculation of the average yield earned by the plan for all contracts.
6. Review the calculation of the average yield allocated to participants for all contracts.
7. Evaluate the fair market valuation of the contract. Review and test the significant assumptions and underlying data used in the valuation. Consider the need to involve valuation specialists.
8. Determine if the certification covers the fair market valuation of the contract and other required disclosures for an ERISA limited-scope audit.

Knowledge check

3. Which of the following is not a disclosure requirement of FASB ASC 962-325 as it applies to accounting for fully benefit-responsive investment contracts in defined contribution benefit plans?

   a. Description of events and circumstances that would allow issuers to terminate the contract at an amount different from contract value.
   b. The amount of expenses charged to the contract.
   c. The total contract value for each type of investment contract.
   d. Description of events that limits the ability of the plan to transact at contract value.

Direct filing entities (DFE)

Some plans participate in certain trusts accounts and other investment arrangements that file Form 5500 as a direct filing entity (DFE). The DOL requires that issuers of pooled separate accounts, common collective trusts, master trusts, or 103-12 entities file a DFE 5500 in order for a plan participating in these investments to utilize one line item reporting on the plan's Form 5500. If the issuer of the pooled investments does not file as a DFE with the Department of Labor (DOL), then the plan is required to present its portion of each of the underlying investments by appropriate investment classification on the Schedule H of Form 5500. If the plan does not list this detail, the DOL would consider the plan's Form 5500 filing incomplete and reject the filing. The plan sponsor should make inquiries with the investment issuer to determine the DFE filing status.

Other investments

Non-readily marketable securities

Some 401(k) plans may invest in securities that do not have a ready market price (specialized or unique investments such as junk bonds, options, limited partnerships, real estate mortgage investment conduits [REMICs], private equity funds, hedge funds, derivative products, and so on). Some factors that may be considered in estimating the fair value of these investments include, but are not limited to, the cost at the date of purchase, the length of time the investment has been held, reported prices and extent of trading of similar investments, a forecast of the expected cash flows from the investment, current interest rates, and the financial condition of the investee or issuer. For these securities, you should confirm the existence of the investment and review and evaluate the plan's methods and procedures for estimating the fair value of such investments, determine whether the plan's methods and procedures for estimating fair value were followed and appear to be reasonable and applied consistently. You should test the underlying documentation supporting the estimates. Auditors should remember that confirmation of the investment does not constitute adequate audit evidence with respect to the valuation. The AICPA Audit and Accounting Guide *Investment Companies* may assist you in understanding and auditing certain investments that may be found in some employee benefit plans.

You may not possess the special skill or knowledge to perform auditing procedures for non-readily marketable securities or derivatives. You may seek guidance from another individual in your firm or from others outside your firm. AU-C section 300, *Planning an Audit* (AICPA, *Professional Standards*), addresses situations in which the engagement team includes a member or consults an individual or organization with expertise in a specialized area of accounting or auditing. If information to be used as audit evidence has been prepared using the work of a management's specialist, then paragraph .08 of AU-C section 500, *Audit Evidence* (AICPA, *Professional Standards*), would apply. AU-C section 620, *Using the Work of an Auditor's Specialist* (AICPA, *Professional Standards*), addresses the auditor's responsibilities relating to the work of an individual or organization possessing expertise in a field other than accounting or auditing when that work is used to assist the auditor in obtaining sufficient appropriate audit evidence.

Derivatives

FASB ASC 815, *Derivatives and Hedging,* establishes accounting and reporting standards for derivative instruments and hedging activities. It requires that an entity (including an employee-benefit 401(k) plan) recognizes all derivatives as either an asset or a liability. It also requires derivatives to be valued at fair value on the statement of net assets available for benefits. Although almost all investments are already valued at fair value, there are certain investments such as hedges or convertible securities that may need to be considered under this standard.

AU-C section 501, *Auditing Derivative Instruments, Hedging Activities, and Investments in Securities* (AICPA, *Professional Standards*), provides guidance on auditing derivative instruments, hedging activities, and investments in securities. The objectives of auditing procedures applied to derivative instruments and related transactions are to provide you with a reasonable basis for concluding

- whether derivatives transactions are initiated in accordance with management's established policies.
- whether information relating to derivatives transactions is complete and accurate.
- whether derivatives accounted for as hedges meet the designation, documentation, and assessment requirements of accounting principles generally accepted in the United States of America.
- whether the carrying amount of derivatives is adjusted to fair value and changes in the fair value of derivatives are accounted for in conformity with accounting principles generally accepted in the United States of America.
- whether derivatives are monitored on an ongoing basis to recognize and measure events affecting related financial statement assertions.

The auditing procedures to be applied to derivative instruments and hedging activities ordinarily should include

- confirming with the counterparty to the derivative.
- confirming settled and unsettled transactions with the counterparty.
- testing the fair value.
- inspecting the derivative contract.
- reading and inspecting related agreements; underlying agreements; and other forms of documentation for amounts reported, unrecorded repurchase agreements, and other evidence.
- inspecting supporting documentation for subsequent realization or settlements after the end of the reporting period.
- reading other information such as minutes of committee meetings.
- testing to verify derivative transactions are initiated in accordance with policies established by the plan's management.

The unique characteristics of derivatives instruments and securities, coupled with the relative complexity of the related accounting guidance, may require you to obtain special skill or knowledge to plan and perform auditing procedures. AU-C section 501 is intended to alert you to the possible need for such skill or knowledge.

Real estate

When real estate is held as an investment in a 401(k) plan (for example, possibly as an investment of a master trust), you should perform special audit procedures to determine that the investment exists, is owned free and clear by the plan or trust, and is fairly valued. You should examine the documents signed at closing to verify cost and ownership. Also, examine the deed, title, and any other evidence that relates to ownership. Evaluate the reasonableness of the fair value based on an independent third-party appraisal (see *Use of Specialists* section), the cost of the real estate, period of time held, and any known reasons regarding the appreciation or depreciation in value of the real estate (for example, area is depressed, real estate prices are decreasing quickly in the area). You also should test investment income from real estate, (such as rents), and payments of related expenses (such as taxes and maintenance).

Loans and mortgages

For 401(k) plans that hold loans and mortgages as investments (not including notes receivable from participants), you should perform the following procedures to determine that the investment exists, is owned by the plan, and is fairly valued:

1. Examine documents, including notes, mortgages, deeds, and insurance policies supporting selected loans and mortgages.
2. Confirm selected loans (including notes receivable from participants as previously described) and mortgages with borrowers.
3. Evaluate the reasonableness of the fair value, including the extent of collateral, if any. Consider the potential effect of defaults on mortgages (especially high interest rate and adjustable rate mortgages) in determining the reasonableness of the fair value of the mortgage.
4. Test to see that interest is recorded properly. (**Note:** Delinquent loans are discussed in chapter 6.)

Knowledge check

4. All of the following are examples of non-readily marketable securities, except which?

    a. Limited partnerships.
    b. Hedge funds.
    c. Reverse repurchase agreements.
    d. Pooled separate account.

ERISA limited-scope auditing procedures

As explained in chapter 1, the plan administrator may make an election to limit the scope of the audit as it relates to investments and related investment income if plan assets are held by a qualifying bank, trust company, or an insurance company that is state or federally chartered and subject to regulation and periodic examination by a state or federal agency. This election permits you not to perform any auditing procedures with respect to investments and related net investment income or loss, notes receivable from participants, and the supplemental schedules related to investment transactions, provided the trustee certifies as to the completeness and accuracy of the plan accounting records. Note that while notes receivable from participants are not characterized as "investments" for financial statement reporting purposes, notes receivable from participants are reported on Form 5500 as investments, and, if held and certified by the trustee, would meet the exemption and not be subject to audit. Normally, the trustee's certification is stamped on the face of the trustee report with a trust officer's signature attesting to the completeness and accuracy of the report.

The ERISA limited-scope audit does not remove the requirement for the plan to have an audit, nor does it extend to participant account activity or non-investment related areas. You are still responsible for auditing sponsor and employee contributions, withdrawals, administrative expenses, as a whole, and for auditing all components of participant account activity that would include the aforementioned items such as loan activity, forfeitures, and other allocations. Plan investments not held by a qualifying institution should be tested with appropriate audit procedures as previously described. In deciding the type of report to be issued when only a portion of the assets is certified by a qualifying institution, you should consider the proportion of assets for which the auditor's scope was limited. If you decide those amounts are material to the plan financial statements, your report on the plan's financial statements should be a limited-scope report. See chapter 7, "The Auditor's Report and Financial Statement Disclosures," for additional information and report examples.

Even though the trustee has certified to the completeness and accuracy of the investments on the trustee report, you are still responsible to agree the total investments according to the certified trustee report, by type, to the plan's financial statements. If you become aware that certain certified information is not correct or is incomplete, you have the responsibility to pursue these matters and, if necessary, modify your report on the financial statements or supplemental schedules, or both. Certain alternative investments and fair market valuations of certain investments may not be covered by the certification. Any investments not covered by the certification should be subjected to appropriate audit procedures. See chapter 7 for report examples.

FASB ASC 820 does not change the auditor's responsibility in an ERISA limited-scope audit. However, the majority of the certifying agents will not certify as to which level of the fair value hierarchy a plan's investments fall into. Although third parties may provide pricing information to determine the fair value hierarchy levels, or may even provide preliminary suggestions of the fair value hierarchy levels, it is ultimately the responsibility of the plan's management to understand the basis for the designations to determine whether the plan's investments have been valued and disclosed in accordance with GAAP or whether revisions are necessary. Initial inquiries may provide the auditor an indication of whether or not the investment information has been valued and presented in accordance with GAAP.

Knowledge check

5. If an eligible ERISA limited-scope audit election is made by the plan administrator, which of the following is correct?

    a. You are required to do nothing with regard to notes receivable from participants because the recordkeeper certifies notes receivable from participants.

    b. You are required to do nothing with regard to contributions because the plan sponsor certifies contributions.

    c. You are required to withdraw from the audit due to a scope limitation.

    d. You are required to perform tests for investments not held by a qualifying institution.

Contributions receivable

The basis for determining employer and, if applicable, employee contributions is specified in the plan document. If the sponsor decides to contribute a profit-sharing match, it is possible that the match level cannot be determined until after the end of the plan year. If, for example, the plan document provides that a match of 25 cents per dollar will be contributed if profits exceed $250,000, and it was not determined until two months after plan year-end that profits totaled $275,000, a contribution receivable should be recorded on the plan's financial statements as of the plan year-end. The existence or lack of an accrued liability in the plan sponsor's statement of financial position does not provide enough support for recognition of a receivable by the plan.

To test employer contributions receivable, you should review the contribution provisions of the plan document and verify compliance with the plan instrument (for example, criteria that must be met for an employer or employee (or both) to make a contribution; the formula to determine upper and lower contribution limits; and the rates for determining the contribution). You should compare the amount of the employer contribution recorded in the plan's trustee report to the amount approved by the board of directors of the plan sponsor, if the contribution requires board approval. That approval should be documented in the board minutes. Alternatively, given the period of time after the plan's year-end in which audit procedures are performed, you may be able to test subsequent payments by the employer to the plan.

You should inquire about the timing of employee contributions to the plan. As with the employer contributions mentioned previously, you may test subsequent receipts of employee contributions. Failure by the plan administrator to remit employee contributions to the plan as soon as practicable may constitute a prohibited transaction under DOL regulations. See chapter 5 for additional information.

Notes receivable from participants receivable

Many 401(k) plans offer participants the ability to borrow against the vested portion of their individual accounts. ERISA and the IRS have established guidelines that must be followed for notes receivable from participants. For example, loans cannot be made for longer than five years, unless it is used to purchase a primary residence—in which case, the loan period may be for 10 years or longer. The interest rate must also be reasonable when compared to the prevailing market for interest rates.

You should read the plan document to learn the specific rules for notes receivable from participants available through the plan. Often, the plan document will limit the amount of the loan to no more than 50 percent of the vested portion of the participant's individual account and establish the number of loans that a participant may have, the minimum loan amount, what constitutes a loan in default, and other conditions. When the loan is made, the amount is deducted from the participant's account and then repaid to the participant's account, generally through payroll deductions based on the repayment schedule for the loan. The portion of the loan repayment that represents principal is added to the participant's account. The portion of the payroll deduction representing interest is added to income from notes receivable from participants (income on the loan fund).

FASB ASC 962, *Plan Accounting—Defined Contribution Plans*, requires that loans to participants be reported as notes receivable from participants at the unpaid principal balance, plus any accrued but unpaid interest. In addition, FASB ASC 962-310-50-1 states that the fair value disclosures for financial instruments prescribed in paragraphs 10–16 of FASB ASC 825-10-50 are not required for notes receivable from participants. Notes receivable from participants are considered an investment for Form 5500 reporting purposes.

The total of all notes receivable from participants outstanding is shown as a receivable within the asset total on the Statement of Net Assets Available for Benefits.

Procedures that you may perform to verify the reasonableness of the notes receivable from participants include the following:

1. Examine documentation of notes receivable from participants, if any, supporting the notes receivable and verify that the notes receivable were made in accordance with the plan document and have been properly segregated in the individual's account. Recently, the IRS has stated that participants are not required to sign forms to initiate a participant loan. This may require you to confirm loans with participants.
2. Confirm selected loans with participants. Include in the confirmation the outstanding balance of the loan at the plan year-end date and the interest rate and maturity date of the loan.
3. Verify that interest is properly recorded. Agree the total withholding per pay period and determine the proper split is made between principal and interest in accordance with the repayment or amortization schedule.
4. Verify that the financial statement presentation is proper (that is, reported as plan receivable).
5. Determine whether delinquent loans have been classified as deemed distributions or as distributions. The plan document determines when a loan is in default. For notes receivable from participants in which that participant has a distributable event (that is, employment termination, death, or disability), the plan's sponsor should distribute these loans. The receivable is removed and a distribution is

recorded. For active participants who have not incurred a distributable event, the loan would be deemed distribution. The loan stays recorded as a receivable until a distributable event occurs. In 2002, the DOL updated the instructions to Form 5500 to require deemed distributions to be recorded in the distribution section on the Schedule H. Due to the difference between GAAP requirements and Form 5500 instructions, a reconciling footnote is required for all plans with deemed distributions.

Knowledge check

6. Notes receivable from participants are

    a. Investments of the 401(k) plan.
    b. Receivables of the 401(k) plan.
    c. Exempt from interest.
    d. Not repayable by participants.

Cash balances

Cash balances of employee benefit plans tend to be small, as most funds are invested in the various investment options provided by the plan. Cash balances represent the residual amounts not yet invested. Confirmation of the cash balance is an appropriate audit procedure to verify the existence and value of the cash balances. Disclosure of cash balances representing unallocated funds and the plans for their disposition should be made in the footnotes to the financial statements.

Other assets

It is possible that, as of year-end, the plan has earned investment income that has not yet been remitted to the plan. You should test accrued investment income to determine that it exists and is properly recorded. You should obtain a listing of all accrued investment income amounts held as of the plan's year-end and select accrued investment income amounts (for example, accrued dividends, interest). You should also test subsequent receipts or other records supporting the amounts and the timing of the selected accruals.

Accrued liabilities

A plan may have liabilities for amounts owed for securities purchased by the plan but not yet remitted or expenses for administrative fees (such as trustee fees) that may still be payable at plan year-end. These liabilities should be deducted to arrive at net assets available for benefits.

Note. The plan should not reflect, as benefits payable, amounts allocated to accounts of persons who have elected to withdraw from the plan but have not yet been paid. These amounts should be disclosed only in the plan's financial statements.

Note. Generally, for daily valued plans, there are not any participants who have requested a distribution and not been paid as of the end of the plan year. See chapter 7 for additional information.

In addition, in certain cases, a plan may record liabilities for excess contributions that need to be refunded to plan participants because of plan's failure under the required anti-discrimination tests. Also, in cases of a plan termination or merger, the plan may record amounts payable as distributions to participants or as a transfer payable to another plan. See chapter 6 for a treatment of these situations.

Test accrued liabilities by reference to the underlying supporting documentation or subsequent disbursement made by the plan to extinguish such liabilities.

Knowledge check

7. Which of the following is an example of a liability that should not be included on the statement of net assets?

    a. Accrued expenses for trustee fees for the fourth quarter.
    b. Benefits payable.
    c. Payable for investments purchased not settled.
    d. Excess contributions refundable to participants.

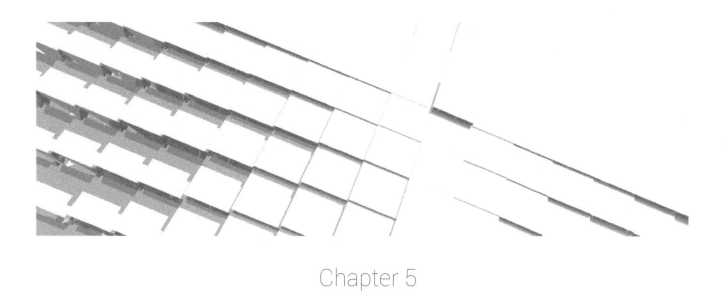

Chapter 5

Auditing the Statement of Changes in Net Assets Available for Benefits

Learning objectives

After completing this chapter, you should be able to do the following:

- Indicate the activity reflected in the Statement of Changes in Net Assets for Benefits.

- Identify the audit procedures required for investment income, investment expenses, and contributions.

Introduction

The Statement of Changes in Net Assets Available for Benefits shows the activity that has occurred (additions and deductions) in the 401(k) plan during the plan year. Additions include net realized gains (interest, dividends, and gains or losses on sales of investments) earned on the investments of the plan as well as unrealized gains or losses (the change in fair value of the investments). Contributions from the plan sponsor or from participants also are additions to the plan. Deductions are usually payments to participants who have retired or terminated employment as well as administrative expenses. Other changes (for example, transfers of assets to or from other plans or demutualization proceeds) should also be presented separately, if they are significant.

It is an acceptable practice for certain types of investments (for example, mutual funds, investments in a master trust, common or collective trust, or pooled separate accounts) to net all the realized gains and losses and the unrealized gains and losses into one net number, called *net investment gain/loss* or *net appreciation/depreciation* in the fair value of investments. Net appreciation or net investment gain would represent an overall addition to the plan's assets; net depreciation or net investment loss would be an overall deduction from the plan's assets. The Statement of Changes in Net Assets Available for Benefits is similar to the income statement for most other entities.

Investment income

Investment income includes interest, dividends, rental income, and other earnings paid on investments that are or were held by the plan during the plan year. It also includes realized and unrealized gains and losses on those investments. Realized gains and losses result when an investment is bought at one price and later sold at a different price. If the selling price is higher than the purchase price, the plan realizes a gain. If the selling price is lower, the plan realizes a loss. In addition, at the end of the plan year, most investments held at year-end will be valued at fair value (certain investment contracts will be presented at contract value). (See chapter 4 for additional information.) If the ending fair value of an investment held at the plan's year-end is higher than the value at the beginning of the year, (or when purchased, if bought during the current fiscal year) then an unrealized gain results—unrealized because the investment is still held at year-end and has not been sold. If the ending value is lower than the value at the beginning of the year, then an unrealized loss results. Another term for unrealized gains and losses is unrealized appreciation/depreciation.

Audit objectives

The audit objectives for investment income are to provide assurance that earnings from the investment vehicles of the plan have been properly recorded in all material respects and allocated to the individual participant account records. Also, you should verify that unrealized and realized gains and losses are properly calculated and recorded in the plan financial statements in accordance with generally accepted accounting principles (GAAP). These principles require that the Statement of Changes in Net Assets Available for Benefits be presented in enough detail to identify the significant changes during the year. These generally should include the following:

- Net appreciation or depreciation in fair value for each significant class of investments, segregated between investments, whose fair values have been measured by quoted prices in an active market and those whose fair values have been otherwise determined.
- Investment income. As noted previously, for certain pooled-type of investments, investment income may be presented as net investment gain or loss.

Suggested audit procedures

In testing investment income in a full-scope audit, you may realize efficiencies to the extent you perform analytical review procedures. You can compare an average rate of return on a particular aggregation of investments from the plan to a stated average rate of return for a similar type of investment as published in an independent source to determine the reasonableness of investment income allocated to the plan. For some investments, it may be more appropriate to perform detail testing. The following represents suggested analytical and detail audit procedures that you may use to audit investment income.

1. Obtain from the trustee a schedule of investments showing beginning and ending balances, investment income, net unrealized gains or losses, and realized gains or losses and agree the plan's

beginning-of-the-year investment balance (fair value) to the prior-year working papers or report. This information previously may have been obtained in connection with the audit of the Statement of Net Assets Available for Benefits—see chapter 4.

2. If you choose to perform analytical review procedures instead of (or in addition to) detail tests, you should perform the following procedures to test investment income:

    a. Segregate investments by significant type (for example, government securities, equities, fixed income securities, mutual funds, temporary investments, and so on).

    b. Determine the average investment balance for each significant type by adding the beginning and ending investment balances together and dividing by two (you may need to refine this simple average to quarterly or monthly amounts if the activity during the year is not reasonably uniform).

    c. Divide the investment income earned on each type of investment by its average investment balance, which will result in an average rate of return on that investment.

    d. Compare the average calculated for the investment type to independent published sources, such as the following:

        i. Equity Investments
            (1) Wall Street Journal
            (2) Standard & Poor's 500 Stock Index
            (3) Wilshire 5000 Stock Index
            (4) Dow Jones Industrial Average
            (5) Dividend amounts agreed to published sources

        ii. Fixed Income Investments
            (1) Moody's Bond Record
            (2) Various Shearson Lehman or Merrill Lynch Indexes
            (3) Interest rates stated on the securities

        iii. Mutual Fund Investments
            (1) Various Lipper Indexes

        iv. Temporary Investments
            (1) Donoghue's 12-month Yield Index

        v. Prior period amounts or return ratios adjusted for known factors during the current period

    Obtain an explanation from the plan administrator or trustee for any significant fluctuation. (Note: The average rate of return that you calculate may differ from the independent source if investment fees are netted against investment income. See the discussion of investment fees.)

3. To perform tests of details, consider the following procedures: Obtain a listing of all investment purchases and sales (such as, proceeds and realized gains or losses) during the year. The trustee usually provides these.

    a. Perform tests of details to test both net realized gains or losses and investment income (such as, interest and dividends) by making a selection of investment sales during the year. Compare selling price to published market price ranges on the applicable trade dates (the date an agreement is made to buy or sell the investment). Depending on the nature of the investment, you should obtain an independent source to compare the selling price. Compare interest, dividends, and net investment gain or loss (for example, for mutual funds) received to an independent source (see previous list). A business library will typically carry reference books that detail dividends declared and paid. The interest rate is generally stated on the investment instrument.

    b. Examine brokers' advices, cash records, or other supporting documentation for the quantity, description, and date of disposition of the investment.

c. In the event that brokers' advices or independent cash records are not available, confirm the sale with the broker or compare prices at which purchases and sales were recorded with published market price ranges on the trade date.

Note: For many pooled investment vehicles (mutual funds, common collective trusts, or pooled separate accounts), quoted returns are often for total return (such as, investment income plus unrealized appreciation or depreciation). In those cases, testing net investment gain or loss in total may be more efficient.

4. Test the calculation of the realized gain or loss on the transaction and agree the realized gain or loss to the listing of investment sales made during the year. Determine what method is used for calculating the realized gain or loss on the transaction, in accordance with the DOL's rules and regulations (for example, realized gains and losses should be based on beginning-of-year market value, not historical cost, for Form 5500). GAAP requires realized gain or loss to be calculated based on historical cost. If realized and unrealized gain or loss is combined into one line on the statement of changes in net assets available for benefits, it does not make any difference which method is used.

5. Recalculate the unrealized gain or loss portion of the net appreciation or depreciation in fair value of investments. To do this, start with the beginning of the year market value of a particular investment. Add to this any purchases of that security and subtract any sales. (For the sales number, use the market value for that security from the beginning of the year, not the actual proceeds received.) This will result in the ending value of the investment. Compare this balance to the ending fair value recorded for that security on the trustee report. If the recorded fair value is higher, the investment has an unrealized gain. If the recorded value is lower, the investment has an unrealized loss. Compare the amount just calculated with the amount recorded by the trustee and evaluate any differences.

You should perform these additional audit procedures if assets are invested in registered investment companies:

a. Obtain the audited financial statements for the mutual fund. Compare the average rate of return stated in, or determined from, the audited financial statements with the average rate of return calculated in step 2. Investigate significant fluctuations with the plan administrator.

b. Determine whether investment expenses related to the mutual fund are charged separately or netted against the investment return. Determine whether this arrangement is consistent with the plan's agreement with the trustee or mutual fund entity.

You should perform these additional audit procedures if assets are invested with insurance companies:

c. Obtain audited financial statements of the insurance investment, if available. (They may be available for certain pooled separate accounts.) Compare the average rate of return for the investment vehicle included in, or determined from, the audited financial statements with the average rate determined in step 2. Investigate significant fluctuations with the plan administrator.

d. Determine whether the investment fees assessed on these investments agree to the investment fee rate stated in the investment contract. Investigate significant fluctuations with the plan administrator.

Knowledge check

1. Performing tests using substantive analytical review to determine the propriety of total investment income earned during the year does not include which?

    a. Separating the investments into similar groupings (such as fixed income, equity, bonds, mutual funds, temporary, and so on) before determining the rate of return.
    b. Comparing the average rate of return to an independent source (for example, WSJ).
    c. Considering using the average balance of investments held during the plan year.
    d. Testing the investment expenses for a sample selection to determine that the amounts are properly assessed.

ERISA limited-scope audit

When the plan administrator has elected to have an ERISA limited-scope audit performed, you should agree the investment income amounts certified on the trustee report to the financial information reported on the financial statements.

Investment expenses

Fees that are assessed by parties involved in the plan for the purchase or sale of securities, investment advice, commission fees, and so on, are considered investment expenses. Investment expenses can be (a) assessed as percentage or basis points on the purchase or selling price of the investment being traded, (b) a flat fee charged per transaction, or (c) a flat fee or percentage (of assets managed) charged per month to manage the account. Some trustees and brokers show the investment fee on a separate invoice or as a separate total on the brokers' advice. However, it is common practice to (a) net the investment fee with proceeds of the sale; (b) delay assessing the fee on a purchase until a sale is transacted, then deduct it from that sale; or (c) deduct the fee automatically on a periodic basis (for example, monthly) from the plan account. In each of these last three examples, the investment fee is not readily available.

You should read the plan document regarding investment fees and then discuss with the plan administrator to determine the method used by the trustee or broker to assess fees. If fees are netted (normally done for mutual funds and common or commingled trust funds), you will be unable to test this amount as the fees will be shown on the trustee statement netted together with the investment income amount. If amounts are not netted, you should test (as you consider necessary) the investment expenses for a sample selection to determine that the amounts are properly assessed.

If assets are invested in common or commingled trust funds (or other funds in which investment fees are netted against investment income), investment fees are generally netted against investment income for these types of investments. If this is true, on the Statement of Changes in Net Assets Available for Benefits, the investment income line should be shown as follows:

Investment income, net of investment expenses $X,XXX

If assets are investments with insurance companies (or other accounts where investment fees are not netted), you should determine that the investment fees assessed on these investments agree to the investment fee rate stated in the investment contract or agreement. Investigate significant fluctuations with the plan administrator.

Contributions from employers

Typically, there are two types of employer contributions: an employer match (of all or part of an employee contribution) and profit-sharing contribution. Some plans provide for no employer contributions, some extend only one type, while still other plans offer both. The plan instrument and related documents should provide the information to determine the proper amount that has been or will be contributed to the plan. For profit-sharing or discretionary plans, you should review board minutes to determine whether, and how much the employer will contribute. You should read these documents to determine the basis for calculating the employer contribution and then recalculate the contribution to make sure that it was made in accordance with the provisions of the plan document.

An employer matching contribution may be calculated based on a stated percentage of the employee contribution. For example, the plan document may read "the plan sponsor will match 50 cents for every dollar contributed by the participant up to 3 percent of his or her regular pay." For an employee who elects to contribute 5 percent of his or her pay to the 401(k) plan, the plan sponsor will contribute 1½ percent of his or her pay (50 cents per $1 × 3%) to the plan.

A profit-sharing contribution may be made when a stated level of profitability is realized by the plan sponsor. An example of this type of contribution may read as follows:

If profits are	Employer match is
$500,000 to $999,999	25 percent
$1,000,000 to $4,999,999	35 percent
$5,000,000 and higher	45 percent

If profits are $678,000 and a participant has contributed $2,750 to the plan, his employer profit-sharing match contribution would be $687.50 ($2,750 × 25%).

For discretionary plans, you should agree the employer match to the amount stated in the board minutes to determine the propriety and timing of the employer contributions.

You should be aware that many plans now accept contributions into a Roth IRA account. Contributions into a Roth IRA are made post-tax (after all federal, state, and the like, taxes are withheld as opposed to a 401(k) contribution that is made pre-tax). However, subsequent distributions from a Roth IRA are not taxable to the participant (401(k) contributions are usually subject to tax upon distribution). Because of these differences, it is imperative that contributions to a Roth IRA and the related earnings on those contributions be maintained in a separate account so that the proper tax treatment can be made by the participant when those monies are distributed.

Audit objectives

The audit objectives for contributions received from employers are to provide assurance that amounts received have been determined and recorded in accordance with the plan documents or minutes of the board. Also, you should verify that employer contributions are properly recorded in the financial statements in conformity with GAAP. (Note that contributions receivable were covered and tested in chapter 4.)

Suggested audit procedures

To verify the auditing objectives are met, you should obtain directly from the plan sponsor a schedule of all employer contributions made to the plan. Select a sample from the list and perform the following:

- Recalculate the contribution to verify that the contribution rate stated in the appropriate documents was applied properly.
- On a sample basis, test postings from the employer contribution listing to the participant records and from these records to the employer contribution listing.

The previous tests should be performed for the various types of employer contributions (for example, matching, profit-sharing, other discretionary).

Ask the plan sponsor about contributions receivable at the plan year-end.

Forfeitures

When participants terminate employment with the plan sponsor, it is possible that employer contributions allocated to their accounts are not fully vested. (See discussion under "Withdrawals" later in this chapter.) Monies not fully vested may be forfeited back to the plan and may be used to offset future employer contributions or to reinstate the employer portion of account balances for participants who previously left the plan within the past five years and have since returned and reinstated their portions of their accounts. Forfeited monies may also be reallocated to the remaining plan participants or used to pay plan expenses. The plan document must state how plan forfeitures are to be used.

Forfeitures result when a participant, whose account has been credited with employer contributions, terminates employment before becoming fully vested in the employer contributions. Vested means entitled to receive all the monies in one's individual account. A participant is always fully vested in his or her own employee contributions. However, many plan sponsors impose incremental vesting percentages that participants have to satisfy to be eligible to receive all the monies the employer has contributed to the participant's account.

The plan document will usually state how forfeitures are to be treated. If the plan document states that forfeited monies are to be used to offset future employer contributions, determine whether forfeited monies were properly used for this purpose. Determine also whether the amount of such forfeitures used to offset current-year employer contributions has been disclosed. Forfeited, nonvested amounts at year-end that will be used to reduce future employer contributions in the subsequent plan year should also be disclosed in the notes to the plan's financial statements. Additionally, consider the appropriateness of how such forfeitures are presented in the statement of net assets available for benefits. Those amounts are essentially unallocated assets that often are identified as prepaid employer contributions. Forfeitures should have no effect on the statement of changes in net assets available for benefits, as they are already assets of the plan. If forfeitures were reallocated to remaining participants, test this reallocation on a sample basis.

Note that in accordance with IRS Revenue Rulings 80-155 and 2002-42, generally, all forfeitures need to be allocated each year. If forfeitures are not allocated, this may be considered an operational defect for the plan.

Knowledge check

2. When testing employer contributions, the auditor should

   a. Recalculate the employer contribution only if no board approval is required.
   b. Verify that the calculation used to make the employer match is in accordance with the plan document.
   c. Determine that the employer contribution does not exceed the contribution from the employee.
   d. Test forfeitures that the plan states should be used for plan expenses paid by the employer.

Individual participant accounts

One of the objectives of auditing procedures applied to individual participant accounts is to provide the auditor with a reasonable basis to conclude whether net assets and transactions have been properly allocated to participant accounts. Participant account balances are an accumulation of transactions and represent the amount the participant is entitled to receive as a benefit payment. Overstated or understated participant account balances may result in errors in allocations or benefits paid to participants. Each type of account activity—such as contributions, income allocation, expense allocation, distributions and forfeitures—should be taken into consideration in the determination of audit procedures. In an ERISA limited-scope audit, the certification of investment activity is at the trust level only and does not apply to the allocation of investment income to participant accounts. This investment allocation should be tested in conjunction with the other individual participant account testing.

Contributions

The plan instrument and related documents provide the information to determine the formula for upper and lower contribution limits and the rates used to calculate the employee contribution. You should read the plan document to determine the basis for calculating the employee contribution, review the employee election form, and then recalculate the contribution to verify that it was made in accordance with the plan document and employee election.

The plan document specifies the aspects of compensation—for example, base wages, overtime, or bonuses—that are to be included in the calculation of contributions. Auditors should test the payroll data to determine if the compensation used in the calculation of contributions matches the plan document definition of eligible compensation. An employer may use any definition of compensation that satisfies IRC Section 414(s), which does not allow a method of determining compensation if that method discriminates in favor of highly compensated employees. Misinterpreting the definition of compensation is one of the most common operational errors for a DC plan.

Audit objectives

The audit objectives for contributions received from participants are to provide assurance that amounts received have been determined and recorded in accordance with the plan document. Also, you should verify that employee contributions are properly recorded in the financial statements in conformity with GAAP and that they are being allocated to the investment vehicles in accordance with the participant's designation. You should determine that employee contributions are being deposited to the participant accounts on a timely basis and in accordance with the plan's policies and procedures.

The objective of auditing procedures for testing individual participant accounts is to provide you with a reasonable basis for concluding whether net assets have been allocated to the individual participant accounts in accordance with the plan instrument and whether the sum of the participant accounts reconciles with the total net assets available for plan benefits.

 Example 5-1

An example of employee contributions follows: Ms. Boyce elects to have 6 percent of her salary withheld from her regular pay. She determines that she wants 50 percent of her contribution invested in the equity fund, 30 percent in the fixed-income fund, and 20 percent in the growth fund. Ms. Boyce's gross monthly pay totals $1,000. Her employee contribution totals $60 ($1,000 × 6%) with $30 going to the equity fund ($60 × 50%), $18 to the fixed income fund ($60 × 30%), and $12 to the growth fund ($60 × 20%).

Suggested audit procedures

1. Obtain from the recordkeeper the individual account records showing beginning and ending balances and current-period additions and deductions by individual account and in total. Test the mathematical accuracy of the report. Agree the total of the ending balances for all participants from the prior-year records to the total of the beginning balances for all participants in the trustee report. IRS Revenue Ruling 70-125 states that the total of the individual participant accounts must equal the total amount of investments in the trustee report. That is, this ruling does not permit unallocated monies to sit indefinitely in a suspense account. The monies must be allocated back to the participants or shown as an asset if the forfeitures will be used to offset future employer contributions.
2. Obtain and review the reconciliation of the recordkeeper account balances to the trust statement balance.
3. Agree or reconcile year-end totals shown in the individual account records (in the aggregate) to the year-end balances in the plan's final accounting records and to the trustee report for the following:
   a. Beginning balances
   b. Employer contributions
   c. Employee contributions
   d. Net investment income
   e. Administrative expenses
   f. Withdrawals
   g. Forfeitures, if applicable
   h. Participant loans
   i. Fund transfers (for example, rollovers, merged plans)
   j. Ending balances
4. To test employee contributions, allocations, and individual account balances efficiently, confirm the information with the participant. (You may use those participants selected for testing of employer contributions.) The confirmation request should include a copy of the participant's account summary as of the end of the plan year, which details the balance in each of the investment accounts. It also should include a summary of the participant's elections. You should try to coordinate the sending of confirmations soon after the participants' year-end account summaries are originally sent to them. This timing may result in a higher response rate from the participants than if the confirmations are sent out several months after the plan year-end.

5. Review the participant election forms to understand how allocations are to be made to individual participant accounts. Evaluate the procedures employed by the plan sponsor or recordkeeper to verify that allocations made to individual participant accounts are appropriate and applied consistently. Review the AT-C section 320, *Reporting on an Examination of Controls at a Service Organization Relevant to User Entities' Internal Control Over Financial Reporting* (AICPA, *Professional Standards*) report, hereinafter referred to as a SOC 1® report (if available) report for the recordkeeper, if applicable.

   a. Determine the plan's policy regarding the timing of deposits to the trustee for employee contributions. DOL regulations require them to be made as soon as such contributions can be segregated by the plan sponsor, but no later than 15 business days following the month in which employee contributions are withheld or received by the employer.

   b. Determine whether any withholdings (for employee contributions to the plan) that were authorized by the participant were withheld and included as an addition to the participant's account. Determine that monies withheld were deposited into the participant's account as soon as practicable. To the extent monies are held by the sponsor and not deposited in a timely manner to the participant's account, this represents a prohibited transaction that should be reported on a supplemental schedule to be attached to Form 5500. (See chapter 6 for additional information.)

   c. If the plan allows the participant to determine to which investment vehicle his or her monies are contributed (for example, participant-directed fund), verify that the participant contribution was allocated in accordance with instructions made by the participant. Consider the frequency that the participants can change their investment option elections and whether there are any records of these changes. To the extent voice response systems are utilized, see suggested procedures in chapters 1 and 3.

   d. Some self-directed funds permit a participant to purchase stocks, securities, shares in mutual funds, and so on—in essence, any security or other investment that is available through the stock market and brokers-dealers, in addition to, or in lieu of offering a selected number of investment options to the participants. If this investment option exists for the plan being audited, you should test that monies withheld from each participant selected previously were appropriately used to purchase the securities chosen by the participant.

   e. For plan transfer amounts, determine whether amounts from the individual participant account records were properly (1) authorized by the individual, (2) recorded in the proper amount on a timely basis, and (3) recorded in the individual's account in the other plan (or fund) in the same period.

6. If you elect not to verify employee contributions, allocations, and account balance information through the use of confirmations or if a confirmation is not received back from the participant, you may select activity in individual participant accounts for testing by sampling individuals from the current-period additions column of the current-year individual account records. (Remember, you may use the same participants selected for employer contribution testing to achieve efficiencies.) For those selections, you may perform the following to test current-period additions:

   For employee contribution amounts, (a) agree such amounts recorded in the individual's account to payroll records of amounts withheld, and (b) determine whether the amount of withholdings were authorized by the individual. Investment income allocated to the individual accounts was tested earlier in this chapter.

   It should be noted that, many times, participant data is only maintained electronically, and original paper documents may have been destroyed. In such cases, the auditor may need to obtain an understanding of the process and the controls used to capture the data, including a walk-through. If the auditor is unable to obtain the necessary evidence regarding participant data or participant accounts on which financial statement amounts are based, there may be a limitation on the scope of the audit. Restrictions on the scope of the audit, whether imposed by the client or circumstances, such as the inability to obtain sufficient appropriate audit evidence, may require the auditor to conclude that a modification to the auditor's opinion on the financial statements, in accordance with AU-C section 705, is necessary.

7. Make a selection of employees from the year-to-date payroll disbursement records.

   Note: Efficiencies can be achieved to the extent that you make selections in conjunction with participant eligibility testing covered in the following text.

   Obtain the employee's personnel file and determine whether the employee is an eligible participant (that is, meets age and service requirements) and whether the employee elected to participate in the plan. For employees who are eligible and elected to participate in the plan, perform the following (as applicable) to test current-period additions for understatement:

   a. Determine that any withholdings (for employee contributions to the plan) that were authorized by the participant were withheld and included as an addition to the participant's account. Determine that monies withheld were deposited into the participant's account as soon as practicable. (To the extent monies are held by the sponsor and not deposited in a timely manner to the participant's account, this represents a prohibited transaction.)
   b. Recalculate the withholding using the participant's deferral election and the plan definition of eligible compensation.

   Note: Any differences other than rounding should be investigated. It is inappropriate to apply the financial statement defined materiality to individual account testing.

   c. If the plan allows the participant to determine to which investment vehicle his or her monies are contributed (for example, participant-directed fund), verify that the participant contribution was allocated to the various investment vehicle(s) in accordance with instructions made by the participant.
   d. Some self-directed funds permit a participant to purchase stocks, securities, shares in mutual funds, and so on; in essence, any security or other investment that is available through the stock market and brokers dealers rather than offer a selected number of investment options to the participants. If this is true of the plan being audited, you should test that monies withheld from each participant selected previously were appropriately used to purchase the securities selected by the participant.
   e. For plan transfer amounts, determine whether amounts from the individual participant account records were properly (1) authorized by the individual, (2) recorded in the proper amount on a timely basis, and (3) recorded in the individual's account in the other plan (or fund) in the same period.

Knowledge check

3. Which of the following statements is incorrect regarding employee contributions?

    a. The plan document sets forth minimum contribution limits.
    b. Employee contributions are not subject to forfeiture.
    c. Employee contributions may not be invested in plan sponsor stock, even if that is an investment option of the plan.
    d. Employee contributions should be deposited to the trustee as soon as practicable.

Participant eligibility

In conducting an audit of a 401(k) plan, you should consider whether the plan participants have met the appropriate criteria for participation in the plan. Essentially, you should perform participant eligibility testing to determine whether the active employees of the plan sponsor have met the criteria established by the plan document to participate, whether they have elected to participate, and whether an individual account record exists for the participant based on the election made to participate. You should also determine for terminated employees of the plan sponsor that they have received distributions from the plan upon their termination of employment by the plan sponsor, or if they had sufficient account balances that allow them to continue to invest their money in the plan.

You may test participant eligibility either while testing internal controls for the plan (see chapter 3) or while testing participant contributions. If testing eligibility while testing contributions, you should, for the selections made for detail contribution testing purposes, determine whether the participants selected have satisfied the criteria in the plan document for participation. Note that many plans have been amended to use automatic enrollment.

You may consider making selections from the employer's records of terminated employees to test that distributions have been made appropriately to terminated participants of the plan. In utilizing the same selections for testing participant eligibility as for testing contributions, you can add some efficiency to the audit process. If you are testing only participants who are contributing to the plan, you should complete some additional procedures to verify eligible individuals are not being excluded from the plan.

Participant eligibility testing requires obtaining information from the plan sponsor and recordkeeper to effectively test eligibility. You will need to review information from the plan sponsor's payroll and personnel files to determine the length of time the participant has been employed by the plan sponsor, whether the participant is an active employee, and whether the participant satisfies any other conditions stipulated by the plan document for participation. You also will need to review the recordkeeping statements in order to determine whether an individual account record has been established for the participant.

For a plan with a voice response recordkeeping system, testing of participant eligibility should not be affected by the voice response feature. The recordkeeper should be able to provide evidence of individual account records for active, eligible participants as well as evidence of account distributions for terminated participants. In addition, for plans that permit terminated participants to maintain their account balances in the plan for a period of time, you should determine that the recordkeeper has appropriately classified the participant as terminated.

As with all of the other areas of auditing a 401(k) plan, testing participant eligibility may provide you with an opportunity to generate suggestions for improving the administration of the plan, which should be presented to the plan administrator, or other appropriate individuals in a management commentary letter as explained in chapter 3.

Contributions from other identified sources

While it is rare, on occasion a plan may receive contributions from state subsidies or federal grants. You should (1) agree the contributions from these other sources to supporting documentation indicating the source; (2) test the amounts; and (3) determine how the contributions are to be allocated to the participant accounts to verify that allocations were made in accordance with the contributor's instructions.

Withdrawals

On September 29, 2017, H.R.3823-Disaster Relief and Airway Extension Act became law. This act includes the following actions in regards to retirement plans:

- Waives 10 percent penalty on early distributions (up to a maximum of 100k)
- Applies to taxpayers who lived in a federally declared disaster area
- Applies to distributions made in 2016 and 2017
- The amount distributed may be repaid
- Income inclusion over three-year period

These actions are intended to aid in the relief of disaster area victims in regards to several natural disasters that occurred in 2017.

The balance in a participant's individual account represents the participant's accumulated benefits and determines the amount of benefits due the participant on termination, retirement, death, disability, age 70½, and qualified domestic relations orders. Many plans utilize a vesting schedule, providing that a participant be in the plan for a minimum number of years before becoming fully vested in the employer contributions allocated to his or her account. (Note that the participant is always 100-percent vested in his or her employee contributions.) You should read the plan document to determine the basis for calculating the vesting percentage for employer contributions and then recalculate that percentage and benefit amount to verify that it was made in accordance with the plan document. You also should test to verify that payments are being made only to qualified participants who have met the requirements for the particular type of distribution. For example, if the withdrawal is due to termination, then you should review the plan sponsor's records to verify the individual had terminated his or her employment. Certain plans may also allow withdrawals for hardship and at age 59½. (See the following section, "Loans," for distributions to participants prior to retirement.)

Knowledge check

4. When testing benefit payments made to terminated participants, the auditor should do all of the following, except

    a. Determine that the benefit payment is made in accordance with plan provisions.
    b. Determine if a forfeiture results from any portion of the employer contribution.
    c. Determine if a forfeiture results from any portion of the employee contribution.
    d. Verify that the participant has terminated employment and is eligible to receive a benefit payment.

5. When testing benefit payments, the auditor should consider all of the following, except

    a. Whether procedures exist to investigate long outstanding benefit checks.
    b. Confirming benefit payments directly with the participant.
    c. Verifying that a lump sum or installment distribution was made to the terminated or retired participant.
    d. Whether the participant has reached at least age 65 to qualify for benefit payments.

Loans

As stated in the previous chapter, many 401(k) plans allow participants to borrow against the vested portion of their individual accounts, prior to termination or retirement. ERISA and the IRS have established guidelines that must be followed regarding loan term, interest rate, and so on.

The plan document will state the rules related to participant loans. For example, loans typically may not exceed 50 percent of the participant's vested account balance, cannot be made for longer than 5 years, unless it is used to purchase a primary residence, and the interest rate must be comparable to the prevailing market for interest rates.

Audit objectives

The audit objectives for withdrawals and loans are to provide assurance that (1) payments are made in accordance with plan provisions and related documents; (2) payments are made only to persons entitled to receive them (that is, only to persons who meet the plan's criteria for loans; are terminated, retired, or their beneficiaries); and (3) transactions are recorded in the proper account, amount, and period.

Suggested audit procedures

Consider using the same participants that were used for employer and employee contribution testing, if these selections provide sufficient coverage of loans. Select activity in individual participant accounts for testing by sampling from the current-period deductions columns of the current-year individual accounts records. For those selections, you may perform the following to test current-period deductions:

1. Examine the participant's file to determine that the participant is eligible to receive a benefit payment (terminated, retired, deceased, and so on) or loan. You should examine evidence of age and employment history, as well as the documentation supporting the withdrawal or loan.
2. Review the benefit election form to verify that the participant has selected an appropriate form of payment (for example, lump sum or installment) based on provisions set forth in the plan document. (Note that some plans will require a participant to take a lump-sum distribution rather than installments if the total vested participant account balance falls below a certain minimum amount.)
3. Review the plan administrator's authorization of the distribution. Some distributions are processed automatically by the recordkeeper, such as termination of employment. Other distributions must be authorized by the plan administrator or sponsor. Hardship withdrawals must meet certain plan provision requirements in order to comply with the IRC. Qualified domestic relations orders (for example, the dissolution of a marriage) have several legal requirements that must be met in order for the distribution to meet the requirement of the IRC.
4. Determine the reasonableness of the withdrawal or loan based on the plan instrument and related documents including the vesting schedule and forfeiture policy. Recompute the forfeiture, if any, on the employer contributions allocated to the selected participant's account.
5. Compare the withdrawal or loan amount to cash disbursement records or trustee reports. If the participant is being paid out over a period of time (for example, five years), agree the benefit payment

to the prior year or determine the propriety of the payment amount based on the total benefit payable divided by the number of years over which the payment will be made.

6. Confirm withdrawal or loan directly with the participant.
7. If confirmations are not received back from the participant, then examine canceled checks—noting agreement to trustee reports of date, amount, and payee. Verify that the endorsement on the check agrees to that on the participant's application for benefit payment.
8. Test that loan repayments and interest income are properly calculated and recorded.
9. Determine whether the plan administrator has procedures for investigating long-outstanding checks. Long-outstanding checks may be indicative of duplicate payments or deceased or missing participants.

Administrative expenses

Agreements with recordkeepers, investment advisors, and others provide the basis for determining the appropriate amount of administrative expenses to be paid and who is liable for paying these expenses (that is, the plan sponsor or the participants). You should read these agreements to verify that payments are made in accordance with these agreements and amounts are paid by the proper parties.

Administrative expenses may be assessed in a number of ways. Two examples are (1) fees based on a percentage of the total net assets that are being invested, or (2) fees based on the total number of participants. In the case of fees as a percent of total net assets, if total net assets were $3,500,000 and the fees were assessed at 0.5 percent, total fees due would be $17,500 (3,500,000 × 0.005).

Although plan expenses are typically small when compared to total pan assets, it is important to perform procedures to assess these expenses. Payments of improper expenses from plan assets could be considered a breach of the fiduciary duties of the plan administrator and may be considered a nonexempt transaction. See chapter 6 for further considerations over the tax-exempt status of a plan.

Audit objectives

The audit objectives for administrative expenses are to provide assurance that (1) administrative expenses are in accordance with agreements, (2) payments are properly classified as administrative expenses, and (3) transactions are recorded in the proper amounts and period.

Suggested audit procedures

1. Analyze administrative expenses to determine which parties provide administrative services. Examine supporting invoices or documentation and calculation of the expenses. You may be able to review administrative expenses analytically, depending on the nature and contractual arrangements that exist.
2. Review the terms of the plan instrument to determine that administrative expenses were properly authorized.
3. If the plan has an agreement with a contract administrator, review the contract to verify that the services contracted for were performed and that payments were made in accordance with the agreement.
4. Determine that fees charged by the recordkeeper, investment advisors, and others comply with their respective agreements.
5. Determine that administrative expenses are paid by the appropriate party (for example, plan sponsor or participants).
6. Obtain a listing of administrative expenses and review the nature and type of expenses to verify that they are allowable under the plan document.

Number of years of employment	Vesting percentage
0–1	0 %
1–2	20 %
2–3	40 %
3–4	60 %
4–5	80 %
5 or more	100 %

Under the vesting chart, if Mr. Adams terminated employment after working just over two years, what percentage of the employer contributions that had been allocated to his account during those two years would he be entitled to receive? What would happen to the remaining percentage of the employer contribution?

 Case study discussion question participant eligibility

XYZ, Inc. (Company) is a manufacturer of high-end electronic goods—including televisions, DVD players, and stereos. The Company sponsors a 401(k) plan. The 401(k) plan administrator, Gary, was just recently hired. Gary previously served as a 401(k) plan administrator at ABC, Inc. for seven years.

In an attempt to familiarize himself with the 401(k) plan, Gary has been reading the 401(k) plan document. During his examination of the plan document, he noted that the eligibility requirements were that employees must be 21 years old and have completed at least 6 months of service. Gary remembered a conversation in his orientation meeting with the company about the 401(k) plan and was told that he could begin participation in the 401(k) plan immediately.

The 401(k) plan was scheduled for an audit at the end of the month. Given Gary's previous plan administrator experience, he knew that the determination of plan eligibility was important. He decided to make a sample selection of participants to see if the proper eligibility requirements were being applied.

Help Gary determine whether the five selections are eligible to participate in the plan as of and for the year ended December 31, 2014. In addition, determine each selection's date the eligibility requirements were fully satisfied

Selections:

2014 Selections		
NAME	DOB	DOH
John Doe	11/23/1976	1/1/2014
Sam Jones	1/5/1980	10/1/2014
Jane Smith	6/4/1968	5/1/2012
Mike Miller	7/18/1994	2/1/2014
Jennifer Murry	9/8/1993	1/1/2014

Case study discussion question participant eligibility (continued)

Debrief:

The 401(k) plan document should contain a definition of "employee" and provide requirements for when employees must become plan participants eligible to make elective deferrals. In this case, the plan document includes eligibility requirements that state employees must be 21 years old and have completed at least 6 months of service. To reduce the risks of including ineligible employees and omitting eligible employees, the plan sponsor should make sure the accuracy of employee data such as dates of birth, hire, and termination; number of hours worked; compensation for the year; 401(k) election information and any other information necessary to properly administer the plan.

Using the plan definition of eligible employee along with the plan age and service requirements, the plan sponsor should determine each employee's eligibility.

A retirement plan doesn't qualify for tax-preferential treatment unless it meets the eligibility and participation standards. These general rules are as follows:

- A plan may not require an employee to be older than 21 to participate in a plan.
- There are two ways to credit service to an employee:
  - **Hours of service**: A 401(k) plan may not require more than a year of service as a condition of becoming eligible to participate.
    - A **year** of service means a calendar year, plan year, or any other consecutive 12-month period during which the employee completes at least 1,000 hours of service starting on the employment commencement date.
  - **Elapsed time**: Under the elapsed time method, an employee's eligibility to participate isn't based upon the completion of a specified number of hours of service. Instead, it is generally determined in reference to a 12-month period.
- An eligible employee must enter the plan within six months after satisfying any eligibility requirements under the plan.
- The plan document may impose rules that are more liberal by allowing a younger age and lesser service requirement. For example, a plan may allow a person to participate immediately upon becoming an employee.
- The plan document contains the definitions and requirements for becoming a participant in the plan.

In addition to identifying eligible employees, the plan sponsor must also give them the opportunity to make a salary deferral election. The plan sponsor should retain copies of who is notified regarding eligibility and when.

Potential consequences of violating the plan document provisions include things such as the following:

- Making participants whole for missed contributions and lost earnings when they were not allowed to participate
- Refunding contributions made by ineligible employees
- Amending the plan to incorporate other employee groups
- Losing the plan's tax exempt status
- Entering a correction program with the IRS or DOL

Case study discussion question participant eligibility (continued)

Selections:

John Doe—Mr. Doe is over the age of 21 and he completed 6 months of service during the year, therefore he was eligible to participate during the year ended December 31, 2014. He reached eligible status on July 1, 2014.

Sam Jones—Mr. Jones is over the age of 21, however, he did not complete 6 months of service during the year. Therefore, he was not eligible to participate during the year ended December 31, 2014. He will reach eligible status on April 1, 2012.

Jane Smith—Ms. Smith is over the age of 21 and she completed 6 months of service during the year, therefore she was eligible to participate during the year ended December 31, 2014. She reached eligible status on prior to the plan year—November 1, 2012.

Mike Miller—Mr. Miller has completed 6 months of service during the year; however, he has not reached the age of 21 and, therefore he was not eligible to participate during the year ended December 31, 2014. He will reach eligible status upon turning 21 years of age on July 18, 2015.

Jennifer Murry—Ms. Murry turned 21 years of age on September 8, 2014, and completed her 6 months of service during the year. Therefore, she was eligible to participate in the plan during the year ended December 31, 2014. She reached eligible status on September 8, 2014.

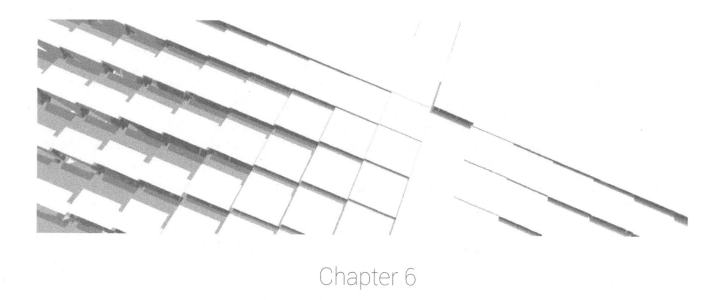

Chapter 6

Other Auditing Considerations

Learning objectives

After completing this chapter, you should be able to do the following:

- Identify the IRC requirements for qualified (tax-exempt) status.

- Recognize representations from plan management.

- Recall the components of Form 5500 and identify the supplemental schedules that are part of Form 5500 filing.

- Recognize party in interest transactions and identify prohibited transactions.

- Recall unique aspects of initial audits.

- Identify provisions affecting employee benefit plans as they relate to Form 11-K filings with the SEC.

Introduction

A 401(k) plan must meet certain requirements to keep a qualified (tax-exempt) status. Although the auditor is not responsible for performing the tests that demonstrate the plan's compliance with these requirements, the auditor should perform procedures relative to the plan's tax status. Form 5500 is the annual report that summarizes certain data for each employee benefit plan to report that data to the respective governmental agencies.

Plan tax status

Generally, the financial statements of a 401(k) plan do not record any income tax liability or provision for income tax expense, as the plan should be designed and operated in accordance with the Internal Revenue Code (IRC) requirements to maintain its qualified, tax-exempt status. In the majority of plans, plan management requests a determination letter from the IRS saying that as of a certain date and point in time, the plan document has been found to be in accordance with the appropriate IRC requirements so that the plan has qualified tax-exempt status. (For plans whose plan document is created from a standardized and non-standardized prototype, the plans may rely on the opinion letter received by the prototype's sponsor. Thus, the determination letter will be issued to the prototype's issuer.) Effective January 1, 2017, the IRS has substantially changed the determination letter program. With limited exceptions, determination letters will only be issued covering the formation of a new retirement plan or the termination of an existing retirement plan. The expiration date included on determination letters issued before this change in the determination letter program will no longer apply. This change only affects plans that are individually designed.

However, the existence of such a letter for a 401(k) plan does not necessarily guarantee that the plan is qualified. For a plan to continue to maintain its qualified status, the plan must operate the plan in accordance with the plan document and it must comply on an annual basis with certain operating tests such as tests of coverage, nondiscrimination, and maximum benefit limitation. With 401(k) plans, the plan recordkeeper will usually be responsible for performing those operating tests, so you should request copies of the test results from the recordkeeper.

In applying auditing procedures in the area of a plan's tax status, you should consider the following:

- Whether the trust established under the plan is qualified under the IRC as being exempt from federal income taxes and whether any transactions or events have occurred during the plan year that may affect that tax-exempt status
- If the plan has lost its tax-exempt status, then the plan has appropriately recorded any income tax liability and expense for any realized investment income earned by the plan and has disclosed that matter in accordance with generally accepted accounting principles (you should consider the provisions of FASB *Accounting Standards Codification*® [ASC] 450, *Contingencies*, in this situation).
- Whether a receivable from the plan sponsor should be recorded on the plan's financial statements if the plan has any income tax exposure

To perform the audit procedures regarding the plan's tax status, you should know enough about matters that could negatively affect the 401(k) plan's tax status, and you should be familiar with certain provisions of the IRC that relate to this type of plan.

Unrelated business taxable income

Although qualified benefit plans are not generally subject to taxation, certain activities or types of investments may be taxable. In general, unrelated business taxable income (UBTI) of a tax-exempt entity is subject to taxation. *UBTI* is defined as:

Gross income derived from an unrelated trade or business that is regularly carried on, less allowable deductions directly connected with the trade or business.

With respect to qualified retirement plans, *unrelated trade or business* is defined by the IRC as any trade or business regularly carried on by the trust, a partnership, or an S corporation of which the trust is an investor.

A qualified plan may have UBTI due to business activity of its investments when those investments pass through their activity to the investor. Nonleveraged investments, such as government securities, stocks and debt instruments of corporations, mutual funds, and insurance company annuity contracts do not typically generate UBTI. However, other nonleveraged investments, such as investments in partnerships; real estate investment trusts; or options to buy or sell securities, such as short sales or repurchase agreements, may generate UBTI. Further, direct or indirect leveraged investments, even in passive investments such as stocks, bonds, or real estate, can generate UBTI. In practice, the most common plans that generate UBTI are health and welfare (H&W) plans with voluntary employees' beneficiary association (VEBA) trusts because the funding restrictions can convert even passive investment income into UBTI. For an H&W plan, UBTI generally arises if the VEBA trust assets exceed the amount reasonably necessary to cover unpaid accrued claims, resulting in the excess accumulations being subject to UBTI. With the increase of investments in hedge funds, private equity funds, and other less traditional investment arrangements, more retirement plans are facing an obligation for unrelated business income tax.

Examples of activities that may produce unrelated business income include the following:

1. Income from investments in partnerships and certain other alternative investments that are pass-through entities for tax purposes and that conduct a trade or business or whose activities include one or more of items (3) to (5)
2. Rents from debt-financed property
3. Rents based on a percentage of net income rather than gross income
4. Rents on personal property
5. Unrelated debt-financed income

For all benefit plans, UBTI can arise from general investment activity. The plan should have procedures in place to determine whether an investment is likely to yield UBTI. When UBTI is present, procedures should be in place to determine whether a tax return (Form 990-T) is required and whether estimated payments must be made. Further, when the UBTI arises from pass-through investments, procedures should be in place to determine whether tax positions taken by the pass-through entity satisfy the standards of FASB ASC 740.

Income taxes

FASB ASC 740-10 clarifies the accounting and provides implementation guidance for uncertainty in income taxes recognized in an entity's financial statements. In certain situations, uncertain tax positions may be associated with the determination of UBTI or the tax-exempt status of the plan.

The following are examples of possible uncertain tax positions associated with UBTI:

- Aspects of the definition of *unrelated business income* are subject to judgment concerning whether an activity is considered a trade or business or is regularly carried on.
- Once a source of unrelated business income is identified, there may be uncertainty in computing the amount of gross income from the activity, determining allowable expenses or attributing expenses to the proper time period, determining the amount of reportable income and when it is reported, and determining the classification of income.
- When the enterprise generating UBTI operates in multiple states, uncertain tax positions may arise about whether the state taxes UBTI of an Employee Retirement Income Security Act (ERISA) plan, the right to tax exists within such state, or the apportionment of income among states has been properly determined.

A plan's status as tax exempt is a tax position that may be subject to uncertainty. If the plan has entered into a correction program, as provided by the Employee Plans Compliance Resolution System, such program may aid the plan administrator in assessing that there is no uncertainty with respect to the plan's tax-exempt status. They provide no relief on tax issues associated with UBTI.

FASB ASC 740-10 prescribes a recognition threshold and measurement attribute for the financial statement recognition and measurement of a tax position taken or expected to be taken in a tax return. FASB ASC 740-10 also provides guidance on derecognition, classification, interest and penalties, accounting in interim periods, disclosure, and transition. According to the FASB ASC glossary, the term *tax position* refers to a position in a previously filed tax return or a position expected to be taken in a future tax return that is reflected in measuring current or deferred income tax assets and liabilities for interim or annual periods. A tax position can result in a permanent reduction of income taxes payable, a deferral of income taxes otherwise currently payable to future years, or a change in the expected realizability of deferred tax assets.

FASB ASC 740-10-50-15 states that all entities should disclose all of the following at the end of each annual reporting period presented:

- The total amounts of interest and penalties recognized in the statement of operations and the total amounts of interest and penalties recognized in the statement of financial position
- For positions for which it is reasonably possible that the total amounts of unrecognized tax benefits will significantly increase or decrease within 12 months of the reporting date:
  - The nature of the uncertainty
  - The nature of the event that could occur in the next 12 months that would cause the change
  - An estimate of the range of the reasonably possible change or a statement that an estimate of the range cannot be made
- A description of tax years that remain subject to examination by major tax jurisdictions

The following are examples of substantive audit procedures for auditing a qualified retirement plan's tax status:

- Reviewing the IRS tax determination letter on an individually designed plan or IRS opinion letter on a prototype or volume submitter plan or, when not available, reviewing an opinion letter from the plan's qualified tax counsel or other ERISA adviser

- Determining whether plan amendments have been made that are required as a result of changes in the laws and regulations
- Inquiring of the plan administrator whether plan operations have been revised to comply with current law changes, even if plan amendments are not yet required. Consider reviewing correspondence from the plan's legal counsel, third-party administrator, or other ERISA or tax adviser
- For individually designed plans or other plans in which there have been substantial departures from the approved language, if a determination letter has not been received or a request for a determination letter has not been made, and an opinion letter from the plan's tax counsel is not available, reviewing those aspects of the plan document is relevant to the determination of its tax-exempt status
- Inquiring of the plan administrator, trustee, or other appropriate plan representative about the plan's or trust's operations or changes in plan or trust design that may cause the plan or trust to lose its tax-exempt status
- Inquiring of plan management about the performance and results of required compliance testing for the specific type of plan
- Reviewing the results of auditing procedures applied in other areas of the audit and considering the findings in relation to tax qualification requirements, as applicable. For example, procedures performed for contributions and distributions when it was found that the plan failed to comply with plan provisions
- Inquiring of plan management, plan administrator, and/or counsel whether the sponsor is part of a controlled group of organizations and whether this has been taken into consideration in the performance of the required compliance testing.
- Inquiring about the procedures applied by the plan administrator in determining UBTI, such as the review of Schedule K-1s received from investments in pass-through entities, partnerships, LLCs, or subchapter S corporations for potential tax accruals
- To the extent UBTI is generated by investments of the plan or pass-through entities, inquiring about the procedures to determine whether any uncertain tax positions have been taken relating to the UBTI either at the trust or investment entity level that could have a material effect at the plan level
- Inquiring of the plan administrator whether Form 990-T has been filed and whether any required state filings have been made
- Obtaining a copy of Form 990-T and related state filings, UBTI calculations, and supporting detail for the year and testing as necessary
- Verifying that UBTI for the year and the associated income tax accrual at year-end have been recorded in accordance with the applicable financial reporting framework
- Obtaining a representation from management that the plan is qualified, and the associated trust is tax exempt under the appropriate sections of the IRC

Knowledge check

1. What should a plan do to maintain its qualified tax status?

    a. Comply with certain operating tests every three years.
    b. Obtain a determination letter.
    c. Operate the plan in accordance with the plan document.
    d. Represent to the auditors that the plan is qualified.

2. Related to income tax exposure, the auditor should consider all of the following except which?

   a. Whether tax has been recorded for unrelated business taxable income even if the plan is qualified.
   b. Whether the plan has appropriately recorded any income tax liability and expense for any realized investment income earned by the plan and has disclosed that matter in accordance with generally accepted accounting principles.
   c. Whether a receivable from the plan sponsor should be recorded on the plan's financial statements.
   d. Whether a determination letter was obtained.

3. Which of the following is NOT important to the plan auditor regarding consideration of the plan's tax status and the plan administrator's monitoring of the tax status?

   a. Consideration of whether refunds for the plan year were required as a result of the discrimination testing.
   b. Existence of a determination letter for the plan.
   c. Whether or not the plan administrator has consulted an ERISA attorney regarding a payment made from the plan to the plan sponsor.
   d. Whether the employer makes a discretionary contribution to the plan.

Testing for discrimination

The most common tests that a 401(k) plan must pass each plan year are the ACP (actual contribution percentage) and ADP (actual deferral percentage) tests, which are tests designed to limit the disparity between elective deferrals by highly compensated employees and elective deferrals made by non-highly compensated participants. The ADP test compares the actual percentages of compensation deferred or contributed to the plan by highly compensated employees to the percentages deferred by the non-highly compensated participants. The ACP test measures the average amount of matching and after-tax contributions made to the plan by highly compensated employees to those of the non-highly compensated participants. You should be familiar with the general provisions of the tests to be able to determine on reviewing them whether they appear to be unreasonable.

Importance of using correct compensation

Independent auditors are not expected to test the underlying calculations for the nondiscrimination tests but, rather, are expected to inquire if the testing was performed in accordance with the respective requirements using the appropriate data. Appropriate data includes the compensation used. You are not expected to recalculate the test results (unless separately engaged by the plan administrator to do so), but should be familiar with the general concepts of the tests. You can refer to the actual IRC provisions for additional specifics regarding the tests.

Safe harbor methods

Beginning with the 1999 plan year, a plan may eliminate the need to perform the ADP test, thanks to new safe harbor methods announced by the IRS. A plan must make this election and notify participants before the beginning of the plan year.

The safe harbor methods have strict contribution requirements, mandate immediate vesting for the safe harbor contributions, restrict withdrawals, and lay down stringent notification requirements to participants.

The safe harbor methods allow for two different contribution formulas. A 3-percent profit-sharing contribution may be made to each participant based on the participant's compensation, or the plan may match 100 percent of the first 3 percent contributed by the employee and 50 percent of the contributions from 3 percent to 5 percent. These safe harbor contributions must immediately vest 100 percent in the participants' accounts.

A participant may not withdraw the safe harbor contributions until either age 59 1/2 or until employment is terminated. Also, safe harbor contributions are not available for hardship distributions.

If all the earlier requirements are met, the plan is not required to perform the ADP testing.

A plan can avoid performing the ACP test if, in addition to the earlier requirements, the plan also provides that no contribution of greater than 6 percent will be matched by the sponsor and the matching percentages are similar for all employees.

Consequences of violations

If you identify any possible violations of laws or regulations that could affect the plan's tax status, you need to consider their possible effects on the plan and consider the need to disclose such matters in the notes to the plan's financial statements. If you determine that the plan's tax-exempt status may be in jeopardy, you should consider the potential audit implications at both the plan level and for the plan sponsor. The following may be necessary: disclosures in the plan's—and plan sponsor's—financial statements; the recording of any amounts for income tax liability (to the extent the plan would lose its tax-exempt status, the investment earnings of the plan would become taxable); and expenses or penalties that may be levied by the IRS.

In addition, the plan sponsor may reimburse the plan for any tax expenses so that the recording of a receivable from the sponsor may be appropriate. You should also consider if any such matters represent fraud or errors that you may need to report to higher levels of plan management and possibly disclose as reportable conditions and also report to the Department of Labor (DOL) as nonexempt transactions via Schedule G, Part III of Form 5500. See the following section for a discussion of the supplemental schedules including Schedule G, Part III for nonexempt transactions.

You also should obtain from plan management a representation in the management representation letter concerning compliance with the laws and regulations that, if violated, could result in the disqualification of the plan.

ERISA requires that the notes to the plan's financial statements disclose "information concerning whether or not a tax ruling or determination letter has been obtained." FASB ASC 740 requires disclosure of the federal income tax status of a plan only if a favorable tax determination letter has not been obtained or maintained.

In certain instances, the plan may not yet have requested a determination letter. This may be the case particularly if it is newly established, is a prototype plan, or has perhaps changed significantly as the result of a plan merger (for example, the plan merged with another savings plan as the result of a business combination). In such cases, you should review the sections of the plan document relevant to its tax-exempt status and perform the other procedures described previously.

In addition, in certain cases you may determine that the plan's tax status may be in jeopardy and the plan may have entered into a Voluntary Compliance Program, Closing Agreement Program, or other such voluntary program with the IRS, to correct deficiencies in either the plan design or its operation so that it does not become a taxable entity.

Failure to pass nondiscrimination tests

In certain cases, a plan may not pass the required nondiscrimination tests for a given plan year. A plan may fail these tests as a result of excess contributions to the plan by highly compensated employees who participate in the plan. Once the plan administrators have been made aware of the failure of the test, they usually take corrective action by refunding the required amount of money to those employees, so that the plan will then pass the nondiscrimination test.

As an alternative, the employer may make a contribution to non-highly compensated employees called a qualified non-elective contribution. In many cases, such refunds or additional contributions to participants occur after the end of the plan year currently under audit. In these instances, the plan's financial statements should reflect an offset to contributions or a separate line item in the Statement of Net Assets Available for Benefits for the amounts to be refunded. The amount may be described as Excess Contributions Refundable to Participants and should be explained in a note to the plan's financial statements.

If the plan administrator does not take the required corrective action to enable the plan to pass the required nondiscrimination tests, the plan's tax-exempt status may be jeopardized. You should then consider that when analyzing the plan's financial position, tax status, the related note disclosures, and the opinion to render on the plan's financial statements.

In addition, during the planning phase of the engagement when you are documenting the understanding of the plan's internal control structure, you may want to consider asking plan management how often the discrimination tests are performed for the plan. With larger 401(k) plans, these tests are often performed quarterly or semiannually so as to monitor more closely the plan's compliance with the required tests. To the extent that the plan continually fails the discrimination tests, you may want to recommend to plan management that the discrimination tests be performed more often during the plan year so that management can monitor the test results more frequently. This may facilitate corrective action to be taken by plan management during the plan year. Finally, by making such inquiries of plan management during the internal control phase of the engagement, you may be able to determine if participants have made changes to the amount they are contributing to the plan. This information may be useful when auditing contributions made to the plan during the plan year.

Knowledge check

4. Which of the following most accurately describes what occurs when a plan fails to pass the required nondiscrimination tests?

   a. The plan is automatically disqualified and the plan is no longer tax exempt.
   b. The plan administrators usually take corrective action by refunding the required amount of money to those employees so that the plan will then pass the nondiscrimination test.
   c. The plan administrators note such failure and proceed with plans to correct in some future years.
   d. The plan is required to resubmit for a new IRS determination letter.

Commitments and contingencies

The procedures that you should perform in connection with identifying possible commitments and contingencies that may affect the plan's financial statements are very similar to the procedures that you would perform when auditing any other type of entity. Such procedures include the following, as suggested by the AICPA Audit and Accounting Audit Guide *Employee Benefit Plans*:

- Discussing possible areas of commitments and contingencies with the sponsoring employer, plan administrator, or other parties performing the plan's management functions
- Reviewing minutes of various committees of the plan during and subsequent to the period being audited for discussion of possible contingent liabilities or commitments
- Analyzing legal expenses for the period and reviewing invoices and statements from legal counsel for indications of possible contingencies. The legal expenses of a single-employer plan may be paid directly by the employer, in which case the auditor may consider reviewing those expenses
- Obtaining a representation letter from the appropriate persons, normally the plan's administrator or other parties performing the plan's management function (see AU-C section 580, *Written Representations* [AICPA, *Professional Standards*])
- Inquiring as to any audits or investigations that the DOL, IRS, or other regulatory agency has made of the plan's activities or filings since the last audit (such reviews might arise, for example, from enforcement activities, from a request for an advisory opinion, or from a request for a prohibited transaction exemption). Obtain and review for financial statement implications any report of an audit or investigation not reviewed as part of the audit planning process, including the effect of transactions noted therein that give rise to potential receivables arising from breaches of fiduciary duties or prohibited transactions. Consider whether this information obtained from the inquiry should be included in the representation letter
- Inquiring as to any possible mergers or spinoffs affecting the plan

Representations from plan counsel

To obtain the appropriate representations from plan counsel, you should ask plan management to send an audit inquiry letter to all attorneys who have been consulted on litigation, claims, and assessments relating to the plan. The matters normally included as part of the letter would include a list prepared by plan management (or alternatively, by counsel if requested by plan management) that describes and evaluates pending or threatened litigation, claims, and assessments and unasserted claims for which the attorney has been engaged and to which the attorney has devoted a substantive amount of attention. In addition, as suggested by the AICPA Audit and Accounting Guide *Employee Benefit Plans*, the audit inquiry letter should include a "pending or threatened litigation" or "unasserted claims and assessments" section that should request the attorney specifically to address the following matters or should expressly state that plan management has advised the auditor that there are no such matters:

- Breach of fiduciary responsibilities
- Prohibited party in interest transactions and other transactions prohibited by ERISA. Parties in interest are defined in ERISA Section 3(14) and regulations under that section
- Loans or leases in default and reportable to the DOL, including late remittances of employee deferral contributions or loan repayments

- Events reportable to the PBGC
- Events that may jeopardize the plan's tax qualification status.
- Legal actions brought by the plan on behalf of plan participants and beneficiaries
- Review or inquiry by the DOL, IRS, or other regulatory agency of the plan's activities or filings since the last audit. A review or an inquiry might arise, for example, from enforcement activities; from a request for an advisory opinion; or from a request for a prohibited transaction exemption.

The American Bar Association has approved a "Statement of Policy Regarding Lawyers' Responses to Auditors' Requests for Information," which is described in AU-C section 501, *Inquiry of a Client's Lawyer Concerning Litigation, Claims, and Assessments* (AICPA, *Professional Standards*). All audit inquiry letters to plan counsel should be made in the context as described in AU-C section 501. If the plan sponsor has not utilized the services of a lawyer, consider including such a statement in the management representation letter.

Once you have received the response from plan counsel to the letter of audit inquiry, you should evaluate the matters covered in the letters and determine whether any disclosures or accruals for commitments and contingencies are required under generally accepted accounting principles. In this regard, you should follow the guidance in FASB ASC section 450, *Contingencies*. You also should document the basis for conclusions reached in the decisions made to disclose or accrue amounts for commitments and contingencies.

Knowledge check

5. To the extent that plan management has informed the auditor that legal counsel was not consulted during the plan year, the auditor should perform which of the following?

    a. The auditor should obtain a representation from plan management regarding the absence of legal matters affecting the plan.
    b. The auditor is not required to perform any further procedures.
    c. The auditor should disclose such in the notes to the plan's financial statements.
    d. The auditor should inform the DOL.

Subsequent events

Similar to the procedures to follow regarding commitments and contingencies, the procedures that you should undertake in documenting subsequent events for the audit of a 401(k) plan are similar to those that you are required to perform under the provisions of FASB ASC 855, *Subsequent Events,* when auditing any other type of entity. AU-C section 560, *Subsequent Events and Subsequently Discovered Facts* (AICPA, *Professional Standards*), addresses the auditor's responsibilities relating to subsequent events and subsequently discovered facts in an audit of financial statements.

FASB ASC 855 was amended by FASB ASU No. 2010-09, *Subsequent Events (Topic 855): Amendments to Certain Recognition and Disclosure Requirements.* FASB ASU No. 2010-09 changed the criteria for determining whether an entity would evaluate subsequent events through the date that financial statements are issued or when they are available to be issued. Plans that file their financial statements with the SEC using Form 11-K should evaluate subsequent events through the date the financial statements are issued. These plans will not be required to disclose the date through which management has evaluated subsequent events in the financial statements. SEC registrants continue to have responsibilities for evaluating subsequent events as previously required. All other plans that do not file with the SEC should evaluate subsequent events through the date that the financial statements are available to be issued. Plans not filing with the SEC using Form 11-K should disclose both of the following:

1. The date through which subsequent events have been evaluated.
2. Whether that date is either of the following:
   a. The date the financial statements were issued.
   b. The date the financial statements were available to be issued.

An example disclosure is as follows:

> For the year ended December 31, 20XX, subsequent events were evaluated through [Month XX, 20XX], the date the financial statements were available to be issued.

Note: Plans which file on Form 11-K with the SEC would not include the earlier sentence regarding the date subsequent events were evaluated. FASB ASU No. 2010-09 determined that SEC filers are required to evaluate subsequent events through the date the financial statements are issued (versus available to be issued) and exempts SEC filers from disclosing the date through which subsequent events have been evaluated.

Note: The financial statements as issued and included in a registrant's filing may be attached to Form 5500 filing for DOL reporting purposes, and do not require further evaluation of subsequent events nor notation of the date through which subsequent events have been evaluated.

Subsequent events procedures that you should perform include the following (though you should perform any additional procedures appropriate under the circumstances):

1. Review any trustee and recordkeeper statements available subsequent to the audit date for evidence of unusual transactions or fluctuations. You should discuss any such transactions or fluctuations with the appropriate level of plan management. Examples of unusual transactions would be a significant decline in the market value of the investments, unusual volumes of investment acquisitions or dispositions, or the failure of an insurance company in which the plan holds an investment.
2. Review minutes of committee meetings through the date of the auditor's report.
3. Obtain supplemental legal representations if there is a significant period between the date of the plan's legal counsel's response and the date of the auditor's report.
4. Ask the plan administrator (or other appropriate individual who is responsible for the administration of the plan) about any of the following occurrences since the end of the plan year:
   a. Abnormal disposal or purchase of investments since year-end
   b. Significant amendments to the plan document
   c. Any change in the amount of the employer matching contribution to be allocated to participants' accounts that may require disclosure in the footnotes
   d. If the plan requires that certain performance targets are met in order for participants to receive the employer matching contribution, whether the plan in fact met the target for the year under audit.
   e. Any new commitments or contingencies that may affect the plan, as well as an update to the litigation matters identified during the audit. Note that if a significant amount of time has passed from the date of the legal representations you received until the date the report on the plan's financial statements is actually issued (normally a period that exceeds two weeks), you should update the legal representation letter with plan management or plan counsel
   f. Any investigations by the DOL, IRS, or other regulatory agency since the end of the plan year. The IRS will often request to perform an audit of the plan sponsor's employee benefit plans in connection with an audit of the plan sponsor's federal income tax filings
   g. Any plans by management to terminate or merge the plan or spinoff plan assets that may result from an acquisition or disposition of a division or company by the plan sponsor and cause the immediate vesting of employer matching contributions
   h. Adverse financial conditions of the plan sponsor

After completing the subsequent events procedures, you should evaluate the information you obtain from this process and determine whether any matters require disclosure or accrual in the plan's financial statements. You should refer to the guidance in FASB ASC 855, in making that determination, and you should document in the working papers the basis for the conclusions you reached.

Knowledge check

6. If a significant period of time has lapsed between the last day of fieldwork and the report issuance date, subsequent events procedures should be performed through which date?

   a. Through the issuance date or the date the report was available to be issued even though such procedures were already performed through the last day of fieldwork.
   b. Through the issuance date or the date the report was available to be issued unless such procedures were already performed through the last day of fieldwork.
   c. Through the last day of fieldwork.
   d. Within four weeks of the issuance date or the date the report was available to be issued.

Representations from plan management

In connection with the audit of a 401(k) plan, you should obtain written representations from plan officials, which should include the plan administrator, who is responsible for the plan's investment and management functions. In addition to the plan administrator's signature, you may also consider obtaining the signatures of the following officials based on specific circumstances: chief financial officer, the chief human resources officer, a member of the board of trustees, or a union official for a multiemployer plan. The representation letter should cover all financial statements and periods included in your report. It should be typed on the plan sponsor's letterhead and dated as of the independent auditor's report date. The representation letter should be tailored to meet specific circumstances of the engagement. Note: The guidance for management representation letters is found in AU-C section 580.

Following is an example management representation letter for a full-scope, defined contribution pension plan that is based on the example provided in the AICPA Audit and Accounting Guide *Employee Benefit Plans*.

Sample management representation letter (401(k) plan)

[*Entity Letterhead*]

(*To Auditor*)

[*Date*]

This representation letter is provided in connection with your audits of the financial statements of Sample Company Employee Benefit Plan (the Plan), which comprise the statements of net assets available for benefits as of December 31, 20X2 and 20X1, and the related statements of changes in net assets available for benefits for the year ended December 31, 20X2, and the related notes to the financial statements, for the purpose of expressing an opinion on whether the financial statements present fairly, in all material respects, the net assets available for benefits and changes in net assets available for benefits of the Plan in accordance with accounting principles generally accepted in the United States of America (U.S. GAAP).[1]

---

[1] For ERISA limited-scope engagements, includes the following in the first paragraph of this letter:
We understand that, at our instruction, you did not perform any audit procedures with respect to information prepared and certified to by [*name of qualifying institution*], the trustee, in accordance with the Department of Labor's Rules and Regulations for Reporting and Disclosure under the Employee Retirement Income Security Act of 1974, other than comparing such information with the financial statements and supplemental schedules. Because of the significance of the information you did not audit, we understand that you will not express an opinion on the financial statements and schedules as a whole. We understand the form and content of the information included in the financial statements and supplemental schedule[s], other than that derived from the information certified or provided by [*name of qualifying institution*], was audited by you in accordance with GAAS, and was subjected to tests of our accounting records and other procedures as you considered necessary to enable you to express an opinion as to whether they are presented in compliance with the DOL's Rules and Regulations for Reporting and Disclosure under ERISA.

Certain representations in this letter are described as being limited to matters that are material. Items are considered material, regardless of size, if they involve an omission or misstatement of accounting information that, in the light of surrounding circumstances, makes it probable that the judgment of a reasonable person relying on the information would be changed or influenced by the omission or misstatement.

We confirm that, to the best of our knowledge and belief, having made such inquiries as we considered necessary for the purpose of appropriately informing ourselves [*as of (date of auditor's report)*], the following representations made to you during your audit:

Financial statements

1. We have fulfilled our responsibilities, as set out in the terms of the audit engagement dated [*insert date*], for the preparation and fair presentation of the financial statements (including disclosures) in accordance with U.S. GAAP.
2. We acknowledge our responsibility for the design, implementation, and maintenance of internal control relevant to the preparation and fair presentation of financial statements that are free from material misstatement, whether due to fraud or error.
3. We acknowledge our responsibility for the design, implementation, and maintenance of internal control to prevent and detect fraud.
4. Significant assumptions used by us in making accounting estimates, including those measured at fair value, are reasonable. The methods and significant assumptions used to estimate fair values of financial instruments are as follows: [*describe methods and significant assumptions used to estimate fair values of financial instruments*]. The methods and significant assumptions used result in a measure of fair value appropriate for financial measurement and disclosure purposes.
5. We are responsible for the estimation methods and assumptions used in measuring assets and liabilities reported or disclosed at fair value, including information obtained from brokers, pricing services, or other third parties. Our valuation methodologies have been consistently applied from period to period. The fair value measurements reported or disclosed represent our best estimate of fair value as of the measurement date in accordance with the requirements of Financial Accounting Standards Board (FASB) *Accounting Standards Codification* (ASC) 820, *Fair Value Measurement*. In addition, our disclosures related to fair value measurements are consistent with the objectives outlined in FASB ASC 820.
6. Related party relationships and transactions have been appropriately accounted for and disclosed in accordance with the requirements of U.S. GAAP.
7. Transactions with *parties in interest*, as defined in Section 3(14) of the Employee Retirement Income Security Act of 1974 (ERISA) and regulations thereunder, including sales, purchases, loans, transfers, leasing arrangements, and guarantees, and amounts receivable from, or payable to, related parties have been appropriately disclosed.
8. All events subsequent to the date of the financial statements and for which U.S. GAAP requires adjustment or disclosure have been adjusted or disclosed.
9. The effects of uncorrected misstatements are immaterial, both individually and in the aggregate, to the financial statements as a whole. A list of the uncorrected misstatements is attached to the representation letter.
10. The effects of all known actual or possible litigation and claims have been accounted for and disclosed in accordance with U.S. GAAP.
11. We have no intentions to terminate the plan.
12. Guarantees, whether written or oral, under which the plan is contingently liable to a bank or another lending institution have been properly recorded or disclosed in the financial statements.

13. We have properly reported and disclosed amendments to the plan instrument, if any.
14. We acknowledge our responsibility for the presentation of the supplementary information in accordance with the applicable criteria and we believe the supplementary information, including its form and content, is fairly presented in accordance with the applicable criteria. The methods of measurement or presentation have not changed from those used in the prior period.

Information provided

15. We have provided you with
    a. access to all information, of which we are aware that is relevant to the preparation and fair presentation of the financial statements such as records, documentation, and other matters;
    b. additional information that you have requested from us for the purpose of the audit;
    c. unrestricted access to persons within the plan from whom you determined it necessary to obtain audit evidence;
    d. all minutes of the meetings [name of plan administrative committee or trustee] or summaries of actions of recent meetings for which minutes have not yet been prepared; and
    e. amendments made to the plan instrument, trust agreement, or insurance contracts during the year, including amendments to comply with applicable laws.
16. All transactions have been recorded in the accounting records and are reflected in the financial statements.
17. Financial instruments with off-balance-sheet risk and financial instruments with concentrations of credit risk have been properly recorded or disclosed in the financial statements.
18. The plan or trust has satisfactory title to all owned assets that are recorded at fair value [state exceptions, if any], and all liens, encumbrances, or security interest requiring disclosure in the financial statements have been properly disclosed.
19. We have disclosed to you the results of our assessment of the risk that the financial statements may be materially misstated as a result of fraud.
20. We have no knowledge of any fraud or suspected fraud that affects the plan and involves
    a. management,
    b. employees who have significant roles in internal control, or
    c. others when the fraud could have a material effect on the financial statements.
21. We have no knowledge of any allegations of fraud, or suspected fraud, affecting the plan's financial statements communicated by employees, former employees, participants, regulators, beneficiaries, service providers, third-party administrators, or others.
22. We have disclosed to you all known instances of noncompliance or suspected noncompliance with laws and regulations whose effects should be considered when preparing financial statements.[2]
23. We are not aware of any pending or threatened litigation and claims whose effects should be considered when preparing the financial statements.
24. There are no other matters (for example, breach of fiduciary responsibilities, nonexempt transactions, loans or loans in default, events reportable to the Pension Benefit Guaranty Corporation, or events that may jeopardize the tax status) that legal counsel have advised us must be disclosed.
25. We have disclosed to you the identity of the plan's related parties and parties in interest and all the related party and party in interest relationships and transactions of which we are aware.
26. We have apprised you of all communications, whether written or oral, with regulatory agencies concerning the operation of the plan.

---

[2] For example, there have been no communications from regulatory agencies concerning noncompliance with, or deficiencies in, financial reporting practices that could have a material effect on the financial statements in the event of noncompliance.

27. The plan has complied with all aspects of debt and other contractual agreements that would have a material effect on the financial statements in the event of noncompliance, including the release of unallocated shares held in employee stock ownership plans.
28. All required filings with the appropriate agencies have been made.
29. The plan (and the trust established under the plan) is qualified under the appropriate section of the Internal Revenue Code and intends to continue as a qualified plan (and trust). The plan sponsor(s) has operated the plan and trust or insurance contract in a manner that did not jeopardize this tax status.
30. The plan has complied with the Department of Labor's regulations concerning the timely remittance of participants' contributions to trusts containing assets for the plan.[3]
31. The plan has complied with the fidelity bonding requirements of ERISA.
32. There are no
    a. *nonexempt party in interest transactions* (as defined in ERISA Section 3[l4] and regulations under that section) that were not disclosed in the supplemental schedules or financial statements.
    b. investments in default or considered to be uncollectible that were not disclosed in the supplemental schedules.
    c. *reportable transactions* (as defined in ERISA Section 103[b][3][H] and regulations under that section) that were not disclosed in the supplemental schedules.

_____

[*Name of Plan Administrator and Title*]

_____

[Name of Plan Financial Officer and Title]

_____

[3] This step would be applicable for a contributory plan.

Illustrative attachment to management representation letter[4]

	Sample company employee benefit plan summary of uncorrected misstatements year ended December 31, 20X2			
	Statement of net assets available for benefits December 31, 20X2		Statement of changes in net assets available for benefits December 31, 20X2	
Proposed adjustments	Assets	Net assets	Contributions	Net increase
Year 20X2 contributions made during 20X2 but not accrued at 12/31/X2	($800,000)	($800,000)	($800,000)	($800,000)
Totals[5]	$76,900,000	$76,900,000	$20,000,000	$40,000,000
Percentage effect of adjustments on total[6]	(1.04%)	(1.04%)	(4.00%)	(2.00%)

The following is a list of additional representations that may be required or appropriate for employee benefit plans, as applicable:

a. When engaged to report on whether the supplemental schedules are fairly stated, in all material respects, in relation to the financial statements as a whole, in accordance with paragraph .07g of AU-C section 725, *Supplementary Information in Relation to the Financial Statements as a Whole* (AICPA, *Professional Standards*), the auditor should obtain written representations from management
   i. that management acknowledges its responsibility for the presentation of the supplementary information in accordance with the applicable criteria.
   ii. that it believes the supplementary information, including its form and content, is fairly presented in accordance with the applicable criteria.
   iii. that the methods of measurement or presentation have not changed from those used in the prior period or, if the methods of measurement or presentation have changed, the reasons for such changes.

---

[4] In accordance with paragraph .14 of AU-C section 580, *Management Representations* (AICPA, *Professional Standards*), a summary of the uncorrected misstatements should be included in, or attached to, the written representation. The summary should include sufficient information to provide management with an understanding of the nature, amount, and effect of the uncorrected misstatements. Similar items may be aggregated. The attachment presented here is for illustrative purposes only and not necessarily the only possible presentation.

[5] This information is not required by AU-C section 580.

[6] See footnote 5.

---

  iv. about any significant assumptions or interpretations underlying the measurement or presentation of the supplementary information.

  v. that when the supplementary information is not presented with the audited financial statements, management will make the audited financial statements readily available to the intended users of the supplementary information no later than the date of issuance by the entity of the supplementary information and auditor's report thereon.

b. Whether financial circumstances are strained, with disclosure of management's intentions and the plan's ability to continue as a going concern,[7] or whether there is knowledge of any matters affecting the plan sponsor that could be significant to the plan

c. Whether the possibility exists that the value of specific significant long-lived assets may be impaired[8]

d. Whether the work of a specialist has been used by the plan[9]

e. Whether receivables have been recorded in the financial statements and the adequacy of allowances for receivables, as appropriate

f. Whether plan management has apprised the auditor of all communications, whether written or oral, with regulatory agencies concerning the operation of the plan

g. The effect of a new accounting standard update is not known

h. The information contained in the notes to the financial statements when the notes are in the opinion of plan management (or plan sponsor) (for example, when the tax status note states that the plan administrator believes that the plan is designed, and is currently being operated, in compliance with the applicable requirements of the Internal Revenue Code and, therefore, believes that the plan is qualified, and the related trust is tax exempt).

i. Management has determined the fair value of significant financial instruments that do not have readily determinable market values,[10] including the reasonableness of significant fair value assumptions, such as whether they appropriately reflect management's intent and ability to carry out specific courses of action on behalf of the entity when relevant to the use of fair value measurements or disclosures.

j. The appropriateness of the measurement methods, including related assumptions, used by management in determining fair value and the consistency in application of the methods

k. The completeness and adequacy of disclosures related to fair values

l. Whether subsequent events require adjustment to the fair value measurements and disclosures included in the financial statements other than normal market fluctuations

m. If the engagement is an ERISA limited-scope audit, the plan administrator's responsibilities as they relate to the completeness and accuracy of the trustee certification

n. Whether plan management has obtained and reviewed a SOC 1® report (if available), and is performing the applicable user controls

o. When the plan uses the liquidation basis of accounting (because liquidation was determined to be imminent in accordance with FASB ASC 205-30) it is important that the written representations be revised. For example, the management representation letter may reflect the date at which liquidation became imminent and a description that caused liquidation to be considered imminent in accordance with FASB ASC 205-30; the periods that the financial statements are presented on the liquidation basis of accounting; when the plan for liquidation was approved; a statement that management has assessed the likelihood of parties blocking the plan's liquidation and the conclusion of that assessment (for example, it is remote that the plan's liquidation will be blocked or that the plan will

---

[7] See exhibit B, "Illustrative Specific Written Representations," of AU-C section 580 for sample wording of this representation.

[8] See footnote 7.

[9] See footnote 7.

[10] See footnote 7.

return from liquidation); a statement that management is responsible for the significant assumptions and methods used to determine the amounts expected to be collected during liquidation and that the assets reflect their best estimate of the amount of cash or other consideration that the plan expects to collect in settling or disposing of those assets in carrying out its liquidation; and other considerations based on the requirements in FASB ASC 205-30.

Knowledge check

7. Which of the following represents accurate statements regarding the plan's management representation letter?

    a. You should obtain written representations from the trustee.
    b. The representation letter should cover all financial statements.
    c. The representation letter should be typed on the auditors' letterhead and dated as of the plan's financial year end.
    d. The representation letter should be general.

Form 5500 and supplemental schedules

Form 5500 is an annual report developed jointly by the IRS and the DOL. Its purpose is to summarize certain data for each employee benefit plan and report that data to the respective governmental authorities. A discussion of filing the final Form 5500 for a terminated plan is also provided.

Plan administrators must generally file a Form 5500 for 401(k) plans that are covered by ERISA. The return is due whether or not the plan is qualified, even if benefits no longer accrue, or contributions were not made this plan year (or both). A frozen plan (also called a wasting trust) is one in which participants no longer accrue benefits but the plan will remain in existence as long as necessary to pay benefits that have already accrued.

As part of Form 5500 filing, a 401(k) plan (as well as every other type of employee benefit plan) is required by Section 103(c)(5) of ERISA and Section 2520 of the DOL Regulations to submit certain supplemental schedules that must be attached to the filing and that should be covered by the auditor's report on the plan's financial statements. The instructions to Form 5500 provide that in some cases, it is permissible to omit from the filing certain schedules for a plan that invests in particular investment arrangements that are either required, or may elect, to file the information directly with the DOL. These exceptions will be considered in the discussion of the individual supplemental schedules.

The DOL has the responsibility to enforce Title I of ERISA, which, in part, establishes the rights of the participants and the duties of the fiduciaries. The Employee Benefits Security Administration (EBSA), which is an agency of the DOL, is responsible for enforcing the rules that discuss appropriate conduct of plan managers, the investment of plan money, the reporting and disclosure of plan information, and rights of the participants.

Form 5500 filing deadline

The deadline for filing Form 5500 is 7 months after the plan year-end. An extension of time for filing the report can be requested from the IRS by filing Form 5558, Application for Extension of Time to File Certain Employee Plan Returns, prior to the original due date. This extension, when properly completed and signed, automatically provides an additional 2 ½ months to satisfy the filing requirement. Because this is an automatic extension approval, the IRS will not return a copy of the request. When the return is filed, a photocopy of the extension request must be included in the filing. (On Form 5500, the box in Part 1, item D must be checked when an application for an extension of time was filed.) The plan administrator has the fiduciary responsibility to make sure Form 5500 is completed properly and submitted on a timely basis.

An automatic extension to file Form 5500 until the due date of the sponsor's federal income tax return is granted if all of the following conditions are met:

- The plan year and the employer's tax year are the same.
- The employer has been granted an extension of time to file its federal income tax return to a date later than the normal due date for filing Form 5500.
- A copy of the IRS extension of time to file the federal income tax return is attached to Form 5500 when it is filed with the IRS.

EFAST2—electronic filing of Form 5500

All pension plans, welfare plans, and direct filing entities (DFEs) subject to ERISA must file electronically.

Under the Department of Labor's Final Rule on Annual Reporting and Disclosure, Form 5500 Annual Returns and Reports must be filed electronically.

Under the all-electronic EFAST2, filers choose between using EFAST2-approved vendor software or the EFAST2 web-based filing system (IFILE) to prepare and submit Form 5500 or Form 5500-SF. Completed forms are submitted via the Internet.

EFAST2 electronic credentials must be obtained to sign and submit Form 5500 or Form 5500-SF, or to prepare a return or report in IFILE. EFAST2 electronic credentials can be obtained by registering on the EFAST2 Website (www.efast.dol.gov).

An individual (for example, officer of an employer, preparer) may register for electronic credentials. The following types of electronic credentials are available: (1) filing author, (2) filing signer, (3) schedule author, (4) transmitter, and (5) third-party software developer. A filing author prepares a 5500 under IFILE. A preparer using third-party software does not need filing author credentials. A filing signer has an obligation to review the 5500 and the signature indicates a belief that the submission is true, correct, and complete. The employer continues to be responsible for the timeliness of the filing.

An employer no longer attaches the Form 5558 to a filing. However, the employer continues to use the form to obtain an extension to file.

A copy of the audited financial statements for the 401(k) plan must be submitted along with Form 5500, which is filed with the IRS by the plan administrator. The audited financial statements must be on the accountant's letterhead, signed, and saved in a PDF file. The preparer then attaches the file to the 5500.

Common problem areas

The most common problem areas identified with Form 5500 and 5500-SF filings are as follows:

- A missing or invalid signature of the Plan Administrator or Plan Sponsor
- Failure to attach an accountant's opinion
- The inclusion of an attachment that was not able to be processed
- Failure of a final plan filing to satisfy the termination criteria
- Indication that a plan's filing was beyond the due date

Filing tips

The plan administrator should do the following:

- Register for credentials with EFAST2 in order to electronically sign Form 5500, even if using third-party software (unless the plan administrator is using the e-signature option).
- Know that if the plan administrator cannot remember the answer to the EFAST 2 website security question, the plan administrator will not be able to log into the EFAST2 website account. As a result, the plan administrator could lose access to filings being created or information regarding filings previously submitted.
- Remember that any filings registered to a revoked account that have not been submitted for processing cannot be retrieved.
- Make sure that if the plan administrator is not attaching an accountant's opinion with Form 5500, the plan administrator does not fill out Schedule H, Part III, Lines 3a, 3b, or 3d. Doing so will result in a filing status of "Filing Error."
- Make sure that the plan administrator's accountant's reports are in PDF format and not encrypted or password protected. EFAST2 cannot process these attachments if they are encrypted or password protected.

Filing amended returns

Delinquent and amended Form 5500 and Form 5500-SF filings must be submitted electronically through EFAST2. To submit a delinquent or amended Form 5500 or Form 5500-SF for the plan's prior years, filers must submit the filing using current filing year Form 5500, schedules, and instructions, except as provided in the following list. The current filing year forms take the place of the pages that would have been included in the prior year's filings. The electronic filing on the current filing year Form 5500 or Form 5500-SF, however, must indicate, in the appropriate space at the beginning of Form 5500, the plan year for which the annual return and report is being filed.

Filers using EFAST2 must use the following correct-year schedules (that is, the plan year for which the annual return and report relates), completed in accordance with the related correct-year instructions:

- Schedule B, SB, or MB (Actuarial Information)
- Schedule E (ESOP Annual Information)
- Schedule P (Annual Return of Fiduciary of Employee Benefit Trust)
- Schedule R (Retirement Plan Information)
- Schedule T (Qualified Pension Plan Coverage Information)

To obtain correct-year schedules and related instructions, go to the EFAST2 website, www.efast.dol.gov, and print the schedules and instructions of the form year that corresponds to the plan year for which you are filing.

It is important to note that filers do not attach any Schedule SSA to any filing with EFAST2. Rather, this information should be submitted on the most current year Form 8955-SSA to the IRS (along with all required attachments). Additional information is available at www.irs.gov/ep.

Agreement of financial statements to Form 5500

Before issuing the audit report, you should determine whether the amounts presented in the financial statements agree to those reported on Form 5500. If there are any differences in the amounts included in the audited financial statements from those reported on Form 5500, other than differences in grouping the investments, those differences must be disclosed in the footnotes to the financial statements. Note that the different treatment of participant loans between the audited financial statements and Form 5500 does not represent a reconciling item. The DOL may reject a Form 5500 filing that does not properly reconcile variances between the audited financial statements and what is reported on Form 5500.

Financial statements and auditor's report issued prior to Form 5500

If the financial statements and auditor's report are issued prior to your review of Form 5500, you should inform the plan administrator that the financial statements and auditor's report are not to be attached to Form 5500 filing until you review Form 5500. If differences between the financial statements and Form 5500 are noted, the notes to the financial statements must be updated to include an explanation of the differences, and the report should be reissued and dual-dated with respect to the note explaining the differences.

Form 5500

The form can best be compared to the Form 1040 for individual taxpayers because it has a one-page main form with basic information to identify the plan. The one-page main form also includes a checklist that guides the preparer to select up to 12 detailed schedules that must be filed if that particular item is applicable to the filer's specific type of plan. This format allows the filer to customize their Form 5500 filing by including only the main form and those additional schedules that are applicable to their plan.

Form 5500 uses computer scannable forms and electronic filing technologies to help reduce costs.

The following is a brief description of the form and the schedules that may be required to be attached:

- Form 5500—This form provides information about the plan itself—for example, the type of plan, the name of the plan, the plan sponsor, plan administrator, the name, address, and EIN of the preparer, as well as a checklist to determine what additional schedules are required to be attached. This includes investments with insurance companies such as guaranteed investment contracts (GICs).
- Schedule A—This form provides information on contracts with insurance companies. A separate Schedule A must be completed and filed for each and every insurance contract in which the plan invests.
- Schedules SB and MB—Note that these forms replace Schedule B. Schedule B was eliminated in 2008. These forms (SB—Single Employer Defined Benefit Plan Actuarial Information and MB—Multiemployer Defined Benefit Plan and Certain Money Purchase Plan Actuarial Information) include actuarial information for all defined benefit pension plans that are subject to minimum funding standards and must be reported on this form (not applicable for 401(k) plans).

- Schedule C—Schedule C lists service organization information for the 40 highest paid service organizations. Service organizations whose compensation for all services to the plan during the plan year that did not exceed $5,000 may be omitted.
- Schedule D—All direct filing entities (DFEs) and those who participate in certain pooled investment or insurance arrangements must file this form. These arrangements include MTIAs (master trust investment accounts), CCTs (bank common or collective trusts), PSAs (pooled separate accounts), and 103-12 IES (103-12 investment entities).
- Schedule G—Schedule G will report information on nonexempt transactions and loans, leases, and fixed income investments in default. The Schedule G will be required to be used to report the information required. Form 5500 no longer requires late remittances of participant contributions (which are prohibited transactions) to be reported on Schedule G. However, the instructions require such to be reported on a supplemental schedule to be attached to Form 5500 and reported on by the auditor. The DOL has posted examples and frequently asked questions at the following website: www.dol.gov/ebsa/faqs/faq_compliance_5500.html.
- Schedule H—This is where the financial statements and related information for large plans (generally 100 or more participants) must be reported.
- Schedule I—This is where the financial statements and related information for small plans (generally fewer than 100 participants) must be reported.
- Schedule R—Schedule R reports certain information on plan distributions, funding, and the adoption of amendments increasing or decreasing the value of benefits in a defined benefit pension plan, as well as certain information on employee stock ownership plans (ESOPs), and multiemployer defined benefit plans (not applicable for 401(k) plans).
- Schedule SSA—Information that is required by the Social Security Administration. Separated participants who have rights to future benefits under this plan must be reported on Schedule SSA. Note that this schedule can no longer be filed through EFAST2 but rather must be submitted by the preparer on paper directly to the IRS.

Supplemental schedules

When applicable, the following schedules must be attached to Form 5500, which is filed with the IRS by the plan administrator.

- Schedule of Assets (held at end of year), Schedule H, Line 4i. This schedule lists the assets held in the plan for investment purposes. The following information should be included:
  - Identity of the issuer, borrower, lessor, or similar party
  - Description of the investment (including the maturity date, rate of interest, collateral, par or maturity value).
  - Cost (the original or acquisition cost of the asset—this may be excluded for participant-directed investments).
  - Current value

  Participant loans may be aggregated and presented with a general description of terms and interest rates. If a person is known to be a party in interest to the plan, place an asterisk to the left of that line, which indicates the party in interest.

- Schedule of Assets (acquired and disposed of within year). Schedule H, Line 4i. Include the following:
  - Identity of the issue, borrower, lessor, or similar party

- Description of the investment (including the maturity date, rate of interest, collateral, par, or maturity value)
- Costs of acquisitions
- Proceeds of dispositions (sales)

Note that this schedule is rarely filed because of the variety of investments that are exempt from being reported on this schedule. The original purpose of this schedule was to identify the churning of investments. The exemptions include the following:

- Debt obligations of the United States
- Interests issued by a company registered under the Investment Company Act of 1940
- Bank certificates of deposit with a maturity of not more than one year
- Commercial paper with a maturity of not more than nine months, if it is (1) ranked in the highest category by at least two nationally recognized statistical rating services and (2) issued by a company required to file reports with the SEC under Section 13 of the Securities Exchange Act of 1934
- Participation in a bank common or collective trust
- Participation in an insurance company pooled separate account
- Securities purchased from a person registered as a broker and dealer under the Securities Exchange Act of 1934 and listed on a national securities exchange registered under Section 6 of that act or quoted on NASDAQ
- Any investment assets reported in any of the other supplemental schedules

- Schedule of Reportable Transactions. Schedule H, Line 4j lists investments that were purchased or sold during the year whose value at the time of the transaction exceeds 5 percent of the current value of plan assets at the beginning of the plan year. For a plan in its first year of existence (that is, current value of plan assets at the beginning of the plan year equals zero), the threshold is calculated as 5 percent multiplied by the current value of plan assets at the end of the first plan year. Include the following:
  - Identity of party involved
  - Description of asset (including interest rate, and maturity in the case of a loan)
  - Purchase price
  - Selling price
  - Lease rental
  - Expenses incurred with transaction
  - Cost of asset (original or acquisition cost)
  - Current value of asset on transaction date
  - Net gain (or loss). For Form 5500 purposes, net gain (or loss) is calculated using the investment's revalued cost. Revalued cost is the investment's market value at the beginning of the year or the purchase price if the investment was purchased during the year.

Reportable transactions are not required to be compiled for participant-directed investments.

- Schedule of Loans or Fixed Income Obligations in Default or Classified as Uncollectible. Schedule G, Part I. This schedule lists loans or fixed-income obligations for which unpaid amounts are overdue. All loans that were renegotiated during the year must be included on this schedule. Do not include on this schedule participant loans that are secured by the remaining account balance. Include the following information:
  - Identity and address of obligor
  - Original amount of loan
  - Principal received during the plan year
  - Interest received during the plan year

- Unpaid balance at the end of the year
- A detailed description of the loan including dates of making and maturity, interest rate, the type and value of collateral, any renegotiation of the loan and the terms of the renegotiation, along with other material items
- Principal amount overdue
- Interest amount overdue
- Schedule of Leases in Default or Classified as Uncollectible. Schedule G, Part II. Include the following information:
  - Identity of lessor and lessee
  - Relationship to plan, employer, employee organization, or other party in interest
  - Terms and description (type of property, location, and date it was purchased, terms regarding rent, taxes, insurance, repairs, expenses, renewal options, date property was leased)
  - Original cost
  - Current value at time of the lease
  - Gross rental receipts during the plan year
  - Expenses paid during the plan year
  - Net receipts
  - Amount in arrears

If a person is known to be a party in interest to the plan, place an asterisk to the left of that line, which shows the party in interest.

- Schedule of nonexempt transactions. Schedule G, Part III. This schedule lists any and all prohibited transactions that occurred during the plan year regardless of the dollar value of the transactions. The following information should be shown:
  - Identity of party involved
  - Relationship to plan, employer, or other party in interest
  - Description of transactions including maturity date, rate of interest, collateral, par or maturity value
  - Purchase price
  - Selling price
  - Lease rental
  - Expenses incurred in connection with the transaction
  - Cost of asset (original or acquisition cost)
  - Current value of asset
  - Net gain (or loss) on each transaction
  - Late contributions are no longer reported on Schedule G

IRS Form 5330 may have to be filed and an excise tax on the transaction may have to be paid by the plan sponsor, which is a tax imposed by the IRS on all prohibited transactions.

Information for supplemental schedules from trustee or custodian

The information required to be included in the supplemental schedules should be available to the auditor in the trustee statements received from the trustee or custodian of the plan investments. In certain cases, the trustee or custodian will actually include within the trustee statement, sections that contain certain of the supplemental schedules that they have prepared based on the investments held at year-end, investment transactions during the plan year, and so on. In such cases, you should review the information included within the schedule and determine whether the information provided appears reasonable and consistent given the other auditing procedures that you applied in testing the plan's investments.

To the extent that the plan's assets are held by more than one trustee or custodian, each of the trustees or custodians may independently prepare supplemental schedules for inclusion in the plan's Form 5500 filing, such as a separate schedule of reportable transactions in which the 5-percent threshold calculation is based on each trustee's or custodian's portfolio of plan assets. In such a situation, the plan administrator may combine the information provided by the trustees or custodians and file one schedule (and would use in the example mentioned a 5-percent threshold based on total plan assets as of the beginning of the year). The other alternative would be to file the two separate schedules, which might be the easiest approach, and would therefore provide more information to the DOL than is literally required.

In the event that you are performing an ERISA limited-scope audit with respect to plan investments, you should still compare the information provided by the trustee or custodian to the supplemental schedules, and if you identify something that appears unreasonable, such as the value of the investments reported in the schedule of assets (held at end-of-year), Schedule H, Line 4i not approximating those presented in the plan's financial statements, you should follow up on such matters with the plan administrator, trustee or custodian, or both of the plan assets.

In the case where the trustee or custodian has not directly prepared the supplemental schedules, the plan sponsor should prepare them or separately engage you to assist in compiling such information based on the summary of plan transactions and other information included in the trustee or custodian statements. The preparation of the plan's supplemental schedules by the auditor performing the audit of the plan's financial statements is beyond the scope of the audit as described in the auditor's report to the plan's financial statements. The last section of this chapter will discuss the procedures that you should apply and modifications that you should make in your report on the plan financial statements if the trustee or custodian has not provided the information required by any of the supplemental schedules.

Mandatory form of supplemental schedules

Finally, you should be aware that the columnar headings for the supplemental schedules are stipulated by the DOL regulations, and the supplemental schedules included in your report on the plan financial statements should substantially follow the columnar headings. Otherwise, the plan's Form 5500 filing may be rejected by the DOL and returned to the plan administrator for correction to conform to the DOL's rules and regulations. As with all of the schedules covered in this chapter, to the extent that a column is not applicable, it may be omitted from the schedule filed with the DOL. Also, there is no materiality threshold (except for the 5-percent threshold used to determine transactions to be reported on the Schedule of Reportable Transactions, Schedule H, Line 4j) that applies to the supplemental schedules, and therefore, all required schedules should be prepared, as applicable.

Absence of a required schedule or omission of required data from schedule

As mentioned previously, in some cases, certain required schedules or data required to be included in one or more of the schedules have been omitted because the trustee or custodian has indicated that such information is not available. When you encounter this situation of an omitted schedule or data, you have the option of adding an explanatory paragraph to the opinion to disclose the omission or to express a qualified or an adverse opinion of the supplemental schedules as appropriate. The type of audit report that should be issued under these circumstances depends on both the type of audit being performed, as well as the nature of the omitted information as discussed in the following text. The following tables are excerpts from the AICPA Audit and Accounting Guide *Employee Benefit Plans*.

	Effect on report
Error, omission, or inconsistency	Full-scope audit
DOL-required information omitted from supplemental schedule (for example, historical cost information for nonparticipant-directed transactions) and the omission or inconsistency is not considered a material misstatement.	Other-matter paragraph
The required schedule is omitted (for example, Schedule H, Line 4j—Schedule of Reportable Transactions) and the omission or inconsistency is not considered a material misstatement.*	Other-matter paragraph
The required schedule is materially misstated in relation to the financial statements as a whole (full-scope audit).	Qualified or adverse regarding schedules

* See the AICPA Audit and Accounting Guide *Employee Benefit Plans* when the Schedule of Nonexempt Transactions is omitted.

Error, omission, or inconsistency	Effect on report	
	ERISA limited-scope audit	
	Exception in information certified by trustee or custodian	Exception in information not certified by trustee or custodian but other procedures have been performed
DOL-required information omitted from supplemental schedule (for example, historical cost information for nonparticipant-directed transactions).	Other-matter paragraph	Qualified or adverse regarding the form and content of the schedules. (Report on form and content in compliance with DOL rules and regulations.)
The required schedule is omitted (for example, Schedule H, Line 4j— Schedule of Reportable Transactions).*	Other-matter paragraph	Qualified or adverse regarding the form and content of the schedules. (Report on form and content in compliance with DOL rules and regulations.)
The required schedule is materially inconsistent with financial statements or misstatement of fact.	Other-matter paragraph	Qualified or adverse regarding the form and content of the schedules. (Report on form and content in compliance with DOL rules and regulations.)

* See the AICPA Audit and Accounting Guide *Employee Benefit Plans* when the Schedule of Nonexempt Transactions is omitted.

Final return/report for a terminated plan

For a terminated plan, once all assets have been distributed to the participants, their beneficiaries, or to another employee benefit plan, check the "final return/report" box at the top of the form for Form 5500 filed for that plan. Because all the monies have been distributed, this year of complete distribution is the final year that a Form 5500 will be required to be filed for that plan. If amounts still remain to be paid to participants or to be transferred into another plan at the end of a plan year, some assets of the terminating plan still remain and the final Form 5500 cannot be filed. A Form 5500 will be filed for the current plan year (and all future years) until the assets of the plan equal zero. The final return and report is due seven months from the end of the month in which all the assets are distributed. The same extensions that apply to an annual Form 5500 also apply to the final Form 5500 filing.

Knowledge check

8. Which of the following most accurately describes the auditor's responsibility relating to a plan's Form 5500 filing?

   a. Before issuing the audit report, the auditor should verify that all areas of Form 5500 are complete and accurate as it is the auditor's responsibility to make sure Form 5500 is completed accurately and filed timely.

   b. Before issuing the audit report, the auditor should determine whether the amounts presented in the financial statements agree to those reported on Form 5500. If there are any differences in the amounts included in the audited financial statements from those reported on Form 5500 (other than differences in grouping the investments and classification of participant loans), then those differences must be disclosed in the footnotes to the financial statements.

   c. Before issuing the audit report, the auditor should prepare Form 5500 on behalf of the plan.

   d. The auditor has no responsibility in relation to the plan's Form 5500.

Terminating plans

In recent years, many employee benefit plans have been terminated as a result of business acquisitions or dispositions entered into by the plan sponsor. For purposes of this discussion, a terminating plan includes all plans for which a termination decision has been made regardless of whether the terminating plan will be replaced. You should be aware that there may be significant accounting implications if a plan is to be terminated and not replaced such as those involving the valuation of assets and vesting of employer matching contributions. Depending on the circumstances of the plan termination, you may need to take such matters into consideration.

When the decision to terminate a plan is made by the plan sponsor, disclosure of the relevant circumstances regarding the plan termination should be included in the plan's financial statements for every set of financial statements issued for the plan until all assets are distributed. In addition, you should consider including an emphasis-of-matter paragraph in your report mentioning the fact that the plan will be terminating and directing the reader to the note disclosure for additional information. For example, the emphasis-of-matter paragraph to your report could read as follows: "As stated in Note X to the Plan's financial statements, the Board of Directors elected to terminate the Plan effective December 31, 20XX."

The decision to terminate a plan may be made in various ways. Sometimes those charged with governance will pass a resolution or amend the plan document to provide documentation to help determine when the decision to terminate the plan was made.

Decision to terminate made before plan year-end

If the decision to terminate a plan is made before the end of the plan year, the termination is considered to be a type I subsequent event that should be disclosed in the notes to the plan's financial statements. It also requires that the plan's financial statements be presented on the liquidation basis of accounting. Interpretation No. 1, "Reporting on Financial Statements Prepared on a Liquidation Basis of Accounting," of AU-C section 700, *Forming an Opinion and Reporting on Financial Statements* (AICPA, *Professional Standards*, AU-C section 9700 par. .01–.05), contains applicable guidance regarding the auditor's reporting responsibilities when using the liquidation basis of accounting.

For terminating plans assets, changing to the liquidation basis will usually cause little or no change in values, most of which are fair values. An example of plan investments that may not be currently carried at fair value is certain investments in insurance contracts. That is, investments in fully benefit-responsive insurance contracts are presented at contract value, which may be different from fair value for the liquidation basis of accounting. The final Form 5500 for the plan will be required to be filed 7 months after the date of the final asset distribution to participants (as of the end of the 7th month), although the plan administrator can request an extension of 2½ months for the filing.

Note that in April 2013, FASB issued ASU No. 2013-07, *Presentation of Financial Statements (Topic 205): Liquidation Basis of Accounting*, which improves financial reporting by clarifying when and how public and private companies and not-for-profit organizations should prepare statements using the liquidation basis of accounting. See the following section for more information.

Decision to terminate made after plan year-end

If the decision to terminate a plan is made after the end of the plan year but before the issuance of your report on the plan's financial statements, the termination is considered to be a type II subsequent event that should be disclosed in the notes to the plan's financial statements. The disclosures required in this circumstance are discussed in FASB ASC 855, *Subsequent Events*. You also should consider the effect of the termination on the vesting of employer matching contributions and may consider disclosure of this matter in the footnotes to the plan's financial statements.

Terminating plans—accounting and reporting update

In accordance with FASB ASC 962-40-25 (paragraphs 1–2), if the liquidation of a plan is deemed to be imminent (as defined in FASB ASC 205-30-25-2) before the end of the plan year, the plan's year-end financial statements should be prepared using the liquidation basis of accounting in accordance with FASB ASC 205-30. Plan financial statements for periods ending after the determination that liquidation is imminent are prepared using the liquidation basis of accounting.

Determining whether liquidation is imminent is a matter of judgment, based on facts and circumstances. In accordance with FASB ASC 205-30-25-2, liquidation is imminent when either of the following occurs:

- A plan for liquidation has been approved by the persons with authority to make such a plan effective, and the likelihood is remote that any of the following will occur:
  - Execution of the plan will be blocked by other parties.
  - The entity will return from liquidation.
- A plan for liquidation is imposed by other forces (for example, involuntary bankruptcy), and the likelihood is remote that the entity will return from liquidation.

For a single-employer defined contribution (DC) plan, this means that the likelihood would need to be remote that other parties, such as the IRS, would block the liquidation. Such evaluation often depends on whether the termination is a standard termination, or a distressed or involuntary termination. The approval for the termination of a defined benefit (DB) plan is different and often more complex than that of a DC plan. For all types of plans, consultation with legal counsel, plan actuaries (if applicable), and service organizations (for example, trustees or recordkeepers) may be necessary in order to make a judgment about whether the likelihood is remote that other parties would block the termination of a plan. This evaluation may change over time, depending upon the stage of the termination process.

FASB ASC 205-30 requires financial statements prepared using the liquidation basis of accounting to present relevant information about an entity's expected resources in liquidation by measuring and presenting assets at the amount of the expected cash proceeds from liquidation. The entity should include in its presentation of assets any items it had not previously recognized under U.S. GAAP, but that it expects to either sell in liquidation or use in settling liabilities.

The entity should recognize and measure its liabilities in accordance with GAAP that otherwise applies to those liabilities. The entity should not anticipate that it will be legally released from being the primary obligor under those liabilities, either judicially or by creditor(s). The entity also is required to accrue and separately present the costs that it expects to incur and the income that it expects to earn during the expected duration of the liquidation, including any costs associated with sale or settlement of those assets and liabilities. Additionally, FASB ASC 205-30-25 requires disclosure about an entity's plan for liquidation, the methods and significant assumptions used to measure assets and liabilities, the type and amount of costs and income accrued, and the expected duration of the liquidation process.

The AICPA Employee Benefit Plans Expert Panel developed Technical Questions and Answers (Q&As) 6931.18–.29 to provide nonauthoritative guidance when applying FASB ASC 205-30 to the accounting for primarily single employer defined benefit pension and defined contribution retirement plans. Although the information contained in these Q&As may be specific to a single-employer DB or DC plan, the information may be relevant when considering the termination of all types of plans including single employer health and welfare plans and multiemployer plans.

These questions and answers discuss the different types of plan terminations and the related processes that may be helpful when determining whether liquidation is imminent, and address numerous issues, such as whether the liquidation basis of accounting applies to partial plan terminations or plan mergers, the presentation of fully benefit-responsive investment contracts, and the presentation of comparative financial statements.

Knowledge check

9. If a decision is made to terminate a plan before the end of the plan year, which of the following is appropriate?

    a. Only note disclosure of the planned termination.
    b. Note disclosure of the planned termination and the financial statements are presented on the liquidation basis of accounting.
    c. Only financial statements are presented on the liquidation basis of accounting.
    d. No disclosure or change in accounting basis is required.

Plan mergers

As mentioned previously, the employee benefit industry has experienced an increasing number of plan mergers as a result of business combinations by plan sponsors. Because the effective date of a plan merger is often different from the date that plan assets are actually transferred from one plan to another, confusion may exist with respect to the actual date of the merger—which also affects the date of the merging plan's final Form 5500 filing.

In general, you should speak with plan management about the intended date of the merger, review plan documents and amendments and excerpts from sales and purchase agreements covering specifics of the merger, and review minutes and correspondence to assist in determining the effective merger date. In addition, you should bear in mind that the merging plan is required to file a Form 5500 with the DOL until all assets have been transferred to the successor plan. (Note that it is possible for a plan to have more than one trust associated with it; that is, the ongoing plan could be modified to have the trust from the plan that is merging become part of it, thus facilitating a faster merger.) The final Form 5500 is due seven months following the date of the asset merger date (as of the end of the month of that transfer) with a 2½-month extension available by request of the plan administrator.

Disclosure in financial statements

Once plan management has decided to merge the plan, the plan's financial statements should disclose the significant details surrounding the plan merger, such as the effective date of the merger, expected date of final asset transfer, and in what type of plan the current participants will be able to participate. If you have been engaged to audit the successor plan during the plan year that the assets from the other plan were transferred to the plan, you should perform adequate procedures to test that individual participant account balances were transferred at the correct market value and that the participants' ending balance from the prior plan agrees to the participants' beginning balance in the plan. You should make a sample selection of participant balances to perform these procedures.

Knowledge check

10. In the case where a plan is going to merge with another employee benefit plan, the plan's final Form 5500 is due to be filed how many months after the effective date of the plan merger if the effective date of the merger is the same date that the asset transfer occurred?

    a. 2 ½ months.
    b. 5 months.
    c. 7 months.
    d. 9 months.

Party in interest transactions

A party in interest is defined by ERISA Section 3(14) to include the following:

- The plan's fiduciaries and employees
- The person or people who provide services to the plan
- The employer whose employees are covered by the plan
- The person who owns 50 percent or more of such an employer or employee association
- The relatives of any of the previously listed persons

Parties in interest to an employee benefit plan are essentially equivalent to related parties for other audit entities.

Events considered prohibited transactions

The types of transactions that are generally considered to be prohibited transactions between the plan and a party in interest are defined by ERISA Section 406(a) as follows:

- A sale, exchange, or lease of property
- A loan or other extension of credit (this includes untimely deposits to the trust of employee salary deferral deposits)
- The furnishing of goods, services, or facilities
- A transfer of plan assets to a party in interest for the use or benefit of a party in interest
- An acquisition of employer securities or real property in violation of the 10-percent limitation

Exempt transactions

However, certain situations do permit a plan fiduciary to receive reasonable compensation for services provided to a plan, or to receive benefits from the plan as long as the benefits received are in accordance with the provisions of the plan document and are consistent with those received by other plan participants. For example, a party in interest such as a sister (an active employee of the plan sponsor) of an officer of the plan sponsor (who serves as one of the plan's trustees) may be entitled to receive the employer matching contribution credited to her individual account exactly as all other eligible plan participants' individual accounts are credited with their appropriate share of the employer matching contribution—provided the sister satisfies all criteria to receive the matching contribution.

The DOL has issued various prohibited transaction exemptions for certain transactions between parties in interest like the types of transactions previously described. Transactions considered to be exempt party in interest transactions are not required to be reported to the DOL on a supplemental schedule. However, in accordance with GAAP, to the extent that such exempt party in interest transactions are material to the plan's financial statements, they must be disclosed in the notes to the plan's financial statements in accordance with FASB ASC 850, *Related Party Disclosures*. Note that for purposes of clarification, employee contributions and employer contributions made to the plan are not normally considered to be party in interest transactions.

During an audit of a 401(k) plan, as with audits of other types of employee benefit plans, you are required to be aware of the possible existence of party in interest transactions that could affect the plan's financial statements. Certain transactions between the plan and a party in interest may be considered to be a prohibited transaction required to be reported in the notes to the plan's financial statements and also included in a supplemental schedule to Form 5500, Schedule of Nonexempt Transactions. Transactions reported on the Schedule of Nonexempt Transactions are also subject to an excise tax under the IRC. When a nonexempt transaction is identified, plan officials should consult with legal counsel to determine if the plan sponsor is required to file Form 5330, Return of Excise Taxes Related to Employee Benefit Plans, with the IRS and whether the plan sponsor is required to pay the excise tax on the transaction.

In October 2014, the SEC approved AS 2410, *Related Parties* (AICPA, *PCAOB Standards and Related Rules*). This standard establishes requirements regarding the auditor's evaluation of a company's identification of, accounting for, and disclosure of relationships and transactions between the company and its related parties. AS 2410 is effective for auditors of financial statements for fiscal years beginning on or after December 15, 2014.

Plans that are required to file Form 11-K are deemed to be issuers and must submit to the SEC an audit in accordance with the auditing and related professional practice standards promulgated by the PCAOB.

No materiality threshold in prohibited transactions

Auditors should also consider that there is no materiality threshold that applies to prohibited transactions, and all prohibited transactions must be reported to the DOL. In other words, even if you identify a prohibited transaction that is clearly immaterial to the plan's financial statements that transaction is still required to be reported on the supplemental schedule. If you decide that the plan has entered into a nonexempt transaction, and the transaction has not been properly disclosed in the supplemental schedule, then you should express either a qualified opinion or an adverse opinion on the plan's financial statements if the nonexempt transaction is material to the plan's financial statements. If the nonexempt transaction has not been properly disclosed in the supplemental schedule and the nonexempt transaction is not material to the plan's financial statements, you should consider modifying your report by adding an other-matter paragraph to describe the situation.

Procedures to identify parties in interest

In terms of procedures you should apply to identify the parties in interest, you should perform generally the same types of procedures that you would perform during the audit of any other type of entity in obtaining a related party listing. Here are some audit procedures that may assist you to identify parties in interest:

- Evaluate the plan's procedures for identifying and reporting party in interest transactions.
- Obtain a listing of all known parties in interest and ask whether there were any transactions with them during the plan period.

- Review filings with the DOL and other regulatory agencies by the plan sponsor to identify names of known parties in interest.
- Review prior-year working papers for the names of known parties in interest.
- Inquire of the predecessor auditor for known parties in interest and any transactions with those parties in prior years, if applicable.
- Inquire of the plan administrator whether any prohibited transactions have been identified as a result of a governmental examination (such as DOL or IRS examination).
- Review agreements with service organizations.

Certain procedures that you may perform to identify transactions that may indicate a previously unknown party in interest relationship include the following:

- Provide members of the audit engagement with the names of known parties in interest so that during the audit, the members may become aware of transactions with those parties.
- Review the minutes of the board of trustees of the plan and other executive meetings for information about transactions approved or considered at their meetings.
- Review correspondence from, and forms filed with, the DOL and other regulatory agencies for information about transactions with parties in interest.
- Read conflict-of-interest statements obtained by plan officials, if any.
- Review the extent and nature of business transacted with the plan's major investees, suppliers, borrowers, lessees, and lenders for indications of previously undisclosed relationships.
- Consider whether transactions are occurring but are not being accounted for in the plan records—for example, receiving or providing services at no charge or the absorbing of plan expenses by a major stockholder of the plan sponsor.
- Review accounting records for large, unusual, or nonrecurring transactions or balances, paying particular attention to transactions recorded at or near the end of the plan period.
- Review invoices from law firms that have performed regular or special services for the plan for indications of the existence of parties in interest transactions.
- Review confirmations of loans receivable and payable for indications of guarantees. When guarantees are indicated, determine their nature and the relationships, if any, of the guarantors to the reporting entity.
- Review the schedule of employee contributions and agree to deposit dates to make sure timely deposits of monies withheld from employees.

When you have identified parties in interest, test material transactions with those parties. Apply the procedures you consider necessary to be satisfied as to the purpose, nature, and extent of these transactions and their effect on the financial statements. The procedures should go beyond inquiry of management and should be directed toward obtaining and evaluating sufficient competent evidential matter. Procedures that should be considered include the following:

- Obtain an understanding of the business purpose of the transaction.
- Examine invoices, executed copies of agreements, contracts, and other pertinent documents.
- Determine whether appropriate approval was obtained for the transaction.
- Test for reasonableness the compilation of amounts to be disclosed or considered for disclosure.
- Inspect or confirm and obtain satisfaction concerning the transferability and value of collateral.

If you feel you should take additional steps to understand fully a particular party in interest transaction, consider the following procedures (which might not otherwise be necessary to comply with generally accepted audited standards):

- Confirm transaction amount and terms, including guarantees and other significant data, with the other party or parties to the transaction.
- Inspect evidence in possession of the other party or parties to the transaction.
- Confirm or discuss significant information with intermediaries—such as banks, guarantors, agents, or attorneys—to obtain a better understanding of the transaction.
- Refer to financial publications, trade journals, credit agencies, and other information sources when there is reason to believe that unfamiliar customers, suppliers, or other business enterprises with which material amounts of business have been transacted may lack substance.
- With respect to material uncollected balances, guarantees, and other obligations, obtain information about the financial capability of the other party or parties to the transaction. You may obtain such information from audited financial statements, income tax returns, and reports issued by regulatory agencies, taxing authorities, financial publications, or credit agencies. You should decide on the degree of assurance required and the extent to which available information provides such assurance.

Implications of prohibited transaction determination

If you detect prohibited transactions, you should challenge other aspects of the audit, especially the reliability of other representations made by management. The implications of particular prohibited transactions will depend on the relationship of those who perpetrated the acts and concealment, if any, of the transactions to specific control procedures and the level of management or employees involved. You should consult plan counsel if you suspect or note prohibited transactions.

As mentioned previously, because of the complexity of certain transactions with parties in interest to the plan, it may be difficult for you to determine whether such transactions are in fact prohibited transactions. In such cases, you should discuss the circumstances of the transactions with the plan administrator and plan counsel to obtain an opinion about the substance of the transaction. To the extent you identify prohibited transactions, you also should consider whether the transactions represent illegal acts that will require further action by you and may require additional disclosures in the plan's financial statements. You also should consider that certain prohibited transactions will require the plan sponsor (or other party) to make the plan and participants whole for any investment earnings lost because of the plan's entering into a prohibited transaction. This may result in receivables to be recorded on the plan's Statement of Net Assets Available for Benefits, such as for additional contributions that will be made to the plan by the plan sponsor for lost investment earnings.

To the extent you conclude that the plan has entered into a prohibited transaction that has not been adequately reported in the plan's financial statements and the required supplemental schedule, you should either (a) express a qualified opinion or an adverse opinion on the supplementary schedule if the transaction is material to the financial statements or (b) modify the report on the supplementary schedule by adding a paragraph to disclose the omitted transaction if the transaction is not material to the financial statements. If the plan sponsor does not accept your report as modified, you should withdraw from the engagement and communicate the reasons for withdrawing to management and those charged with governance. Finally, you should notify the plan administrator or other appropriate party of the prohibited transactions or other illegal acts identified during the course of the audit.

Knowledge check

11. The auditor is not permitted to apply the concepts of materiality in determining whether a prohibited transaction is required to be reported to the DOL on a supplemental schedule. Which of the following does not constitute a prohibited transaction to be included?

    a. An employer contribution to the plan made in accordance with the plan document.
    b. A sale, exchange, or lease of property between the plan and a party in interest.
    c. A loan or other extension of credit (this includes untimely deposits to the trust of employee salary deferral deposits) between the plan and a party in interest.
    d. The furnishing of goods, services, or facilities between the plan and a party in interest.
    e. A transfer of plan assets to a party in interest for the use or benefit of a party in interest.

Initial audit of the 401(k) plan

An initial audit of the 401(k) plan will occur in the first year of the plan or in the year when the number of participants increases to 100 (120 if the plan chooses to utilize the DOL's 80-120 rule) for plans that have been in existence for more than one year.

If you did not audit the plan's financial statements in the prior year, you should perform procedures to obtain reasonable assurance that the accounting principles used by the plan in the current and the prior year are consistent. If the plan has maintained adequate records, you ordinarily should be able to apply auditing procedures to determine that generally accepted accounting principles have been applied consistently.

During the initial audit of a plan's financial statements, you should pay close attention to certain areas. Participant records as they relate to the eligibility of participants, benefit eligibility, the completeness of participant data and records of the prior year (if the plan has been in existence more than one year), and account balances should be considered. The nature, timing, and extent of auditing procedures you apply are a matter of judgment and will vary with such factors as the complexity of the plan's operations, and, if the plan is more than one year old, the adequacy of past records and the significance of beginning balances.

ERISA requires that audited plan financial statements present comparative Statements of Net Assets Available for Benefits, unless this is the first year of the plan. When comparative statements are issued, the current-year balances should be audited and the prior-year balances, which are presented for comparative purposes only, should be either compiled, reviewed, or audited. In the current-year report, you should state what level of testing (compilation, review, or audit) was performed on the prior-year balances. If the prior-year balances are compiled, a separate compilation report must be issued for the prior year.

Although a compilation or review of the prior year is acceptable, paragraph .04 of AU-C section 510 states that the objective of the auditor in conducting an initial audit engagement, including a reaudit engagement, is to obtain sufficient appropriate audit evidence regarding opening balances about whether (*a*) opening balances contain misstatements that materially affect the current period's financial statements and (*b*) appropriate accounting policies reflected in the opening balances have been consistently applied in the current period's financial statements or changes thereto are appropriately accounted for and adequately presented and disclosed in accordance with the applicable financial reporting framework. Accordingly, the nature, timing, and extent of audit procedures performed to obtain such evidence may be significantly different and more extensive for a plan that has never been audited previously than for one that has.

For existing plans that have gone from not requiring an audit to now requiring one, audit work is necessary to test the opening account balances. If the plan sponsor has adequate records, you should review and test those so you are comfortable with the reasonableness of the opening account balances. You should consider confirming the opening balances with the trustee and plan participants and performing an analytical review of the significant accounts that make up the Statement of Changes in Net Assets Available for Benefits.

If records were not adequately retained or they are difficult to locate, you should consider confirming the year-end balances and reconciling back to the beginning-of-year balances. Regardless of the testing method, you should perform sufficient auditing procedures on the beginning balance of net assets available for benefits to obtain reasonable assurance that there are no material misstatements in these beginning balances that may impact the current year's statement of changes in net assets available for benefits.

Auditors of employee benefit plans often perform audits of plans that previously audited by another firm. When the plan has been previously audited by another auditor, the auditor communicates with the predecessor auditor. The auditor should request management to authorize the predecessor auditor to respond fully to the auditor's inquiries regarding matters that will assist the auditor in determining whether to accept the engagement. If management refuses to authorize the predecessor auditor to respond or limits the response, the auditor should inquire about the reasons and consider the implications of that refusal in deciding whether to accept the engagement.

The auditor should evaluate the predecessor auditor's response, or consider the implications if the predecessor auditor provides no response or a limited response, in determining whether to accept the engagement. The communication with the predecessor auditor may be either written or oral. Matters subject to the auditor's inquiry of the predecessor auditor may include:

a. information that might bear on the integrity of management.
b. disagreements with management about accounting policies, auditing procedures, or other similarly significant matters.
c. communications to those charged with governance regarding fraud and noncompliance with laws or regulations by the entity.
d. communications to management and those charged with governance regarding significant deficiencies and material weaknesses in internal control.
e. the predecessor auditor's understanding about the reasons for the change of auditors. (The DOL also requires that auditor changes and the reason for the change be reported on Form 5500, Schedule C, Service Provider Information.)

When performing an initial audit engagement, the auditor should read the most recent financial statements, if any, and the predecessor auditor's report thereon, if any, for information relevant to opening balances, including disclosures, and consistency in the application of accounting policies. In instances in which the prior period financial statements were audited by a predecessor auditor, the auditor should request that plan management authorize the predecessor auditor to allow a review of the predecessor auditor's audit documentation and for the predecessor auditor to respond fully to inquiries by the auditor, thereby providing the auditor with information to assist in planning and performing the engagement. The predecessor auditor may request a consent and an acknowledgment letter from plan management to document this authorization in an effort to reduce misunderstandings about the scope of the communications being authorized. In addition, before permitting access to the audit documentation, the predecessor auditor may request written confirmation of the auditor's agreement regarding the use of the audit documentation.

Areas of special consideration in an initial audit of a plan's financial statements include the completeness and accuracy of participant data and records of prior years, especially as they relate to

a. participant contributions and eligibility.
b. the amounts and types of benefits.
c. the eligibility for benefits.
d. participant account balances.
e. census data maintained by the actuary.

Form 11-K: The Sarbanes-Oxley Act of 2002

The Sarbanes-Oxley Act of 2002 (the Act) dramatically affects the accounting profession and affects not just the largest accounting firms, but any CPA actively working as an auditor of or for a publicly traded company or any CPA working in the financial management area of a public company. Although most of the provisions of this legislation are specific to auditors of public companies, even practitioners not performing audits may be affected by the Act. Therefore, all CPA firms should become familiar with the provisions of the Act and the PCAOB.

Major provisions affecting employee benefit plans include the following:

- Auditors of public companies are required to register with the PCAOB. This includes auditors of employee benefit plans whose plan sponsors file annual reports on Form 11-K with the SEC.
- Auditor independence
  - Section 201—*Services Outside the Scope of Practice of Auditors*—The independence provisions of the Act and the SEC rules prohibit a registered firm from performing specified non-audit services for audit clients. Nonaudit services are services other than those provided in connection with an audit or a review of the financial statements. It should be noted that independence would be impaired if an auditor prepares financial statements for a client that are filed with the SEC.
  - Section 202—*Pre-Approval Requirements*—The rule requires an audit committee to establish policies and procedures for the pre-approval of services to be provided by the auditor.
  - Section 203—*Audit Partner Rotation*—To maintain independence, partners must rotate after serving for five consecutive years and are subject to a five-year "timeout" period after the rotation. This requirement also includes concurring review partners and extends to both 11-Ks as well as other types of benefit plans if there is a Form 11-K filing.
  - Section 204—*Auditor Reports to Audit Committees*—Auditors are currently required by GAAS to communicate specified matters related to the conduct of an audit to those who have responsibility for oversight of the financial reporting process, which is often the sponsor's audit committee. SAS No. 114 and S-X Rule 2-07 communications need to be completed prior to the issuance of the audit report and filing of the Form 11-K.
  - PCAOB Rule 3526, *Communication with Audit Committees Concerning Independence* (AICPA, *PCAOB Standards and Related Rules*, Select Rules of the Board)—This rule requires the registered public accounting firm to (1) describe in writing, to the audit committee of the issuer, all relationships between the registered public accounting firm or any affiliates of the firm and the potential audit client or persons in financial reporting oversight roles at the potential audit clients that, as of the date of the communication, may reasonably be thought to bear on independence; (2) discuss with the audit committee of the issuer the potential effects of any relationships that could affect independence, should a member of the registered public accounting firm be appointed as the issuer's auditor; and (3) document the substance of these discussions. These discussions should occur at least annually.
- Corporate responsibility
  - Section 302—*Corporate Responsibilities for Financial Reports*—Requires a certification of the financial statements and other financial information; this requirement does not apply to annual reports on Form 11-K.
  - Based upon discussions currently with the SEC, Section 906 does not apply to Form 11-K filings. Plan sponsors should consult with their SEC counsel.
- Management assessment of internal controls
  - Section 404—Requires each issuer that files period reports with the SEC to (1) establish and maintain a system of internal control over financial reporting, (2) include in its annual report a report by management on the system of internal controls, and (3) accompany the report with an

attestation report on the system of internal controls. Based upon discussions with the SEC, Section 404 is not applicable to Forms 11-K.

Additional requirements

Note: On March 31, 2015, the PCAOB adopted amendments to reorganize its auditing standards (see PCAOB Release No. 2015-002). The reorganization and related amendments are effective as of December 31, 2016. These amendments do not impose new requirements on auditors or change the substance of the requirements for performing and reporting on audits under the standards of the PCAOB. The standards are now organized into a logical structure by topic areas that generally follow the flow of the audit process, rather than numbered consecutively by standard.

- AS 1215—*Audit Documentation.* This standard establishes general requirements for documentation the auditor should prepare and retain in connection with engagements conducted pursuant to the standards of the PCAOB. Audit documentation should be in sufficient detail to provide a clear understanding on its purpose, source, and conclusions reached. Documentation should demonstrate that the engagement complied with the standards of the PCAOB, support the auditor's conclusions, and demonstrate the accounting records agree to the financial statements. AS 1215 also indicates that the audit documentation must contain sufficient information to enable an experienced auditor with no previous connection with the engagement to *(a)* understand the nature timing, extent, and results of procedures performed, evidence obtained, and conclusions reached and *(b)* to determine who performed the work, the date the work was performed, who reviewed the work, and the date the work was reviewed.
- AS 6115—*Reporting on Whether a Previously Reported Material Weakness Continues to Exist.* This standard establishes requirements and provides direction that apply when an auditor is engaged to report on whether a previously reported material weakness in internal control over financial reporting continues to exist as of a date specified by management.
- AS 2201—*An Audit of Internal Control Over Financial Reporting That Is Integrated with An Audit of Financial Statements.* This standard establishes requirements and provides direction that applies when an auditor is engaged to perform an audit of management's assessment of the effectiveness of internal control over financial reporting ("the audit of internal control over financial reporting") that is integrated with an audit of the financial statements.
- AS 2820—*Evaluating Consistency of Financial Statements.* This standard and its related amendments update the auditors' responsibilities to evaluate and report on the consistency of a plan's financial statements and align the auditors' responsibilities with FASB ASC 250, *Accounting Changes and Error Corrections.* This standard also improves the auditor reporting requirements by clarifying that the auditors' report should indicate whether an adjustment to previously issued financial statements results from a change in accounting principles or correction of a misstatement.
- AS 1220—*Engagement Quality Review and Conforming Amendment to the Board's Interim Quality Control Standards.* This standard establishes standards related to an engagement quality review and concurring approval of issuance that is required for each audit engagement and for each engagement to review interim financial information conducted pursuant to the standards of the PCAOB.
  - AS 1220 was effective for the Engagement Quality Reviews (EQR) of audits of all public plans with fiscal years ending on or after December 15, 2009.
  - AS 1220 focuses on the qualifications of the EQR partner and lists nine specific tasks that the reviewer must perform, using language that is more explicit than the interim standard. AS 1220 also calls for specific documentation of the quality review process.

- AS 1101—*Audit Risk.* This standard discusses the auditor's consideration of audit risk in an audit of financial statements as part of an integrated audit or an audit of financial statements only.
- AS 2101—*Audit Planning.* This standard establishes requirements regarding planning an audit.
- AS 1201—*Supervision of the Audit Engagement.* This standard establishes requirements regarding supervision of the audit engagement, including supervising the work of engagement team members.
- AS 2105—*Consideration of Materiality in Planning and Performing an Audit.* This standard establishes requirements regarding the auditor's consideration of materiality in planning and performing an audit.
- AS 2110—*Identifying and Assessing Risks of Material Misstatement.* This standard establishes requirements regarding the process of identifying and assessing risks of material misstatement of the financial statements and discusses the auditor's responsibilities for performing risk assessment procedures. This standard also discusses identifying and assessing the risks of material misstatement using information obtained from performing risk assessment procedures.
- AS 2301—*The Auditor's Response to the Risks of Material Misstatement.* This standard establishes requirements regarding designing and implementing appropriate responses to the risks of material misstatement.
- AS 2810—*Evaluating Audit Results.* This standard establishes requirements regarding the auditor's evaluation of audit results and determination of whether he or she has obtained sufficient appropriate audit evidence.
- AS 1105—*Audit Evidences.* This standard explains what constitutes audit evidence and establishes requirements regarding designing and performing audit procedures to obtain sufficient appropriate audit evidence.
- AS 1301—*Communications with Audit Committees.* This standard requires the auditor to communicate with the company's audit committee regarding certain matters related to the conduct of an audit and to obtain certain information from the audit committee relevant to the audit. This standard also requires the auditor to establish an understanding of the terms of the audit engagement with the audit committee and to record that understanding in an engagement letter.
- AS 2701—*Auditing Supplemental Information Accompanying Audited Financial Statements.* This standard sets forth the auditor's responsibilities when the auditor of the company's financial statements is engaged to perform audit procedures and report on supplemental information that accompanies financial statements audited pursuant to PCAOB standards.
- AS 2410—*Related Parties.* This standard establishes requirements regarding the auditor's evaluation of a company's identification of, accounting for, and disclosure of relationships and transactions between the company and its related parties.

Knowledge check

12. Which of the following requirements of the Sarbanes-Oxley Act of 2002 (Act) is applicable to benefit plans that file Form 11-K?

   a. An opinion on internal controls under Section 404 of the Act.
   b. Certification by management as to the accuracy of the financial statements under Section 302 of the Act.
   c. Required partner rotation after five years.
   d. Reporting on material weaknesses to the SEC.

Communication with those charged with governance

AU-C section 260, *The Auditor's Communication With Those Charged With Governance* (AICPA, *Professional Standards*), requires the auditor to conduct two-way communication with those charged with governance about certain significant matters related to the audit, and also establishes standards and provides guidance about (*a*) the matters to be communicated, (*b*) the people to whom the matters should be communicated, and (*c*) the form and timing of the communication. AU-C section 260 uses the term *those charged with governance* to refer to the person(s) or organization(s) (for example, a corporate trustee) with responsibility for overseeing the strategic direction of the entity and the obligations related to the accountability of the entity. This includes overseeing the financial reporting process.

The auditor should communicate with those charged with governance

- the auditor's responsibilities under GAAS (described in chapter 2),
- the overview of the planned scope and timing of the audit (described in chapter 2), and
- the significant findings from the audit (described following).

In August 2012, the PCAOB adopted AS 1301, *Communications with Audit Committees*. AS 1301 stipulates additional requirements regarding matters to communicate. Refer to AS 1301 for a complete listing of matters to be communicated when performing an audit on a Form 11-K in accordance with standards of the PCAOB.

Significant findings from the audit

The auditor should communicate the following with those charged with governance:

- The auditor's views about qualitative aspects of the plan's significant accounting policies, including accounting policies, accounting estimates, and financial statement disclosures. For example
  - significant difficulties, if any, encountered during the audit;
  - uncorrected misstatements (other than those the auditor believes are trivial), if any;
  - disagreements with management, if any; and
  - other findings or issues, if any, arising from the audit that are, in the auditor's professional judgment, significant and relevant to those charged with governance regarding their oversight of the financial reporting process.

Unless all of those charged with governance are involved in managing the entity, the auditor also should communicate

- misstatements that are material and have been corrected;
- representations that the auditor is requesting of management;
- consultations that occurred with management and other accountants; and
- issues discussed with management and other significant findings or issues that the auditor believes are significant and relevant to those charged with governance.

AU-C section 260 requires the auditor to communicate with those charged with governance uncorrected misstatements and the effect that they may have on the opinion in the auditor's report, and request their correction. In communicating the effect that material uncorrected misstatements may have on the opinion in the auditor's report, the auditor should communicate them individually. Where there are a large number of small uncorrected misstatements, the auditor may communicate the number and overall monetary effect of the misstatements rather than the details of each individual misstatement. The auditor should discuss with those charged with governance the implications of a failure to correct known and likely misstatements, if any, considering qualitative as well as quantitative considerations, including possible implications in relation to future financial statements. The auditor should also communicate with those charged with governance the effect of uncorrected misstatements related to prior periods on the relevant classes of transactions, account balances or disclosures, and the financial statements as a whole. AU-C section 240, *Consideration of Fraud in a Financial Statement Audit* (AICPA, *Professional Standards*), says the auditor also may wish to communicate other risks of fraud identified as a result of the assessment of the risks of material misstatement due to fraud. Such a communication may be a part of an overall communication to the audit committee of the plan and financial statement risks affecting the plan or in conjunction with the auditor communication about the quality of the plan's accounting principles (or both).

Communications required by AU-C section 260 are applicable regardless of a plan's governance structure or size.

The auditor should communicate with those charged with governance the auditor's views about qualitative aspects of the plan's significant accounting practices, including accounting estimates. Certain accounting estimates are particularly sensitive because of their significance to the financial statements and because of the possibility that future events affecting them may differ markedly from management's current judgments. For significant estimates, such communication may include management's identification of accounting estimates, management's process for making accounting estimates, risks of material misstatement, indicators of possible management bias, and disclosure of estimation uncertainty in the financial statements (see AU-C section 260 for further guidance). For example, the auditor may consider communicating the nature of significant assumptions used in fair value measurements, the degree of subjectivity involved in the development of the assumptions, and the relative materiality of the items being measured at fair value to the financial statements as a whole.

The auditor should explain to those charged with governance why the auditor considers a significant accounting practice (including accounting estimates) not to be appropriate and, when considered necessary, request changes. If requested changes are not made, the auditor should inform those charged with governance that the auditor will consider the effect of this on the financial statements of the current and future years, and on the auditor's report.

Although the communication can be oral, it should be in writing when, in the auditor's judgment, oral communication would not be adequate. AU-C section 260 also contains information on the communication process, timing of the communication, adequacy of the communication process, and specific examples of what should be communicated.

When matters required to be communicated have been communicated orally, the auditor should document them. AU-C section 260 requires that the audit documentation include documentation of the significant findings or issues discussed, and when and with whom the discussions took place. When matters have been communicated in writing, the auditor should retain a copy of the communication. Documentation of oral communication may include a copy of minutes prepared by the plan if those minutes are an appropriate record of the communication.

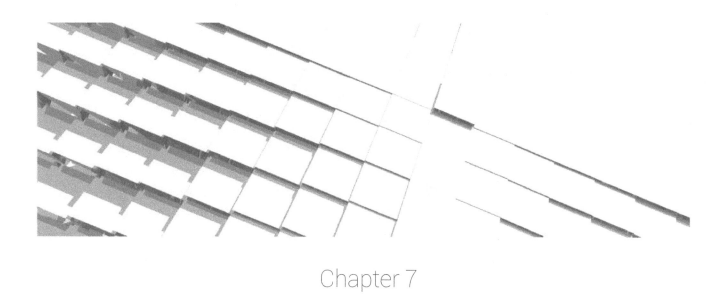

Chapter 7

The Auditor's Report and Financial Statement Disclosures

Learning objectives

After completing this chapter, you should be able to do the following:

- Identify the paragraphs to include in the auditor's reports for various situations encountered in audits of 401(k) plans.

- Indicate the appropriate note disclosures for the financial statements of 401(k) plans.

AICPA auditing standards board proposes significant changes to EBP auditor reporting

In July 2018, the ASB voted to issue a new auditing standard, Statement on Auditing Standards (SAS), *Forming an Opinion and Reporting on Financial Statements of Employee Benefit Plans Subject to ERISA*. Although the ASB voted to issue this SAS as a final standard, it was not issued immediately because the ASB was also deliberating proposed SAS *Auditor Reporting and Amendments—Addressing Disclosures in the Audit of Financial Statements* (Auditor Reporting SAS). The Auditor Reporting SAS was voted as a final standard at the January 2019 ASB meeting and conforming amendments will need to be made to the EBP SAS to align the reporting elements.

This SAS addresses the auditor's responsibility to form an opinion and report on the audit of financial statements of employee benefit plans subject to ERISA, and the form and content of the auditor's report issued as a result of an audit of ERISA plan financial statements, including changes to the form and content of the auditor's report when management elects to have an audit performed pursuant to ERISA section 103(a)(3)(C). This SAS also includes new requirements for engagement acceptance, audit risk assessment and response, communications with those charged with governance, procedures for an ERISA section 103(a)(3)(C) audit, and considerations relating to the Form 5500. For audits of ERISA plan financial statements only, this SAS would apply in place of AU-C section 700, *Forming an Opinion and Reporting on Financial Statements*, and paragraph .09 of AU-C section 725, *Supplementary Information in Relation to the Financial Statements as a Whole*. The SAS also would amend various other AU-C sections in AICPA *Professional Standards*. This SAS should not be adapted for plans that are not subject to ERISA.

When issued, this SAS will be effective for audits of financial statements for periods ending on or after December 15, 2020. Early implementation is not permitted.

This course has not been updated to reflect this new SAS. The Standards Tracker provides a quick reference to recently issued audit and attest standards, complete with effective dates, summaries, and links to the standards themselves and can be accessed at www.aicpa.org/interestareas/frc/auditattest/standardstracker-auditandattest.html.

Introduction

The examples in this chapter incorporate the new auditor's opinion and report formats required by the clarified auditing standards issued by the AICPA Auditing Standards Board (ASB) and codified in *Professional Standards* in AU-C sections 700, *Forming an Opinion and Reporting on Financial Statements*; 705, *Modifications to the Opinion in the Independent Auditor's Report*; 706, *Emphasis-of-Matter Paragraphs and Other-Matter Paragraphs in the Independent Auditor's Report* ; and 725, *Supplementary Information in Relation to the Financial Statements as a Whole*, as established by Statement of Auditing Standard No. 122, which was effective for audits of financial statements for periods ending on or after December 15, 2012.

The AICPA Audit and Accounting Guide *Employee Benefit Plans* contains illustrations of auditor opinions and reports and is an important resource from which the examples in this chapter were based and from which examples of other auditor opinions and reports discussed can be obtained.

This chapter has been designed to provide you with examples and knowledge of various types of auditor reports that will be useful when preparing your report for the plan's financial statements. This chapter provides examples of the standard audit report and an ERISA limited-scope audit example.

In addition, the financial statements of defined contribution 401(k) plans should include various disclosures about the nature of the plan and the financial information presented in the Statements of Net Assets Available for Benefits and Statement of Changes in Net Assets Available for Benefits. This chapter contains descriptions and examples of the types of disclosures that should be included in the notes to the plan's financial statements. Additionally, the AICPA developed *Employee Benefit Plans—Best Practices in*

Presentation and Disclosure, which has a compilation of various note disclosures for all types of employee benefit plans.

New Accounting Standards

> This course has been updated to include the following FASB Accounting Standards Update (ASU) whose provisions are not yet effective. The preparers of this course believe that many plans will want to adopt this new ASU early and therefore the provisions of this ASU have been reflected in the body of this course guide.

For those who are not early adopting this ASU, the AICPA is continuing to offer the 2018 edition of the AICPA Audit & Accounting Guide *Employee Benefit Plans* as a resource for requirements prior to the effective date of this ASU.

ASU No. 2017-06—In February 2017, FASB issued ASU No. 2017-06, *Plan Accounting: Defined Benefit Pension Plans (Topic 960), Defined Contribution Pension Plans (Topic 962), Health and Welfare Benefit Plans (Topic 965): Employee Benefit Plan Master Trust Reporting.*

The ASU relates primarily to the reporting by a plan for its interest in a master trust. The amendments clarify presentation requirements for a plan's interest in a master trust and require more detailed disclosures of the plan's interest in the master trust. The amendments also eliminate a redundancy relating to 401(h) account disclosures.

The amendments in FASB ASU 2017-06 are effective for fiscal years beginning after December 15, 2018, and early adoption is permitted. An entity should apply the amendments retrospectively to each period for which financial statements are presented.

This course has not been updated to include the following FASB ASU whose provisions are not yet effective.

> In August 2018, FASB issued ASU No. 2018-13, *Fair Value Measurement (Topic 820): Disclosure Framework—Changes to the Disclosure Requirements for Fair Value Measurement*, to modify the disclosure requirements on fair value measurements in FASB ASC 820, *Fair Value Measurement*. FASB ASU No. 2018-13 contains amendments that remove, modify or add disclosure requirements including those relating to transfers between levels of the fair value hierarchy, level 3 fair value measurements, and entities that calculate net asset value.
>
> The amendments in FASB ASU No. 2018-13 are effective for all entities for fiscal years beginning after December 15, 2019. Early adoption is permitted. Readers are encouraged to consult the full text of this ASU on FASB's website at www.fasb.org.

The auditor's report

Generally, your report should be addressed to the plan whose financial statements are subject to audit, or to the plan administrator, or to participants and their beneficiaries, or any appropriate combination of addressees. The report should be dated no earlier than the date you have obtained sufficient appropriate audit evidence to support the opinion and should cover the audit period for which financial statements are presented. Specifically, for Form 5500 purposes, the Statement of Net Assets Available for Benefits must be comparative and it is permissible to present only one year for the Statement of Changes in Net Assets Available for Benefits, consistent with the financial information in Form 5500.

Addressing the Auditor's Report—Paragraph .24 of AU-C section 700 states that the auditor's report should be addressed as required by the circumstances of the engagement. For employee benefit plans, the report may be addressed to the plan or trust whose financial statements are being audited, the plan administrator or board of trustees, or participants and beneficiaries.

Dating of the Auditor's Report—The auditor's report should be dated no earlier than the date on which the auditor has obtained sufficient appropriate audit evidence on which to base the auditor's opinion on the financial statements. Paragraph .41 of AU-C section 700 states that this includes evidence that (*a*) the audit documentation has been reviewed; (*b*) all the statements that the financial statements comprise, including the related notes, have been prepared; and (*c*) management has asserted that it has taken responsibility for those financial statements.

Content of the Auditor's Report—The auditor's report should be in writing. The following is a list of elements that should be included in the auditor's report, in accordance with paragraphs .23–.41 of AU-C section 700. See AU-C section 700 for the specific requirements related to each of these elements:

1. *Title* (paragraph .23 of AU-C section 700)
2. *Addressee* (paragraph .24 of AU-C section 700)
3. *Introductory paragraph* (paragraph .25 of AU-C section 700)
4. *Management's responsibility for the financial statements* (paragraphs .26–.28 of AU-C section 700)
5. *Auditor's responsibility* (paragraphs .29–.33 of AU-C section 700)
6. *Auditor's opinion* (paragraphs .34–.36 of AU-C section 700)
7. *Other reporting responsibilities* (paragraphs .37–.38 of AU-C section 700)
8. *Signature of the auditor* (paragraph .39 of AU-C section 700)
9. *Auditor's address* (paragraph .40 of AU-C section 700)
10. *Date of the auditor's report* (paragraph .41 of AU-C section 700)

In Form 5500 filings, the DOL generally rejects auditors' reports that express either a qualified or adverse opinion or disclaimer of opinion (other than the disclaimer opinion permitted for ERISA limited-scope audits). In such situations, the DOL will send a letter to the plan administrator indicating that the plan's Form 5500 filing has been rejected and giving the plan a period of time to correct the deficiencies. This would then permit the auditor to issue an unqualified opinion on the plan's financial statements—provided all of the deficiencies are corrected to the auditor's satisfaction.

Supplemental schedules relating to ERISA and DOL regulations

In addition to the financial statements and related disclosures, which may conform to the requirements of FASB ASC 962, *Plan Accounting—Defined Contribution Pension Plans*, ERISA and DOL regulations require additional information to be disclosed in the financial statements or presented in the supplemental schedules. Some of this information is required to be covered by the auditor's report.

Because the supplemental schedules are required by ERISA and DOL regulations, not a designated accounting standard setter, the supplemental schedules are not considered *required supplementary information*, as defined in AU-C section 730, *Required Supplementary Information* (AICPA, *Professional Standards*); therefore, AU-C section 730 does not apply. Instead, auditors report on whether the supplemental schedules that are required to be covered by the auditor's report are fairly presented in relation to the financial statements as a whole. Therefore, the requirements in AU-C section 725 apply.

When performing a full-scope audit of an employee benefit plan, the auditor is typically engaged to report on whether the supplemental schedules that are required to be covered by the auditor's report are fairly presented in relation to the financial statements as a whole; therefore, the requirements in AU-C section 725 apply as previously noted. Paragraphs .05–.08 of AU-C section 725 require certain audit procedures to be performed in addition to the procedures performed during the audit of the financial statements in order for the auditor to provide such an opinion on the supplemental schedules. AU-C section 725 also provides guidance on the form and content of the report. When the plan presents the supplemental schedules with the financial statements, the auditor should report on the supplementary information in either an other-matter paragraph, in accordance with AU-C section 706, or a separate report on the supplemental schedules.

Paragraph .09 of AU-C section 725 states that the other-matter paragraph or separate report, in those circumstances, should include the following elements:

1. A statement that the audit was conducted for the purpose of forming an opinion on the financial statements as a whole.
2. A statement that the supplementary information is presented for purposes of additional analysis and is not a required part of the financial statements.
3. A statement that the supplementary information is the responsibility of management and was derived from, and relates directly to, the underlying accounting and other records used to prepare the financial statements.
4. A statement that the supplementary information has been subjected to the auditing procedures applied in the audit of the financial statements and certain additional procedures—including comparing and reconciling such information directly to the underlying accounting and other records used to prepare the financial statements or to the financial statements themselves and other additional procedures—in accordance with auditing standards generally accepted in the United States of America.
5. A statement that, in the auditor's opinion, the supplementary information is fairly stated in all material respects in relation to the financial statements as a whole, if the auditor issues an unmodified opinion on the financial statements and the auditor has concluded that the supplementary information is fairly stated in all material respects, in relation to the financial statements as a whole,

6. If the auditor issues a qualified opinion on the financial statements and the qualification has an effect on the supplementary information, a statement that in the auditor's opinion, except for the effects on the supplementary information of (refer to the paragraph in the auditor's report explaining the qualification), such information is fairly stated, in all material respects, in relation to the financial statements as a whole.

When the auditor's report on the audited financial statements contains an adverse opinion or a disclaimer of opinion and the auditor has been engaged to report on whether the supplementary information is fairly stated in all material respects in relation to such financial statements as a whole, the auditor is precluded from expressing an opinion on the supplementary information. See paragraph .11 of AU-C section 725 for further guidance.

Standard report

Following is an example of an auditor's report in which a full-scope audit was performed, which resulted in an unqualified opinion on the plan's financial statements and supplemental schedules. In this case, the plan's financial statements include a comparative Statement of Net Assets Available for benefits and a single-year presentation of the Statement of Changes in Net Assets Available for Benefits. Also, as required by the DOL's rules and regulations, this report also covers the applicable supplemental schedules. (See chapter 6, "Other Auditing Considerations," for additional information.)

As noted in chapter 6, the auditor's report for plans that file Form 11-K with the SEC and are subject to the Sarbanes-Oxley Act of 2002 must follow PCAOB guidance. Currently, to comply with PCAOB guidance, two audit reports must be issued—one that references the PCAOB standards (for filing with the Form 11-K) and one that references GAAS (for filing with Form 5500).

Independent auditor's report

[Appropriate Addressee]

Report on the financial statements[1]

We have audited the accompanying financial statements of ABC 401(k) Plan, which comprise the statements of net assets available for benefits as of December 31, 20X2 and 20X1, and the related statement of changes in net assets available for benefits for the year ended December 31, 20X2, and the related notes to the financial statements.

Management's responsibility for the financial statements

Management is responsible for the preparation and fair presentation of these financial statements in accordance with accounting principles generally accepted in the United States of America; this includes the design, implementation, and maintenance of internal control relevant to the preparation and fair presentation of financial statements that are free from material misstatement, whether due to fraud or error.

Auditor's responsibility

Our responsibility is to express an opinion on these financial statements based on our audits. We conducted our audits in accordance with auditing standards generally accepted in the United States of America. Those standards require that we plan and perform the audit to obtain reasonable assurance about whether the financial statements are free from material misstatement.

---

[1] The subtitle "Report on the Financial Statements" is unnecessary when the second subtitle, "Report on Other Legal and Regulatory Requirements," is not applicable. In this illustration, the heading "Report on the Financial Statements" has been included even though there is no report on other legal and regulatory requirements included in this report.

An audit involves performing procedures to obtain audit evidence about the amounts and disclosures in the financial statements. The procedures selected depend on the auditor's judgment, including the assessment of the risks of material misstatement of the financial statements, whether due to fraud or error. In making those risk assessments, the auditor considers internal control relevant to the entity's preparation and fair presentation of the financial statements in order to design audit procedures that are appropriate in the circumstances, but not for the purpose of expressing an opinion on the effectiveness of the entity's internal control.[2] Accordingly, we express no such opinion. An audit also includes evaluating the appropriateness of accounting policies used and the reasonableness of significant accounting estimates made by management, as well as evaluating the overall presentation of the financial statements.

We believe that the audit evidence we have obtained is sufficient and appropriate to provide a basis for our audit opinion.

Opinion

In our opinion, the financial statements referred to above present fairly, in all material respects, the net assets available for benefits of the Plan as of December 31, 20X2 and 20X1, and the changes in net assets available for benefits for the year ended December 31, 20X2, in accordance with accounting principles generally accepted in the United States of America.

Report on supplementary information[3]

Our audits were conducted for the purpose of forming an opinion on the financial statements as a whole. The supplemental schedules of [identify title of schedules and period covered] are presented for the purpose of additional analysis and are not a required part of the financial statements but are supplementary information required by the Department of Labor's Rules and Regulations for Reporting and Disclosure under the Employee Retirement Income Security Act of 1974. Such information is the responsibility of the Plan's management and was derived from and relates directly to the underlying accounting and other records used to prepare the financial statements. The information has been subjected to the auditing procedures applied in the audits of the financial statements and certain additional procedures, including comparing and reconciling such information directly to the underlying accounting and other records used to prepare the financial statements or to the financial statements

---

[2] In circumstances when the auditor also has responsibility to express an opinion on the effectiveness of internal control in conjunction with the audit of the financial statements, this sentence would be worded as follows: "In making those risk assessments, the auditor considers internal control relevant to the entity's preparation and fair presentation of the financial statements in order to design audit procedures that are appropriate in the circumstances." In addition, the next sentence, "Accordingly, we express no such opinion." would not be included.

[3] The auditor is reporting on the supplemental schedules in an other-matter paragraph, as required by AU-C section 725, *Supplementary Information in Relation to the Financial Statements as a Whole* (AICPA, *Professional Standards*). In accordance with paragraph .08 of AU-C section 706, *Emphasis-of-Matter Paragraphs and Other-Matter Paragraphs in the Independent Auditor's Report* (AICPA, *Professional Standards*), the heading "Other Matter" or other appropriate heading should be used when including an other-matter paragraph in the auditor's report. In this illustration the heading "Report on Supplementary Information" is used rather than "Other Matter."

themselves, and other additional procedures in accordance with auditing standards generally accepted in the United States of America. In our opinion, the information is fairly stated in all material respects in relation to the financial statements as a whole.

[*Auditor's signature*]

[*Auditor's city and state*]

[*Date of the auditor's report*]

Additional communications: Emphasis-of-matter and other-matter paragraphs

When the auditor is forming an opinion and issuing an auditor's report in connection with an audit of financial statements, AU-C section 706 addresses situations when the auditor considers it necessary, or is required, to include additional communications in the auditor's report that are not modifications to the auditor's opinion (emphasis-of-matter paragraphs and other-matter paragraphs). This section of chapter 7 will discuss various examples of such reports of additional communications that are not modifications.

Going concern considerations

During the audit of a non-terminated employee benefit plan, the auditor may become aware that the plan sponsor may not be able to continue as a going concern. Although employee benefit plans are not automatically and necessarily affected by the plan sponsor's financial adversities, this situation may result in the auditor determining it to be a condition or an event sufficient to evaluate whether there is substantial doubt about the plan's ability to continue as a going concern. AU-C section 570, *The Auditor's Consideration of an Entity's Ability to Continue as a Going Concern* (AICPA, *Professional Standards*), addresses the auditor's responsibilities in an audit of financial statements relating to the entity's ability to continue as a going concern and the implications for the auditor's report. This AU-C section applies to all audits of a complete set of general purpose financial statements, regardless of whether the financial statements are prepared in accordance with a general purpose or special purpose framework. This AU-C section does not apply to an audit of a complete set of general purpose financial statements prepared under the liquidation basis of accounting.

See AU-C section 570 for implications for the auditor's report when the auditor concludes that there are conditions, considered in the aggregate, that raise substantial doubt about an entity's ability to continue as a going concern for a reasonable period of time.

Decision to terminate plan

Another situation that warrants a modification to the auditor's report via the addition of an emphasis-of-matter paragraph arises when a 401(k) plan has been terminated or a decision has been made to terminate the plan and liquidation is deemed to be imminent. If a decision has been made to merge a 401(k) plan with another employee benefit plan, this fact does not normally require the modification of the auditor's report via the addition of an emphasis-of-matter paragraph. However, you have the option of adding an emphasis-of-matter paragraph to mention the merger if desired.

As noted in chapter 6, if the liquidation of a plan is deemed to be imminent (as defined in FASB ASC 205-30-24-2) before the end of the plan year, the plan's financial statements should be presented using the liquidation basis of accounting in accordance with FASB ASC 205-30, and this fact should be covered in an emphasis-of-matter paragraph added to the auditor's report. If the decision to terminate a plan is made after the plan's year-end but before the year-end financial statements have been issued, the decision is generally a type two subsequent event requiring the disclosure described in AU-C section 560, *Subsequent Events and Subsequently Discovered Facts* (AICPA, *Professional Standards*).

Knowledge check

1. If a decision has been made before the plan's year-end to terminate the plan and liquidation is deemed to be imminent, what is required in the financial statements?

    a. No special disclosures.
    b. A modified opinion in the auditor's report.
    c. A statement in the notes to the financial statements.
    d. Cash basis of accounting.

Modified reports

When the auditor is forming an opinion and issuing an auditor's report in connection with an audit of financial statements, AU-C section 700 is applicable. AU-C section 705 addresses how the form and content of the auditor's report are affected when the auditor expresses a modified opinion (a qualified, an adverse, or a disclaimer of opinion). The following section provides examples of modified reports.

Information omitted or entire schedule omitted from supplemental schedules

As noted in chapter 6, "Other Auditing Considerations," you may determine that certain parts of the information required by one of the supplemental schedules—or an entire supplemental schedule—has been omitted from the information provided to you by the trustee or custodian of plan assets. Chapter 6 includes a chart depicting the type of auditor's report that you should render, depending on the scope of the audit and the deficiencies in the supplemental schedule that you have identified.

In accordance with paragraph .13 of AU-C section 725, if the auditor concludes (on the basis of the procedures performed) that the supplementary information is materially misstated in relation to the financial statements as a whole, then the auditor should discuss the matter with management and propose appropriate revision of the supplementary information. If management does not revise the supplementary information, the auditor should either

1. modify the auditor's opinion on the supplemental schedules and describe the misstatement in the auditor's report, or
2. withhold the auditor's report on the supplemental schedules if a separate report is being issued on the supplemental schedules.

Note that this is not applicable when the Schedule of Nonexempt Transactions, Schedule G, Part III, has been omitted from the plan's financial statements. This situation and the type of report that should be rendered will be covered next.

Note that if the auditor concludes (on the basis of the procedures performed) that the supplementary information omitted is not materially misstated in relation to the financial statements as a whole, then the auditor should discuss the matter with management and propose appropriate revision of the supplementary information. If management does not revise the supplementary information, the auditor should issue an unqualified opinion with an other-matter paragraph.

Schedule of nonexempt transactions omitted or incomplete

As discussed in chapter 6, ERISA requires that all non-exempt transactions with parties in interest be reported on the supplemental schedule irrespective of the materiality of the transaction to the plan's financial statements. If the plan's financial statements have failed to report a material nonexempt transaction, then you should issue either a qualified or adverse opinion on the supplemental schedule. If the omitted nonexempt transaction is not material to the plan's financial statements, then you should modify your report on the supplemental schedule by including an other-matter paragraph to disclose the omitted or incomplete schedule.

In addition, to the extent that a material nonexempt party in interest transaction that is not disclosed in the supplemental schedule is also considered to be a related party transaction, and that related party transaction is not properly disclosed in the notes to the plan's financial statements, you should express a qualified or adverse opinion on the plan's financial statements as well as on the supplemental schedule. If the client refuses to accept your report as modified, you should withdraw from the engagement and communicate in writing to the plan administrator or board of trustees (for a multiemployer sponsored plan) the reasons for withdrawing

Knowledge check

2. If a material nonexempt party in interest transaction has not been disclosed in the appropriate supplemental schedule and is also considered to be a related party transaction, and that related party transaction is not properly disclosed in the notes to the financial statements, what type of audit report should be rendered when performing a full-scope audit?

    a. Qualified.
    b. Disclaimer.
    c. Unqualified with an other matter paragraph.
    d. Unqualified with an emphasis-of-matter paragraph.

Non-GAAP basis financial statements

Departure from accounting principles generally accepted in the United States of America

In certain instances, you may determine that the plan's financial statements are not in compliance with accounting principles generally accepted in the United States of America because of inadequate disclosures or other deficiencies. DOL regulations permit, but do not require, financial statements included in the annual report (Form 5500) to be prepared on a basis of accounting other than U.S. GAAP. Also, they do not prohibit variances from U.S. GAAP if the variances are described in a note to the financial statements.

A common example of the use of a basis other than U.S. GAAP is financial statements prepared on the modified cash basis of accounting for filing with the DOL. AU-C section 800, *Special Considerations — Audits of Financial Statements Prepared in Accordance With Special Purpose Frameworks* (AICPA, *Professional Standards*), addresses special considerations in the application of AU-C sections 200–700 to an audit of financial statements prepared in accordance with a special purpose framework, which is a cash, tax, regulatory, or contractual basis of accounting. A *cash basis of accounting* is defined as a basis of accounting that the entity uses to record cash receipts and disbursements and modifications of the cash basis having substantial support. For an employee benefit plan, cash basis financial statements that adjust investments to fair value are typically considered to be prepared on a modified cash basis of accounting.

Paragraph .15 of AU-C section 800 states that in an audit of special purpose framework financial statements, the auditor should evaluate whether the financial statements are suitably titled, include a summary of significant accounting policies, and adequately describe how the special purpose framework differs from GAAP.

Paragraph .17 of AU-C section 800 states that in an audit of special purpose financial statements, when the special purpose financial statements contain items that are the same as or similar to those in financial statements prepared in accordance with GAAP, the auditor should evaluate whether the financial statements include informative disclosures similar to those required by GAAP. Paragraph .A21 of AU-C section 800 further notes that disclosures in special purpose financial statements may substitute qualitative information for some of the quantitative information required by GAAP or may provide information that communicates the substance of those requirements. Appendix B, "Fair Presentation and Adequate Disclosures," of AU-C section 800 provides additional guidance on evaluating the adequacy of disclosures in financial statements prepared in accordance with a special purpose framework, including matters related to the presentation of financial statements.

In accordance with paragraph .18 of AU-C section 800, in the case of an auditor's report on special purpose financial statements, the explanation of management's responsibility for the financial statements should also make reference to its responsibility for determining that the applicable financial reporting framework is acceptable in the circumstances when management has a choice of financial reporting frameworks in the preparation of such financial statements.

The auditor's report on special purpose financial statements should include an emphasis-of-matter paragraph, under an appropriate heading, that (*a*) indicates that the financial statements are prepared in accordance with the applicable special purpose framework, (*b*) refers to the note in the financial statements that describes that framework, and (*c*) states that the special purpose framework is a basis of accounting other than GAAP. See paragraph .19 of AU-C section 800.

Knowledge check

3. What should be included in the emphasis-of-matter paragraph within the auditor's report on special purpose financial statements (prepared on the modified cash basis)?

    a. Indication that the financial statements are not prepared using an appropriate basis.
    b. Reference to the note in the financial statements that describes that framework.
    c. Statement that the scope is limited.
    d. Nothing as the modified cash basis is a special purpose framework that is allowed.

Reports filed pursuant to the SEC Form 11-K

As noted in chapter 1 of this course, certain 401(k) plans are required to file a Form 11-K with the SEC. As part of the Form 11-K filing, the plan's financial statements and related auditor's report must be provided. The instructions to the Form 11-K indicate that if a plan is subject to the provisions of ERISA, then the plan's financial statements may be presented to include only the financial statements required by ERISA, namely, a comparative Statement of Net Assets Available for Benefits and the most recent year's Statement of Changes in Net Assets Available for Benefits. The Form 11-K filings for plans filing the financial statements pursuant to the provisions of ERISA must be filed with the SEC within 180 days following the plan's year-end.

A 15-day extension is available through filing a Form 12b-25. The SEC does not accept ERISA limited-scope audit reports. All audit reports filed with a Form 11-K for plans electing to file its ERISA financial statements and having over 100 participants should demonstrate that a full-scope audit was performed for the plan.

Article 6A of Regulation S-X requires that for a Form 11-K filing, the plan's financial statements present a comparative Statement of Net Assets Available for Benefits and three years of data for the Statement of Changes in Net Assets Available for Benefits in addition to the following schedules which must be presented: Schedule I—Investments, Schedule II—Allocation of plan assets and liabilities to investment programs and Schedule III—Allocation of plan income and changes in plan equity to investment programs. Under Article 6A of Regulation S-X, the note disclosures to the plan's financial statements would be for either two or three years depending on the type of disclosure (that is, two years of disclosure for items involving the Statement of Net Assets and three years of disclosure for items involving the Statement of Changes in Net Assets). The filing of Form 11-K under Article 6A of Regulation S-X is due 90 days after the plan's year-end. Because of the additional reporting requirements under Article 6A of Regulation S-X, the majority of plans that are required to file a Form 11-K adopt the reporting format prescribed by ERISA for purposes of such financial statements.

PCAOB adopted Rules 3210 and 3211 and related amendments to its auditing standards (AS 3101, *Reports on Audited Financial Statements*, and AS 1205, *Part of the Audit Performed by Other Auditors*) that require the disclosure of the name of the engagement partner and information about other accounting firms that are participants in audits of issuers. Under the rules, firms are required to file certain information on Form AP, *Auditor Reporting of Certain Audit Participants*, disclosing the following:

- The name of the engagement partner
- The name, location, and extent of participation of each other accounting firm participating in the audit whose work constituted at least 5 percent of total audit hours
- The number and aggregate extent of participation of all other accounting firms participating in the audit whose individual participation was less than 5 percent of total audit hours

Form AP is available in a searchable database on the PCAOB website. Form AP is due to be filed by the 35th day after the date the audit report is first included in a document filed with the SEC and is required to be filed electronically with the PCAOB. In addition to filing Form AP, firms also have the ability to identify the engagement partner and/or provide disclosure about other accounting firms participating in the audit in the auditor's report on a voluntary basis.

Form AP disclosure regarding the engagement partner is required for audit reports of issued on or after January 31, 2017. Disclosure regarding other accounting firms is required for audit reports issued on or after June 30, 2017. Section VI of PCAOB Release No. 2015-008 specifically states that the rules and amendments apply to audits of employee stock purchase plans. Readers are encouraged to consult the full text of PCAOB Release No. 2015-008 and the related rules and auditing standards on the PCAOB's website at www.pcaobus.org.

In June 2017, the PCAOB adopted a new auditor reporting standard, *The Auditor's Report on an Audit of Financial Statements When the Auditor Expresses an Unqualified Opinion*, that replaced portions of AS 3100, *Reports on Audited Financial Statements*. AS 3101 and related amendments requires the auditor to provide new information about the audit and make the auditor's report more informative and relevant to investor's and other financial statement users. The final standard retains the pass/fail opinion of the existing auditor's report but makes significant changes to the existing auditor's report.

The final standard generally applies to audits conducted under PCAOB standards.

In October 2017, the SEC approved the final standard. The final standard and amendments take effect as follows:

- All provisions other than those related to critical audit matters take effect for audits of fiscal years ending on or after December 15, 2017.
- Provisions related to critical audit matters take effect for audits of fiscal years ending on or after June 30, 2019, for large accelerated filers; and for fiscal years ending on or after December 15, 2020, for all other companies to which the requirements apply.

The new standard allows for early adoption.

Based on AICPA staff discussions with the SEC and PCAOB staff to seek clarification of the performance and reporting requirements for audits of Form 11-K filers, firms will need to conduct their audits of plans that file a Form 11-K in accordance with two sets of standards and prepare two separate audit reports: (1) an audit report prepared in accordance with PCAOB standards for Form 11-K filings with the SEC, and (2) a separate audit report prepared in accordance with GAAS for DOL filings. . The following example is appropriate for the Form 11-K filing with the SEC based upon the new standards as detailed previously.

Report of independent registered public accounting firm

[Addressee][4]

Opinion on the financial statements

We have audited the accompanying statements of net assets available for benefits of the ABC 401(k) Plan (the Plan) as of December 31, 20X2 and 20X1, and the related statement of changes in net assets available for benefits for the year ended December 31, 20X2, and the related notes [*and schedules*][5] (collectively referred to as the *financial statements*). In our opinion, the financial statements present fairly, in all material respects, the net assets available for benefits of the Plan as of [*at*] December 31, 20X2 and 20X1, and the changes in net assets available for benefits for the year ended December 31, 20X2, in conformity with accounting principles generally accepted in the United States of America.

Basis for Opinion

These financial statements are the responsibility of the Plan's management. Our responsibility is to express an opinion on the Plan's financial statements based on our audits. We are a public accounting firm registered with the Public Company Accounting Oversight Board (United States) (PCAOB) and are required to be independent with respect to the Plan in accordance with the U.S. federal securities laws and the applicable rules and regulations of the Securities and Exchange Commission and the PCAOB.

---

[4] See paragraph .07 of AS 3101, *The Auditor's Report on an Audit of Financial Statements When the Auditor Expresses an Unqualified Opinion* (AICPA, *PCAOB Standards and Relates Rules*). *PCAOB Staff Guidance Changes to the Auditor's Report Effective for Audits of Fiscal Years Ending On or After December* 15, 2017 (PCAOB Staff Guidance, sec. 300.04) (updated as of December 28, 2017), states:

> AS 3101 requires the auditor's report to be addressed to the shareholders and the board of directors, or equivalents for companies not organized as corporations. For example, if a company is not organized as a corporation, the auditor's report would generally be addressed to (1) the plan administrator and plan participants for a benefit plan; (2) the directors (or equivalent) and equity owners for a broker or dealer; and (3) the trustees and unit holders or other investors for an investment company organized as a trust. The auditor's report may include additional addressees. Since inclusion of additional addressees is voluntary, auditors can assess, based on the individual circumstances, whether to include additional addressees in the auditor's report.

[5] Footnote 15 of PCAOB AS 3101 states:

> Various SEC rules and forms require that companies file schedules of information and that those schedules be audited if the company's financial statements are audited. See, e.g., Regulation S-X Rules 5-04, 6-10, 6A-05, and 7-05, 17 CFR 210.5-04, 210.6-10, 210.6A-05, 210.7-05. See generally, Regulation S-X Rule 12-01, 17 CFR 210.12-01, et seq., which address the form and content of certain SEC-required schedules.

We conducted our audits in accordance with the standards of the PCAOB. Those standards require that we plan and perform the audit to obtain reasonable assurance about whether the financial statements are free of material misstatement, whether due to error or fraud[6].

Our audits included performing procedures to assess the risks of material misstatement of the financial statements, whether due to error or fraud, and performing procedures that respond to those risks. Such procedures included examining, on a test basis, evidence regarding the amounts and disclosures in the financial statements. Our audits also included evaluating the accounting principles used and significant estimates made by management, as well as evaluating the overall presentation of the financial statements. We believe that our audits provide a reasonable basis for our opinion.

Supplemental Information[7]

The [*identify supplemental information, for example title of schedules and period covered*] has been subjected to audit procedures performed in conjunction with the audit of the Plan's financial statements. The supplemental information is the responsibility of the Plan's management. Our audit procedures included determining whether the supplemental information reconciles to the financial statements or the underlying accounting and other records, as applicable, and performing procedures to test the completeness and accuracy of the information presented in the supplemental information. In forming our opinion on the supplemental information, we evaluated whether the supplemental information, including its form and content, is presented in conformity with the Department of Labor's Rules and Regulations for Reporting and Disclosure under the Employee Retirement Income Security Act of 1974. In our opinion, the supplemental information is fairly stated, in all material respects, in relation to the financial statements as a whole.

[*Signature of Firm*]

We have served as the Plan's auditor since [*year*][8].

[*City and State*]

[*Date*]

---

[6] As described in paragraphs .59–.60 of AS 3105, *Departures from Unqualified Opinions and Other Reporting Circumstances* (AICPA, *PCAOB Standards and Related Rules*), this section should be revised in situations in which management is required to report on the effectiveness of internal control over financial reporting but such report is not required to be audited, nor has the auditor been engaged to perform an audit of management's assessment of the effectiveness of internal control over financial reporting. In such circumstances, paragraph .60 of PCAOB AS 3105 provides an example of appropriate language to include in the auditor's report. Footnote 7 to PCAOB Staff Guidance *Changes to the Auditor's Report Effective for Audits of Fiscal Years Ending on or After December 15, 2017* states that a similar paragraph may voluntarily be included in the auditor's report in situations in which management is not required to report on internal control over financial reporting and neither is the auditor.

[7] PCAOB AS 2701 and PCAOB AS 3101 do not specify the location or section title for the auditor's report on supplemental information. The title is an example for purposes of this illustration.

[8] PCAOB Staff Guidance, *Changes to the Auditor's Report Effective for Audits of Fiscal Years Ending on or After December 15, 2017,* provides guidance relating to the determination and reporting of tenure. AS 3101 does not specify a required location within the auditor's report for the statement on tenure. Example auditor's reports included in Appendix B of AS 3101 and PCAOB Staff Guidance, *Changes to the Auditor's Report Effective for Audits of Fiscal Years Ending on or After December 15, 2017*, include the statement on auditor tenure at the end of the report; however, auditors have discretion to present auditor tenure in the part of the auditor's report they consider appropriate.

Knowledge check

4. If a plan is subject to the SEC Form 11-K filing requirements and ERISA, how many years of statements of changes in net assets available for benefits are required to be presented in the plan's Form 11-K filing if the plan has elected to file the Form 11-K under the election of following ERISA?

   a. One.
   b. Two.
   c. Three.
   d. There is no option to file the Form 11-K under the election of following ERISA.

5. In order to comply with the requirements of the DOL and the PCAOB for plans that file a Form 11-K, how many opinions must be issued?

   a. None.
   b. One.
   c. Two.
   d. Three.

ERISA limited-scope reports

The following section of this chapter will address reports for ERISA limited-scope audits where the auditor has not performed auditing procedures with respect to investments and net investment income certified by a qualifying institution as defined by the DOL regulations. In an ERISA limited-scope audit, the plan administrator has restricted the scope of the audit to exclude investments, investment income, and investment expenses; therefore, the audit report reflects that scope restriction *as a disclaimed opinion*.

As explained in chapter 4, in certain situations, plans may hold investment assets, only some of which are covered by the certification of a qualifying institution that would permit an ERISA limited-scope audit to be performed for the plan. In that case, the investments held by the "nonqualifying institution" would have to be audited, and if the plan's assets that are not audited are material to the plan's financial statements as a whole, you should not issue an ERISA limited-scope audit report.

ERISA limited-scope audit considerations of supplemental schedules

When the auditor is engaged to perform an ERISA limited-scope audit, as permitted under 29 CFR 2520.103-8 of the DOL's rules and regulations for reporting and disclosure under ERISA, and consequently disclaims an opinion on the financial statements as a whole, the auditor is precluded from issuing an opinion on the supplemental schedules in relation to the financial statements under AU-C section 725. Therefore, unless the auditor is specifically engaged to perform the procedures required in AU-C section 725, the auditor is not required to follow such AU-C section. However, because the DOL requires supplemental schedules to be presented with the financial statements, the auditor is required to follow the guidance in AU-C section 720, *Other Information in Documents Containing Audited Financial Statements* (AICPA, *Professional Standards*). AU-C section 720 requires the auditor to read the other information in order to identify material inconsistencies, if any, with the audited financial statements. AU-C section 720 also addresses if, on reading the other information, the auditor becomes aware of an apparent material misstatement of fact. (See AU-C section 720 for specific guidance.)

Paragraph .A2 of AU-C section 720 states that the auditor is not required to make reference to the other information in the auditor's report on the financial statements. However, the auditor may include an other-matter paragraph disclaiming an opinion on the other information. For example, an auditor may choose to include a disclaimer on the other information when the auditor believes that the auditor could be associated with the information, and the user may infer a level of assurance that is not intended.

In addition, under an ERISA limited-scope audit, although the auditor is precluded from expressing an opinion on the supplemental schedules in relation to the financial statements, the DOL requires the auditor to offer an opinion on the financial statements and supplemental schedules. This is accomplished by expressing an opinion on the form and content of the information included in the supplemental schedules, other than that derived from the information certified by a qualifying institution. Accordingly, in addition to the requirements in AU-C section 720, the auditor would also need to perform certain audit procedures the auditor deems necessary to provide an opinion that the form and content of the information included in the supplemental schedules, other than that derived from the information

---

certified by a qualifying institution, have been audited and are presented in compliance with the DOL's rules and regulations for reporting and disclosure under ERISA.

The following is an example of the auditor's report for a defined contribution plan, when the plan administrator limits the scope of the audit, as permitted by 29 CFR 2520.103-8 of the Department of Labor's Rules and Regulations for Reporting and Disclosure under the ERISA and the auditor follows AU-C section 720 relating to the supplemental schedules. The example assumes that comparative Statements of Net Assets Available for Benefits and a single-year presentation of the Statement of Changes in Net Assets Available for Benefits are presented in the plan's financial statements.

Independent auditor's report

[Appropriate Addressee]

Report on the financial statements

We were engaged to audit the accompanying financial statements of XYZ 401(k) Plan, which comprise the statements of net assets available for benefits as of December 31, 20X2 and 20X1, and the related statement of changes in net assets available for benefits for the year ended December 31, 20X2, and the related notes to the financial statements.

Management's responsibility for the financial statements

Management is responsible for the preparation and fair presentation of these financial statements in accordance with accounting principles generally accepted in the United States of America; this includes the design, implementation, and maintenance of internal control relevant to the preparation and fair presentation of financial statements that are free from material misstatement, whether due to fraud or error.

Auditor's responsibility

Our responsibility is to express an opinion on these financial statements based on conducting the audits in accordance with auditing standards generally accepted in the United States of America. Because of the matter described in the Basis for Disclaimer of Opinion paragraph, however, we were not able to obtain sufficient appropriate audit evidence to provide a basis for an audit opinion.

Basis for disclaimer of opinion

As permitted by 29 CFR 2520.103-8 of the Department of Labor's Rules and Regulations for Reporting and Disclosure under the Employee Retirement Income Security Act of 1974, the plan administrator instructed us not to perform, and we did not perform, any auditing procedures with respect to the information summarized in Note X, which was certified by ABC Bank, the trustee (or custodian)[9] of the Plan, except for comparing such information with the related information included in the financial

---

[9] The words in this sentence may be modified when the assets are certified by an insurance entity.

statements. We have been informed by the plan administrator that the trustee (or custodian)[10] holds the Plan's investment assets and executes investment transactions. The plan administrator has obtained a certification from the trustee (or custodian)[11] as of December 31, 20X2 and 20X1, and for the year ended December 31, 20X2, that the information provided to the plan administrator by the trustee (or custodian)[12] is complete and accurate.

Disclaimer of opinion

Because of the significance of the matter described in the Basis for Disclaimer of Opinion paragraph, we have not been able to obtain sufficient appropriate audit evidence to provide a basis for an audit opinion. Accordingly, we do not express an opinion on these financial statements.

Other matter

The supplemental schedules [*identify schedules*] as of or for the year ended December 31, 20X2 are required by the Department of Labor's (DOL) Rules and Regulations for Reporting and Disclosure under the Employee Retirement Income Security Act of 1974 and are presented for the purpose of additional analysis and are not a required part of the financial statements. Because of the significance of the matter described in the Basis for Disclaimer of Opinion paragraph, we do not express an opinion on these supplemental schedules.

Report on form and content in compliance with DOL rules and regulations

The form and content of the information included in the financial statements and supplemental schedules, other than that derived from the information certified by the trustee (or custodian),[13] have been audited by us in accordance with auditing standards generally accepted in the United States of America and, in our opinion, are presented in compliance with the Department of Labor's Rules and Regulations for Reporting and Disclosure under the Employee Retirement Income Security Act of 1974.

[*Auditor's signature*]

[*Auditor's city and state*]

[*Date of the auditor's report*]

---

[10] See footnote 7.
[11] See footnote 7.
[12] See footnote 7.
[13] See footnote 7.

Financial statement disclosures

Defined contribution plan financial statements should disclose, if applicable, information regarding the items listed as follows:

- General description of the plan—including participation requirements, participant accounts, determination of employee and employer contributions, vesting requirements, forfeitures, administrative expenses, investment options, and loan provisions.
- Plan amendments adopted during the year and their effect on the plan net assets, if significant.
- Significant accounting policies, which should include the basis of accounting of the financial statements and a description of the valuation techniques and inputs used to measure the fair value less costs to sell, if significant, of investments (as required by FASB ASC 820-10-50) (including the plan's policy regarding the use of derivative financial instruments) and significant assumptions used to measure the reported value of insurance contracts (if any). However, 401(k) plans are exempt from the requirements in item (a) in FASB ASC 820-10-50-2B to disaggregate assets by nature, characteristics and risks. The disclosures of information by classes of assets required by FASB ASC 820-10-50 should be provided by general type of plan assets required by FASB ASC 962-325-45-5. In addition to the requirements in FASB ASC 235, *Notes to Financial Statements,* these disclosures would also include, as applicable
  - Basis of accounting (if other than GAAP)
  - Use of estimates
  - Notes receivable from participants
  - Investment valuation and income recognition
  - Payment of benefits
  - Risks and uncertainties
- Tax status of the plan including disclosure of information concerning whether a tax ruling or determination letter has been obtained.
- Prohibited transactions that have occurred during the year, regardless of materiality.
- Related party transactions that have occurred during the year, if significant.
- Benefit claims payable and reconciliation to Form 5500 if applicable.
- If differences between the financial statement amounts and the amounts in Form 5500 exist, a note reconciling the financial statements to Form 5500.
- Description of the plan sponsor's ability to terminate the plan and any significant matters related to a termination of the plan.
- Plan mergers and terminations that have occurred during the year.
- Subsequent events of the plan or the plan sponsor that may affect the plan as required by FASB ASC 855, *Subsequent Events.* For all entities other than SEC, filers must disclose (1) the date through which subsequent events have been evaluated, and (2) whether that date is the date the financial statements were issued or available to be issued in the originally issued financial statements.
- Commitments and contingencies in accordance with FASB ASC 440, *Commitments,* and FASB ASC 450, *Contingencies* (for example, future capital commitments for investments).
- Risks and uncertainties that may affect the plan either directly or as a result of the plan sponsor being affected (for example, bankruptcy of plan sponsor, plan sponsor going concern issues, litigation).
- Master trust arrangements
- Limited-scope disclosures for plans that are being audited under the ERISA limited-scope audit.
- Unit value disclosures for plans that assign units, except for unit value information for a plan that invests in mutual funds or other external investment funds, which is not required to be disclosed.
- Significant costs of plan administration being absorbed by the employer.

- Amounts allocated to accounts of persons who have elected to withdraw from the plan but have not yet been paid. These amounts should not be reported as a liability on the statement of net assets available for benefits, in financial statements prepared in conformity with GAAP. A note to the financial statements to reconcile the audited financial statements to Form 5500 may be necessary to comply with ERISA.
- The amount and disposition of forfeited nonvested accounts. Specifically, identification of those amounts that are used to reduce future employer contributions, expense, or reallocated to participants' accounts, in accordance with plan documents.
- Amount of unallocated assets and the basis for allocating the amounts.
- Information regarding the purchase of contracts with insurance entities by participants that are excluded from plan assets.
- The following information regarding fully benefit-responsive investment contracts in accordance with FASB ASC 962-325-50-3:
  - Description of the nature of the investment contract (including how the contracts operate) by the type of investment contract (for example, synthetic investment contracts or traditional investment contracts)
  - Description of events that limit the ability of the plan to transact at contract value.
  - Description of events that would allow issuers to terminate the contract at less than contract value.
  - The total contract value of each type of investment contract (for example, synthetic investment contracts or traditional investment contracts)
- FASB ASC 210-20-50 expands the disclosure requirements in FASB ASC 815 about an entity's derivative instruments and hedging activities. The disclosure provisions of ASC 815 apply to employee benefit plan financial statements. The new guidance requires more robust qualitative disclosures and expanded quantitative disclosures.
- If the plan provides for participant-directed and nonparticipant-directed investments programs, the plan should disclose information in the financial statements about the net assets and significant components of changes in net assets relating to the nonparticipant-directed investment program. (Note that if such disclosures are included in the face of the financial statement, no additional disclosures are required.)
- Investments pledged to secure debt of the plan, as well as a description of such investments of the provisions regarding the release of such investments from the pledge and the amounts of investments released from the pledge in the last period presented
- Guarantees by others of debt of the plan
- The following information regarding investments in accordance with FASB ASC 820:
  - Information that enables readers of the financial statements to assess the valuation techniques and inputs used to measure fair value of investments of the plan by identifying the level within the fair value hierarchy into which each investment falls.
  - The amounts of all transfers between level 1 and level 2 or the fair value hierarchy and the reasons for the transfers. Significant transfers into each level should be disclosed separately from transfer out of each level. A reporting entity should disclose and consistently follow its policy for determining when transfers between levels are recognized.
  - For fair value measurements using significant unobservable inputs (level 3), a reconciliation of beginning and ending balances, separately presenting the changes during the period attributable to any of the following:
    - Total gains and losses for the period (realized and unrealized), separately presenting gains or losses included in earnings (or changes in net assets) and gains or losses recognized in other comprehensive income, and a description of where those gains or losses included in earnings

(or changes in net assets) are reported in the statement of income (or activities) or in other comprehensive income
- Purchases, sales, issuances, and settlements
- Transfers in or out of level 3 and the reasons for those transfers. Significant transfers into level 3 should be disclosed separately from significant transfers out of level 3. A reporting entity should disclose and consistently follow its policy for determining when transfers between levels are recognized. The policy about the timing of recognizing transfers should be the same for transfers into level 3 as that for transfers out of level 3.
- The amount of the total gains and losses
- For fair value measurements using significant other observable inputs (level 2) and significant unobservable inputs (level 3), a description of the valuation technique (or multiple valuation techniques) used, and the inputs used in determining the fair values of each class of assets or liabilities. If there has been a change in the valuation technique(s), the reporting entity should disclose that change and the reason for making it.
- For fair value measurements categorized within level 3 of the fair value hierarchy, a reporting entity should provide quantitative information about the significant unobservable inputs used in the fair value measurement. FASB ASC 820-10-50-2(bbb)(2) states that employee benefit plans, other than those plans that are subject to the SEC's filing requirements, are not required to provide quantitative information about the significant unobservable inputs used in the fair value measurement of investments held by an employee benefit plan in their plan sponsor's own nonpublic equity securities, including equity securities of the plan sponsor's nonpublic affiliated entities. However, it is important to note that, as per FASB ASC 820-10-50-2(bbb)(1), both a description of the valuation technique(s) and the inputs used in the fair value measurement are requirements for recurring and nonrecurring fair value measurements categorized within level 2 and level 3 of the fair value hierarchy.
- Because participant loans are no longer measured at fair value, they are not presented in the fair value measurements note and therefore are not included in the hierarchy table as required by FASB ASC 820-10-50.
- Disclosure requirements in FASB ASC 310-10-50 should be considered because participant loans are now reported as notes receivable. The following paragraphs are specifically excluded for participant loans:
  - FASB ASC 310-10-50-6 through 7a
  - FASB ASC 310-10-50-11b and 11c
  - FASB ASC 310-10-50-28 through 30
- FASB ASC 820-10-50-6A requires disclosures for each class of investment about the attributes of investments within the scope of paragraphs 4–5 of FASB ASC 820-10-15, such as the nature of any restrictions on the investor's ability to redeem its investments at the measurement date, any unfunded commitments, and the investment strategies of the investees. These disclosures are required for all investments within the scope of paragraphs 4–5 of FASB ASC 820-10-15 and that are measured using the practical expedient in FASB ASC 820-10-35-59 on a recurring or nonrecurring basis during the period.
- In accordance with FASB ASC 820-10-35-54B an investment within the scope of paragraphs 4-5 of FASB ASC 820-10-15 for which fair value is measured using net asset value per share (or its equivalent) as a practical expedient should not be categorized within the fair value hierarchy. Although the investment is not categorized within the fair value hierarchy, a reporting entity should provide the amount measured using the net asset value per share (or its equivalent) practical expedient to permit reconciliation of the fair value of investments included in the fair value hierarchy to the line items presented in the statement of net assets available for benefits.

- In accordance with FASB ASC 960-325-50-6, FASB ASC 962-325-50-9 and FASB ASC 965-325-50-4, if an investment is measured using the NAV per share (or its equivalent) practical expedient in FASB ASC 820-10-35-59 and that investment is in a fund that files Form 5500 as a direct filing entity, disclosure of that investment's significant investment strategy, as discussed in item (a) in FASB ASC 820-10-50-6A, is not required.

Knowledge check

6. Which of the following is an example of a note to the financial statements that is not required for a 401(k) plan, assuming the situation exists for the plan?

    a. Information regarding an immaterial prohibited transaction.
    b. Tax status of the plan.
    c. Details regarding pending merger related only to the plan sponsor.
    d. Plan sponsor uncertainty for a sponsor with a going concern uncertainty.

7. Risks and uncertainties that are not required to be disclosed in the financial statements include

    a. Litigation.
    b. Plan sponsor going concern.
    c. Plan sponsor filing of bankruptcy.
    d. Plan sponsor's plans to purchase another company that has a 401(k) plan.

8. If a plan provides for participant-directed and nonparticipant-directed investments programs, the plan should disclose information in the footnotes of the financial statements about the net assets and significant components of changes in net assets relating to the nonparticipant-directed investment program, unless which of the following situations exist?

    a. A plan has elected to have an ERISA limited-scope audit.
    b. A plan is under a full-scope audit.
    c. Such disclosures are included in the face of the financial statements.
    d. There are no situations that exempt a plan from the requirement to disclose information in the footnotes of the financial statements about the net assets and significant components of changes in net assets relating to the nonparticipant-directed investment program.

Please note: Based on its effective date, this version of the CPE course has NOT been updated to reflect changes resulting from the following standard. However, due to the breadth of the changes, auditors are encouraged to review these standards now to prepare.

In July 2019, the AICPA Auditing Standards Board (ASB) issued as final standard, Statement on Auditing Standards (SAS) No. 136, *Forming an Opinion and Reporting on Financial Statements of Employee Benefit Plans Subject to ERISA* (EBP SAS). The EBP SAS prescribes certain new performance requirements for an audit of financial statements of employee benefit plans subject to the Employee Retirement Income Security Act of 1974 (ERISA) and changes the form and content of the related auditor's report. **SAS No. 136 is effective for audits of financial statements for periods ending on or after December 15, 2020. Early implementation is not permitted.**

SAS No. 136 is codified in AU-C section 703 of the AICPA *Professional Standards*, and is the foundational section that addresses the auditor's responsibility to form an opinion on the ERISA plan financial statements and prescribes the form and content of the auditor's report for ERISA plan audits.

To enhance the quality of employee benefit plan audits, the EBP SAS specifically addresses requirements for:

- Engagement acceptance
- Audit risk assessment and response, including the auditor's consideration of relevant plan provisions
- Communications of reportable findings with those charged with governance
- The auditor's responsibilities relating to the ERISA- required supplemental schedules and the Form 5500.
- The form and content of the related auditor's report

To access the final EBP SAS in its entirety and related resources, including frequently asked questions, please refer to https://www.aicpa.org/interestareas/frc/auditattest/auditing-standards-information-and-resources.html Note: additional resources will be posted as they become available to assist with implementation, so auditors are encouraged to visit the site periodically.

Appendix A

ERISA AND RELATED REGULATIONS

Appendix A

The following is from appendix A of the 2016 AICPA Audit & Accounting Guide, *Employee Benefit Plans*.

ERISA and related regulations

Introduction

A.01   The following description, prepared with the assistance of the Employee Benefits Security Administration (EBSA), U.S. Department of Labor (DOL), is intended to enable the auditor to familiarize himself or herself with the important provisions of the Employee Retirement Income Security Act of 1974 (ERISA). This is a summary and is not intended to serve as a substitute for the entire act, the related regulations, or the advice of legal counsel. Changes in the statute and related regulations subsequent to publication of this guide also should be considered.

A.02   The primary purpose of ERISA is to protect the interests of workers who participate in employee benefit plans and their beneficiaries. ERISA seeks to attain that objective by requiring financial reporting to government agencies and disclosure to participants and beneficiaries, by establishing standards of conduct for plan fiduciaries, and by providing appropriate remedies, sanctions, and access to the federal courts. Another objective of ERISA is to improve the soundness of employee pension benefit plans[1] by requiring plans (*a*) to vest the accrued benefits of employees with significant periods of service, (*b*) to meet minimum standards of funding, and (*c*) with respect to defined benefit pension plans, to subscribe to plan termination insurance through the Pension Benefit Guaranty Corporation (PBGC).

A.03   ERISA replaced the Welfare and Pension Plans Disclosure Act of 1958, amended certain sections of the Internal Revenue Code (IRC), and generally preempted state laws that related to employee benefit plans.

Coverage under Title I

A.04   Title I of ERISA generally applies to employee benefit plans established or maintained by employers engaged in interstate commerce or in any industry or activity affecting interstate commerce or by employee organizations representing employees engaged in such activities, or by both employer and employee organizations.[2] Most aspects of ERISA do not apply to

   a.   governmental plans, including those of state and local governments.
   b.   church plans unless the plan has made a voluntary election under IRC Section 410(d).

---

[1] Pension plans are broadly defined in the Employee Retirement Income Security Act of 1974 (ERISA) to include all defined benefit and defined contribution plans, including profit-sharing, stock bonus, and employee stock ownership plans.

[2] No correlation exists between coverage under Title I of ERISA and qualification under the Internal Revenue Code (IRC).

---

    c.   plans established and maintained solely for the purpose of complying with applicable workers' compensation, unemployment compensation, or disability insurance laws.

    d.   plans maintained outside the United States primarily for nonresident aliens.[3]

    e.   unfunded excess benefit plans (ERISA section 3[36]).

Participant standards for pension plans (ERISA Section 202)[4]

A.05   ERISA generally provides that a pension plan cannot exclude an employee from participation because of age or service if he or she has completed one year of service and is at least 21 years old. However, a pension plan may defer participation until attainment of age 21 and 2 years of service, provided that benefits vest 100 percent thereafter. In addition, ERISA provides that an individual may not be denied the right to participate in a plan on the basis of having attained a specific age.

Vesting standards for pension plans (ERISA Section 203)

A.06   Pension plan participants' rights to accrued benefits from their own contributions are nonforfeitable. In addition, generally, defined benefit plans are required to provide that the employees' rights to accrued benefits from employer contributions vest in a manner that equals or exceeds either of two alternative schedules: (*a*) graded vesting of accrued benefits, with at least 20 percent vesting after three years of service, at least 20 percent each year thereafter for four years, so that the employee's accrued benefit would be 100 percent vested after seven years; or (*b*) 100 percent vesting of accrued benefits after five years of service, with no vesting required before the end of the five-year period. Defined contribution (individual account) plans are required to provide that the employees' rights to accrued benefits from employer contributions vest in a manner that equals or exceeds either of two faster alternative schedules: (*a*) graded vesting of accrued benefits, with at least 20 percent vesting after two years of service, at least 20 percent each year thereafter for three years, so that the employee's accrued benefit would be 100 percent vested after six years; or (*b*) 100 percent vesting of accrued benefits after three years of service, with no vesting required before the end of the three-year period.

A.07   Tax-qualified plans require more stringent vesting if a termination, partial termination, or discontinuance of contribution to the plan is initiated or if the plan is top-heavy (IRC sections 411[d] and 416).

A.08   For computation of years of service as they relate to an employee's vesting rights, a year of service is defined in ERISA as a 12-month period during which the participant has completed at least 1,000 hours of service (ERISA section 203[b][2]). Regulations that refine that definition are complex. In addition, complex rules apply that define breaks in service.

---

[3] The phrase *plans maintained outside the United States* does not include a plan that covers residents of Puerto Rico, the U.S. Virgin Islands, Guam, Wake Island, or America Samoa.

[4] Reorganization Plan No. 4 of 1978 (Title 43 U.S. *Code of Federal Regulations* [CFR] Part 47713, October 17, 1978) generally transferred from the Secretary of Labor to the Secretary of the Treasury regulatory and interpretative authority for Parts 2 and 3 of Title I of ERISA.

A.09 Sufficient records must be maintained to determine an employee's benefits. ERISA section 105 sets forth the requirements applicable to the furnishing of pension benefit statements to plan participants and beneficiaries. Plan administrators of both individual account plans and defined benefit plans are required to automatically furnish pension benefit statements, at least once each quarter, in the case of individual account plans that permit participants to direct their investments; at least once each year, in the case of individual account plans that do not permit participants to direct their investments; and at least once every three years in the case of defined benefit plans. ERISA section 209 also requires the maintenance of records by employers relating to individual benefit reporting. ERISA section 107 provides general record retention requirements for employee benefit plans.

Minimum funding standards for pension plans (ERISA Sections 301–305)

A.10 ERISA requires that pension plans subject to the minimum funding standards maintain an account called the *funding standard account* (FSA). This account is a memorandum account, and it is not included in the plan's financial statements. Defined benefit pension plans are required to maintain an FSA. Certain defined contribution plans (that is, money-purchase and target-benefit plans) must maintain FSAs, but on a more limited basis. The FSA is used to determine compliance with minimum funding standards set forth in ERISA.

A.11 For most defined benefit pension plans, the sponsor's annual contribution to the plan must be sufficient to cover the normal cost for the period, the amount to amortize initial unfunded past service liability, and increases or decreases in unfunded past service liability resulting from plan amendments, experience gains or losses, and actuarial gains or losses from changes in actuarial assumptions.

A.12 An accumulated funding deficiency is the excess of total charges (required contributions) to the FSA for all plan years (beginning with the first plan year when the funding standards are applicable) over total credits (actual contributions) to the account for those years. Accumulated funding deficiencies, in the absence of a funding waiver issued by the IRS, may result in an excise tax payable by the plan sponsor for failure to meet the minimum funding standards and in possible action by the IRS to enforce the standards. If a deficiency in the FSA exists at the end of the plan year, it is important for the auditor to consider whether a receivable from the employer company (and, possibly, a related reserve for uncollectible amounts) should be reflected in the plan's financial statements.

A.13 The IRS may waive all or part of the minimum funding requirements for a plan year in which the minimum funding standard cannot be met without imposing substantial business hardship on the employer. That waiver is issued, however, only if failure to do so would be adverse to the participants' interests. The IRS determines whether a substantial hardship would occur on the basis of various factors, certain of which are stated in ERISA section 303. This does not change the plan's possible need to record a contribution receivable.

A.14 ERISA section 305 provides rules for multiemployer plans determined to be in endangered status or critical status. The actuary of a multiemployer-defined benefit plan should certify to the Department of Treasury and the plan sponsor whether or not the plan is in endangered status and whether or not the plan is in or will be in critical status, no later than the 90th day of each plan year. In addition, the actuary should certify whether or not the plan is making the scheduled progress in meeting the requirements of the funding improvement plan or rehabilitation plan. Within 30 days of being certified in critical, seriously endangered, or endangered status, the plan sponsor should notify in writing the participants and beneficiaries, the bargaining parties, the PBGC, and the DOL. Not later than 240 days following the required date for the actuarial certification of endangered status, the plan sponsor should adopt a funding improvement plan if the plan is in endangered or seriously endangered status or a rehabilitation plan if in critical status.

Trust requirements (ERISA Section 403)

A.15 Generally, tax laws require that qualified pension, profit-sharing, and stock bonus plans be funded through a trust. The IRC does not contain any such requirement for welfare benefit plans or fringe benefit plans. ERISA section 403 generally requires, however, that the assets of all employee benefit plans, including welfare plans, be held in trust. There are exceptions for certain insurance contracts and 403(b) custodial accounts. Participant contributions, including salary reduction amounts, are considered to be employee contributions under ERISA and generally do constitute *plan assets.* An employer is required to segregate employee contributions from its general assets as soon as practicable, but in no event more than (*a*) 90 days after the contributions are paid by employees or withheld from their wages for a welfare benefit plan or (*b*) the 15th business day following the end of the month in which amounts are contributed by employees or withheld from their wages for a pension benefit plan [ref. DOL Reg. 2510.3-102]. The DOL has announced that it will not presently enforce the trust requirement for cafeteria plans under IRC section 125 to which employees make contributions. This policy also temporarily relieves these contributory welfare plans from compliance with the trust requirements of ERISA with respect to participant contributions used to pay insurance premiums in accordance with the department's reporting regulations.[5]

Voluntary employee benefit associations

A.16 A voluntary employee benefit association (VEBA) is a welfare trust under IRC section 501(c)(9). Generally, plans funded by a section 501(c)(9) trust must be audited if they have 100 or more participants at the beginning of the plan year (see paragraph A.26).

---

[5] See 29 CFR 2520.104-20(b)(2)(ii) or (iii) and 29 CFR 2520.104-44(b)(1)(ii) or (iii), as applicable.

Reporting and disclosure for pension and welfare plans (ERISA Sections 101–111 and 1032–1034)

A.17 ERISA generally requires that the administrator of an employee benefit plan prepare and file various documents with the DOL, the IRS, and the PBGC. Under Title I of ERISA, the plan administrator is required to furnish to the DOL, upon request, any documents relating to the employee benefit plan, including but not limited to, the latest summary plan description (including any summaries of plan changes not contained in the summary plan description), and the bargaining agreement, trust agreement, contract, or other instrument under which the plan is established or operated (ERISA section 104[a][6]). In addition, most plans are required to file an annual report that also satisfies the annual reporting requirements of Titles I and IV of ERISA (sections 104[a][1][A], 1031, and 4065) and the IRC. Title I of ERISA also requires that the plan administrator furnish certain information relative to the employee benefit plan to each participant and beneficiary receiving benefits under the plan. These disclosures include summary plan descriptions, including summaries of changes and updates to the summary plan description (Section 104[b][1]), summary annual reports (section 104[b][3]) (except for defined benefit plans to which ERISA section 101[f] applies), defined benefit plan funding notices (section 101[f]), and, in the case of most pension plans, individual benefit reports describing the participant's accrued and vested benefits under the plan (sections 105 and 209).

Annual report

A.18 The report of most significance to the auditor is the annual report. The annual report required to be filed for employee benefit plans generally is Form 5500, *Annual Return/Report of Employee Benefit Plan*. Form 5500 is a joint-agency form developed by the IRS, DOL, and PBGC, that may be used to satisfy the annual reporting requirements of the IRC and Titles I and IV of ERISA. For purposes of Title I of ERISA only, a plan administrator may, in lieu of filing Form 5500, elect to file the information required by ERISA section 103. However, almost all plan administrators use Form 5500. Use of Form 5500 is required for filings under the IRC and Title IV of ERISA.

Who must file

A.19 An administrator of an employee benefit plan subject to ERISA, and not otherwise exempt, must file an annual report for each such plan every year. The IRS, DOL, and PBGC have consolidated their requirements into Form 5500 to minimize the filing burden for plan administrators and employers. Likewise, direct filing entities (DFE), described as follows, are also required to use Form 5500 when reporting to the DOL. In general, Form 5500 reporting requirements vary depending on whether Form 5500 is being filed for a *large plan*, a *small plan*, or a DFE and on the particular type of plan or DFE involved. Plans with 100 or more participants as of the beginning of the plan year must complete Form 5500 following the requirements for a *large plan*. Plans with fewer than 100 participants should follow the requirements for a *small plan*. (There are three approaches to small-plan filings. The first is Form 5500 with all attachments but replacing Schedule H, "Financial Information," with Schedule I, "Small Plan Financial Information." The second is Form 5500-SF, which is limited to small plans whose investments are limited to those with a readily determinable market value and do not include any employer securities. The final choice is Form 5500-EZ, which is generally limited to plans covering owners only.) DOL regulations permit plans that have between 80 and 120 participants (inclusive) at the beginning of the plan year to complete Form 5500 in the same category (*large plan* or *small plan*) as was filed for the previous year. Form 5500 and Form 5500-SF is filed with the EBSA in accordance with the instructions to the form.

Participants

A.20   ERISA section 3(7) defines a *participant* as any employee or former employee of an employer, or any member or former member of an employee organization, who is or may become eligible to receive a benefit of any type from an employee benefit plan that covers employees of such employer or members of such organization or whose beneficiaries may be eligible to receive any such benefit.

A.21   For IRC section 401(k) qualified cash or deferred arrangement, a *participant* means any individual who is eligible to participate in the plan whether or not the individual elects to contribute or has an account under the plan [ref: DOL Regulation Title 29 U.S. *Code of Federal Regulations* (CFR) Part 2510.3-3(d) and Form 5500 Instructions]. For welfare plans, however, an individual becomes a participant on the earlier of the date designated by the plan as the date on which the individual begins participation in the plan; the date on which the individual becomes eligible under the plan for a benefit subject only to occurrence of the contingency for which the benefit is provided; or the date on which the individual makes a contribution to the plan, whether voluntary or mandatory [ref: DOL Reg. 29 CFR 2510.2-3(d) and Form 5500 Instructions].

Stop-loss coverage

A.22   Many self-funded plans carry stop-loss coverage to limit either the plan's or employer's loss exposure. Stop-loss coverage is a contract with an insurer that provides that the insurer will pay claims in excess of a specified amount. The coverage may be aggregate (that is, the insurer will pay if total claims exceed the specified amount) or specific (that is, the insurer will pay if an individual claim exceeds the specified amount).

Plans required to file the annual report and audited financial statements

A.23   Generally, plans subject to Part 1 of Title I of ERISA require an audit. Certain plans are not covered by ERISA and accordingly are not subject to the federal audit requirement (see paragraph A.04). In addition, it should be noted that the plan administrator's obligation to retain an accountant to audit the plan continues to remain in effect even when the plan loses its tax-qualified status.

Who must engage an independent qualified public accountant

A.24   Employee benefit plans filing Form 5500 as a *large plan* (for example, plans with 100 or more participants as of the beginning of the plan year) are generally required to engage an independent qualified public accountant (IQPA) pursuant to ERISA section 103(a)(3)(A). In counting participants for these purposes, an individual usually becomes a participant under a welfare plan when he or she becomes eligible for a benefit and under a pension plan when he or she has satisfied the plan's age and service requirements for participation (see instructions to Form 5500). An IQPA's opinion, accompanying financial statements and notes, must also be attached to a Form 5500 for a *large plan* unless (*a*) the plan is an employee welfare benefit plan that is unfunded, fully insured, or a combination of unfunded and insured as described in 29 CFR 2520.104-44(b)(1);[6] (*b*) the plan is an employee pension benefit plan whose sole asset(s) consist of insurance contracts that provide that, upon receipt of the premium payment, the insurance carrier fully guarantees the amount of benefit payments as specified in 29 CFR 2520.104-44(b)(2) and Form 5500 instructions;[7] or (*c*) the plan has elected to defer attaching the accountant's opinion for the first of two plan years, one of which is a short plan year of seven months or less as allowed by 29 CFR 2520.104-50[8] (see paragraphs A.85, 29 CFR 2520.104-50, and the instructions to Form 5500).

Pension benefit plans filing Form 5500 as a small plan (for example, those with fewer than 100 participants as of the beginning of the plan year) are exempt from the audit requirement to the extent that at least 95 percent of their assets are *qualifying plan assets*. Plans not satisfying this test may still avoid the audit requirement if the total amount of nonqualifying plan assets are covered by an ERISA section 412 fidelity bond. Small pension plans seeking to avoid the audit requirement must also make certain required disclosures to plan participants.

Pension benefit plans

A.25 An annual report is generally required to be filed even if (*a*) the plan is not qualified, (*b*) participants no longer accrue benefits, and (*c*) contributions were not made for the plan year. The following are among the pension benefit plans for which a Form 5500 annual return or report must be filed:

- Annuity arrangements under IRC section 403(b)(1)
- Custodial accounts established under IRC section 403(b)(7) for regulated investment company stock
- Individual retirement accounts established by an employer under IRC section 408(c)
- Pension benefit plans maintained outside the United States primarily for nonresident aliens if the employer who maintains the plan is a domestic employer or a foreign employer with income derived from sources within the United States (including foreign subsidiaries of domestic employers) and deducts contributions to the plan on its U.S. income tax return
- Church pension plans electing coverage under IRC section 410(d)

---

[6] Single employer welfare plans using an IRC section 501(c)(9) trust are generally not exempt from the requirement of engaging an independent qualified public accountant. See paragraph A.36 for an explanation of the welfare plans considered to be unfunded, fully insured, or a combination of unfunded and insured.

[7] See paragraph A.69*n*.

[8] FN8 29 CFR 2520.104-50 permits the administrator of an employee benefit plan to defer the audit requirements for the first two consecutive plan years, one of which is a short plan year of seven or fewer months' duration and to file an audited statement for that plan year when the annual report is filed for the immediately following plan year, subject to certain conditions.

Pension benefit plans generally provide retirement income and include

- defined benefit plans; and
- defined contribution plans, including profit-sharing plans, money-purchase pension plans, stock-bonus and employee stock-ownership plans, and 401(k), 403(b), and other thrift or savings plans.

General Filing Requirements:

- Plans with 100 or more participants at the beginning of the plan year must file Form 5500, Form 5500-SF, or Form 5500-EZ following the requirements for *large plans.*
- Plans with fewer than 100 participants at the beginning of the plan year must file Form 5500 following the requirements for *small plans.*

Exception:

Pursuant to DOL Regulation 29 CFR 2520.103-1(d), plans that have between 80 and 120 participants (inclusive) at the beginning of the plan year may complete Form 5500 in the same category (*large plan* or *small plan*) as was filed for the previous year. Plans that file Form 5500 as a *small plan* pursuant to the 80/120 rule will not be required to have an audit of their financial statements provided they meet the requirements of DOL Reg. 29 CFR 2520.104.46, as amended (see paragraph A.24).

General Audit Requirements:

- Plans with 100 or more participants at the beginning of the plan year that file Form 5500 as a *large plan* are required to have an annual audit of their financial statements.
- Plans with fewer than 100 participants at the beginning of the plan year that file Form 5500 as a *small plan* may be exempt from the audit requirement provided they meet the requirements of DOL Reg. 29 CFR 2520.104.46, as amended (see paragraph A.24). Plans may only file using Form 5500-SF if they meet the conditions to be exempt from audit.

General Exemptions From Filing and Audit Requirements:

- Plans that are unfunded or fully insured and provide benefits only to a select group of management or highly compensated employees. *Note:* A one-time DOL notification is required for these "top hat" plans [ref: DOL Reg. 29 CFR 2520.104-23].

General Exemptions From Audit Requirement Only:

Plans, irrespective of the number of participants at the beginning of the plan year, that

- provide benefits exclusively through allocated insurance contracts. A contract is considered to be allocated only if the insurance company or organization that issued the contract unconditionally guarantees, upon receipt of the required premium or consideration, to provide a retirement benefit of a specified amount, without adjustment for fluctuations in the market value of the underlying assets of the company or organization, to each participant, and each participant has a legal right to such benefits that is legally enforceable directly against the insurance company or organization;

- are funded solely by premiums paid directly from the general assets of the employer or the employee organization maintaining the plan, or partly from such general assets and partly from contributions from employees;
- forward any participant contributions within three months of receipt; and
- provide for the return of refunds to contributing participants within three months of receipt by the employer or employee organization [ref: DOL Reg. 29 CFR 2520.104-44(b)(2)].

Welfare benefit plans

A.26   These plans are described in section 3(1) of Title I of ERISA. An employee welfare benefit plan includes any plan, fund, or program that provides, through the purchase of insurance or otherwise, medical, surgical, hospital, sickness, accident, disability, severance, vacation, prepaid legal services, apprenticeship, and training benefits for employees.[9]

General Filing Requirements:

- Plans with 100 or more participants at the beginning of the plan year must file Form 5500 as a *large plan*.
- Plans with fewer than 100 participants at the beginning of the plan year must file Form 5500 as a *small plan*, as previously described.

Exception:

Pursuant to DOL Reg. 29 CFR 2520.103-1(d), a plan that covers between 80 and 120 participants at the beginning of the plan year may elect to complete Form 5500 in the same category (*large plan* or *small plan*) as was filed for the previous year. Plans that file Form 5500 as a *small plan* pursuant to the 80/120 rule are not required to have an audit of their financial statements [ref: DOL Reg. 29 CFR 2520.104-46].

General Audit Requirements:

- Plans with 100 or more participants at the beginning of the plan year that file Form 5500 as a *large plan* are required to have an annual audit of their financial statements.
- Plans with fewer than 100 participants at the beginning of the plan year that file Form 5500 as a *small plan* are exempt from the audit requirement.

General Exemptions From Filing and Audit Requirements:

- Plans that are unfunded or fully insured and provide benefits only to a select group of management or highly compensated employees. *Note:* The DOL can require that certain information be provided upon request [ref: DOL Reg. 29 CFR 2520.104-24].
- Plans that have fewer than 100 participants at the beginning of the plan year and do all of the following [ref: DOL Reg. 29 CFR 2520.104-20]:
  - (1) Pay benefits solely from the general assets of the employer or employee organization maintaining the plan; (2) provide benefits exclusively through insurance contracts or policies issued by a qualified insurance company or through a qualified HMO, the premiums of which are paid directly out of the general assets of the employer or employee organization, or partly from general assets and partly from employee or member contributions; or (3) partly as in (1) and partly as in (2).

---

[9] In certain cases, a severance plan will be considered a pension plan. See DOL Reg. 29 CFR 2510.3-2(b).

- Forward any employee contributions to the insurance company within three months of receipt.
- Pay any employee refunds to employees within three months of receipt.

General Exemption From Audit Requirement Only:

Plans, irrespective of the number of participants at the beginning of the plan year, that do all of the following [ref: DOL Reg. 29 CFR 2520.104-44(b)(1)]:

- (1) Pay benefits solely from the general assets of the employer or employee organization maintaining the plan; (2) provide benefits exclusively through insurance contracts or policies issued by a qualified insurance company or through a qualified HMO, the premiums of which are paid directly out of the general assets of the employer or employee organization, or partly from general assets and partly from employee or member contributions; or (3) provide benefits partly from the general assets of the employer or employee organization and partly through insurance (for example, a stop-loss insurance policy purchased or owned by the plan).
- Forward any employee contributions to the insurance company within three months of receipt.
- Pay any employee refunds to employees within three months of receipt.

Plans covered by IRC Section 6058

A.27 Most retirement and savings plans (for example, pension, profit-sharing, or stock bonus plans) are required to file a Form 5500 series return under IRC Section 6058 as well as ERISA. According to Announcement 82-146, however, church plans that have not made a section 410(d) election and governmental plans are not required to file a return.

Cafeteria arrangements (IRC Section 125 plans)

A.28 In Notice No. 2002-24, the IRS eliminated the filing requirement for cafeteria plans maintained pursuant to section 125. It is important to note, however, that this notice does not affect the annual reporting requirements of employee benefit plans under Title I of ERISA. This means that cafeteria plans that incorporate welfare benefits are no longer required to complete a Schedule F, but they may still be required to file a Form 5500 to report on the plan's welfare benefits covered by Title I of ERISA (see paragraph A.26).

PWBA Technical Release 92-1

A.29 In June 1992, the Pension and Welfare Benefits Administration (PWBA [now known as the EBSA]) issued Technical Release 92-1 announcing the DOL's enforcement policy with respect to welfare benefit plans with participant contributions. Cafeteria plans described in section 125 of the IRC may not be required to have an audit if the participant contributions used to pay benefits have not been held in trust. An audit may also not be required for other contributory welfare benefit plans where participant contributions are applied to the payment of premiums and such contributions have not been held in trust. The enforcement policy stated in ERISA Technical Release 92-1 will continue to apply until the adoption of final regulations addressing the application of the trust and reporting requirements of Title I of ERISA to welfare plans that receive participant contributions. See exhibit 2-3, "Welfare Benefit Plans Audit: Decision Flowchart," for further guidance.

Plans excluded from filing

A.30 Plans maintained only to comply with workers' compensation, unemployment compensation, or disability insurance laws are excluded from filing.

A.31 An unfunded excess benefit plan (Section 3[36]) is excluded from filing.

A.32 A welfare benefit plan maintained outside the United States primarily for persons substantially all of whom are nonresident aliens (see footnote 3) is excluded from filing.

A.33 A pension benefit plan maintained outside the United States is excluded from filing if it is a qualified foreign plan within the meaning of IRC section 404A(e) that does not qualify for the treatment provided in IRC section 402(c) (see paragraph A.04*d*).

A.34 A church plan not electing coverage under IRC section 410(d) or a governmental plan is excluded from filing.

A.35 An annuity arrangement described in 29 CFR 2510.3-2(f) is excluded from filing.

A.36 A welfare benefit plan as described in 29 CFR 2520.104-20 is excluded from filing. Such a plan has fewer than 100 participants as of the beginning of the plan year and generally is one of the following:

    a. *Unfunded*. Benefits are paid as needed directly from the general assets of the employer or the employee organization that sponsors the plan.[10]

    b. *Fully insured*. Benefits are provided exclusively through insurance contracts or policies, the premiums being paid directly by the employer or employee organization from its general assets or partly from its general assets and partly from contributions by its employees or members.

    c. *A combination of unfunded and insured*. Benefits are provided partially as needed directly from the general assets of the employer or the employee organization that sponsors the plan and partially through insurance contracts or policies, the premiums being paid directly by the employer or employee organization from its general assets (see paragraph A.69*d*).

A.37 An apprenticeship or training plan meeting all of the conditions specified in 29 CFR 2520.104-22 is excluded from filing (see paragraph A.69*f*).

A.38 An unfunded pension benefit plan or an unfunded or insured welfare benefit plan (*a*) whose benefits go only to a select group of management or highly compensated employees and (*b*) that meets the requirements of 29 CFR 2520.104-23 (including the requirement that a notification statement be filed with the DOL) or 29 CFR 2520.104-24, respectively, is excluded from filing (see paragraph A.69*g*–*h*).

A.39 Daycare centers as specified in 29 CFR 2520.104-25 are excluded from filing (see paragraph A.69*i*).

A.40 Certain dues-financed welfare and pension plans that meet the requirements of 29 CFR 2520.104-26 and 2520.104-27 are excluded from filing (see paragraph A.69*j*).

---

[10] *Directly* means that the plan does not use a trust or separately maintained fund (including a IRC section 501[c][9] trust) to hold plan assets or to act as a conduit for the transfer of plan assets.

A.41 A welfare plan that participates in a group insurance arrangement that files a Form 5500 on behalf of the welfare plan is excluded from filing (see 29 CFR 2520.104-43).

A.42 A simplified employee pension (SEP) described in IRC section 408(k) that conforms to the alternative method of compliance described in 29 CFR 2520.104-48 or -49 is excluded from filing. A SEP is a pension plan that meets certain minimum qualifications regarding eligibility and employer contributions (see paragraph A.69*p−q*).

Kinds of filers

A.43 A *single employer plan* is a plan sponsored by one employer.[11]

A.44 A plan for a *controlled group* is a plan for a controlled group of corporations under IRC section 414(b), a group of trades or businesses under common control under IRC section 414(c), or an affiliated service group under IRC section 414(m). For Form 5500 filing purposes, a controlled group is generally considered one employer when benefits are payable to participants from the plan's total assets without regard to contributions by each participant's employer (ref: Form 5500 instructions].

A.45 A *multiemployer plan* is a plan (*a*) in which more than one employer is required to contribute, (*b*) that is maintained pursuant to one or more collective bargaining agreements, and (*c*) that had not made the election under IRC section 414(f)(5) and ERISA section 3(37)(E).

A.46 A *multiple-employer plan* is a plan that involves more than one employer, is not one of the plans described in paragraphs A.45−.46, and includes only plans whose contributions from individual employers are available to pay benefits to all participants.[12] Participating employers do not file individually for these plans. Multiple-employer plans can be collectively bargained and collectively funded, but if covered by PBGC termination insurance, must have properly elected before September 27, 1981, not to be treated as a multiemployer plan under IRC section 414(f)(5) or ERISA sections 3(37)(E) and 4001(a)(3).

A.47 DFEs include common or collective trusts (CCTs), pooled separate accounts (PSAs), master trust investment accounts (MTIAs), 103-12 investment entities (103-12 IEs), and group insurance arrangements (GIAs). CCTs, PSAs, MTIAs, and 103-12 IEs must generally comply with Form 5500 instructions for large pension plans. GIAs must follow the instructions for large welfare plans.

A.48 A *group insurance arrangement* is an arrangement that provides welfare benefits to the employees of two or more unaffiliated employers (not in connection with a multiemployer plan nor a multiple employer collectively bargained plan), fully insures one or more welfare plans of each participating employer, and uses a trust (or other entity such as a trade association) as the holder of the insurance contracts and the conduit for payment of premiums to the insurance company. If such an arrangement files a Form 5500 in accordance with 29 CFR 2520.103-2, the welfare plans participating in the arrangement need not file a separate report.[13]

---

[11] If several employers participate in a program of benefits wherein the funds attributable to each employer are available only to pay benefits to that employer's employees, each employer must file as a sponsor of a single employer plan.

[12] A separate Schedule T, "Qualified Pension Plan Coverage Information," for each participating employer that provides pension benefits must be attached to the plan's Form 5500.

[13] Also see 29 CFR 2520.104-21 and 2520.104-43.

When to file

A.49 *Plans and GIAs.* The annual report is due by the last day of the seventh calendar month after the end of a plan year (not to exceed 12 months in length), including a short plan year (any plan year less than 12 months). A plan year ends upon the date of the change in accounting period or upon the complete distribution of the assets of the plan. *Direct Filing Entities Other Than GIAs.* The annual report is due no later than 9.5 months after the end of the direct filing entity's year. No extension of time is available to these entities for making their Form 5500 filings.

A.50 A one-time extension of time up to 2.5 months may be granted for filing the annual report of a plan or group insurance arrangement if Form 5558, *Application for Extension of Time to File Certain Employee Plan Returns*, is filed with the IRS before the normal due date of the report. In addition, single-employer plans and plans sponsored by a controlled group of corporations that file consolidated federal income tax returns are automatically granted an extension of time to file Form 5500 to the due date of the federal income tax return of the single employer or controlled group of corporations if certain conditions described in the instructions to the forms are met. A copy of the extension is no longer required to be filed with the annual report, but should be retained in the sponsor's records.

Filing under the statute versus the regulations

A.51 As stated in paragraph A.18, plan administrators may, for purposes of Title I of ERISA, file an annual report containing all of the information required by ERISA section 103 (that is, the statute) or the information required by the regulations. As also noted in paragraph A.18, however, a filing in accordance with ERISA section 103 will not satisfy an administrator's annual reporting obligations under the IRC or Title IV of ERISA; Form 5500 must be filed to comply with those requirements.

    a. *Regulations.* Filing Form 5500 is considerably different than filing pursuant to the statute. The regulations require that the accountant's report
- i. disclose any omitted auditing procedures deemed necessary by the accountant and the reasons for their omission.
- ii. state clearly the accountant's opinion of the financial statements and schedules covered by the report and the accounting principles and practices reflected therein.
- iii. state clearly the consistency of the application of the accounting principles between the current year and the preceding year or about any changes in such principles which have a material effect on the financial statements.[14]
- iv. state clearly any matters to which the accountant takes exception, the exception, and to the extent practical, the effect of such matters on the related financial statements. Exceptions are required to be further identified as (*a*) those that are the result of DOL regulations and (*b*) all others.[15]

---

[14] An accountant's report prepared in accordance with AU-C section 708, *Consistency of Financial Statements* (AICPA, *Professional Standards*), which prescribes that no reference be made to the consistent application of accounting principles generally accepted in the United States in those cases in which there has been no accounting change, will be viewed as consistent with the requirements of ERISA and regulations issued thereunder with regard to the required submission of an accountant's report.

[15] Other requirements are that the report be dated and manually signed, that it indicate the city and state where it is issued, and that it identify (without necessarily enumerating) the statements and schedules covered.

The regulations also require (1) current value,[16] comparing the beginning and end of the plan year; (2) a description of accounting principles and practices reflected in the financial statements and, if applicable, variances from accounting principles generally accepted in the United States of America as promulgated by the Financial Accounting Standards Board (U.S. GAAP); and (3) an explanation of differences, if any, between the information contained in the separate financial statements and the net assets, liabilities, income, expense, and changes in net assets as required to be reported on Form 5500.

b. *Statute.* In particular, a plan administrator electing to comply with the statute must satisfy all the requirements of ERISA section 103 and may not rely on regulatory exemptions and simplified methods of reporting or alternative methods of compliance prescribed with respect to Form 5500. In addition, the statute requires (1) the accountant to express an opinion on whether the financial statements and ERISA section 103(b) schedules conform with U.S. GAAP on a basis consistent with that of the preceding year and (2) current value, comparing the end of the previous plan year and the end of the plan year being reported.

A.52 The statute and the regulations require that the examination be conducted in accordance with U.S. GAAS.

a. Financial information required under both methods includes plan assets and liabilities (aggregated by categories and valued at their current value with the same data displayed in comparative form using the end of the current plan year at either [1] the end of the previous plan year [statute] or [2] beginning of the current plan year [regulations] and information concerning plan income, expenses, and changes in net assets during the plan year.

b. Required supplemental information includes mandatory use of standardized schedules (Form 5500, Schedule G, "Financial Transaction Schedules") as follows (see paragraph A.77):
    i.   Loans or fixed income obligations due in default or uncollectible
    ii. Leases in default or uncollectible
    iii. Nonexempt transactions

    Required information also includes the following nonstandardized schedules:

    iv. Schedule H, line 4a—Schedule of Delinquent Participant Contributions
    v.   Schedule H, line 4i—Schedule of Assets (Held at End of Year)
    vi. Schedule H, line 4i—Schedule of Assets Held (Acquired and Disposed of Within Year), if filing under the alternative method[17]
    vii. Schedule H, line 4j—Schedule of Reportable Transactions (that is, transactions that exceed 3 percent [statute] or 5 percent [regulations] of the current value of plan assets at the beginning of the year).[18]

---

[16] *Current value*, as used in this guide, means fair market value where available and otherwise the fair value as determined in good faith by a trustee or a named fiduciary (as defined in section 402[a][2]) pursuant to the terms of the plan and in accordance with regulations of the Secretary, assuming an orderly liquidation at the time of such determination (section 3[26] of ERISA).

[17] Any assets held for investment purposes in a 401(h) account should be shown on Schedule H, line 4i—Schedule of Assets (Held at End of Year), and Schedule H, line 4j—Schedule of Reportable Transactions, for the pension plan.

[18] Plans filing their annual reports under the statutory method are required to report transactions that exceed 3 percent of the fair value of plan assets at the beginning of the year, whereas plans that file pursuant to the alternative method of compliance prescribed in the Department of Labor's (DOL's) regulations are required to report transactions that exceed 5 percent of the fair value of plan assets at the beginning of the year.

  c. Notes to the financial statements, when applicable, should be provided concerning
    i. a description of the plan, including significant changes in the plan and effect of the changes on benefits.
    ii. the funding policy and changes in funding policy (including policy with respect to prior service cost) and any changes in such policies during the year (only applicable under the statutory method for pension plans).
    iii. a description of material lease commitments and other commitments and contingent liabilities.
    iv. a description of any agreements and transactions with persons known to be parties in interest.
    v. a general description of priorities in the event of plan termination.
    vi. whether a tax ruling or determination letter has been obtained.
    vii. any other information required for a fair presentation.
    viii. an explanation of differences, if any, between the information contained in the separate financial statements and the net assets, liabilities, income, expense, and changes in net assets as required to be reported on Form 5500, if filing under the alternative method (see paragraph A.51).

Investment arrangements filing directly with the DOL

A.53 Generally, when the assets of two or more plans are maintained in one trust or account or separately maintained fund, all annual report entries, including any attached schedules, should be completed by including the plan's allocable portion of the trust, account, or fund. Certain exceptions have been made, however, for plans that invest in certain investment arrangements that are either required to, or may elect to, file information concerning themselves and their relationship with employee benefit plans directly with the DOL as discussed subsequently. Plans participating in these investment arrangements are required to attach certain additional information to Form 5500 as specified in subsequent paragraphs. For a definition of plan assets and the look-through provisions, see 29 CFR 2510.3-101.

CCTs and PSAs

A.54 For reporting purposes, a *CCT* is a trust maintained by a bank, trust company, or similar institution that is regulated, supervised, and subject to periodic examination by a state or federal agency for the collective investment and reinvestment of assets contributed thereto from employee benefit plans maintained by more than one employer or a controlled group of corporations, as the term is used in IRC section 1563.

  For reporting purposes, a *PSA* is an account maintained by an insurance carrier that is regulated, supervised, and subject to periodic examination by a state agency for the collective investment and reinvestment of assets contributed thereto from employee benefit plans maintained by more than one employer or controlled group of corporations, as that term is used in IRC section 1563.

  Although CCTs and PSAs are not required to file directly with the DOL, their filing or lack thereof directly affects the participating plan's filing responsibilities. If the CCT or PSA does elect to directly file, participating plans must

  a. file a Form 5500, completing items 1c(9) or 1c(10) and items 2b(6) or (7) on Schedule H, and
  b. complete Part I of Schedule D, "DFE/Participating Plan Information."

If the CCT or PSA does not file directly with the DOL, plans participating in these arrangements must

a. file a Form 5500, allocating and reporting the underlying assets of the CCT or PSA in the appropriate categories on a line by line basis on Part I of Schedule H, and
b. complete Part I of Schedule D.

CCTs and PSAs that elect to file directly with the DOL must do so by filing a Form 5500, including Schedule D and Schedule H.

See paragraph A.69*b–c* and 29 CFR 2520.103-3, -4 and -5, and 2520.103-9.[19]

Master trust

A.55 For reporting purposes, a master trust is a trust for which a regulated financial institution serves as trustee or custodian (regardless of whether such institution exercises discretionary authority or control with respect to the management of assets held in the trust) and in which assets of more than one plan sponsored by a single employer or by a group of employers under common control are held.[20] Participating plans are required to complete item 1c(11) and item 2b(8) on Schedule H and Part I of Schedule D.

The following information is required to be filed by the plan administrator or by a designee directly with the DOL no later than 9.5 months after the end of the master trust's year. Form 5500 filing of each plan participating in the master trust will not be deemed complete unless all of the following information is filed within the prescribed time:

a. Form 5500
b. Schedule A, "Insurance Information," for each insurance or annuity contract held in the master trust (see paragraph A.74)
c. Schedule C, "Service Provider Information," Part I, if any service provider was paid $5,000 or more (see paragraph A.75)
d. Schedule D, Part II (see paragraph A.76)
e. Schedule G (see paragraph A.77)
f. Schedule H (see paragraph A.78)

See paragraph A.69*a* and 29 CFR 2520.103-1(e).

Plans versus trusts

A.56 Under ERISA, the audit requirement is applied to each separate plan and not each separate trust. As a result, each plan funded under a master trust arrangement is subject to a separate Form 5500 and audit requirement, unless otherwise exempt.

---

[19] For reporting purposes, a separate account that is not considered to be holding plan assets pursuant to 29 CFR 2510.3-101(h)(1)(iii) should not constitute a pooled separate account.

[20] A *regulated financial institution* means a bank, a trust company, or a similar institution that is regulated, supervised, and subject to periodic examination by a state or federal agency. Common control is determined on the basis of all relevant facts and circumstances.

103-12 Investment entities

A.57   For purposes of the annual report, entities described subsequently that file the information directly with the DOL as specified subsequently constitute "103-12 Investment Entities" (103-12 IEs).[21] Plans may invest in an entity, the underlying assets of which include *plan assets* (within the meaning of 29 CFR 2510.3-101) of two or more plans that are not members of a related group of employee benefit plans. For reporting purposes, a *related group* consists of each group of two or more employee benefit plans (a) each of which receives 10 percent or more of its aggregate contributions from the same employer or from a member of the same controlled group of corporations (as determined under IRC Section 1563[a], without regard to IRC Section 1563[a][4] thereof) or (b) each of which is either maintained by, or maintained pursuant to, a collective bargaining agreement negotiated by the same employee organization or affiliated employee organizations. For purposes of this paragraph, an *affiliate* of an employee organization means any person controlling, controlled by, or under common control with such organization.

The following information for the fiscal year of the 103-12 IE ending with or within the plan year must be filed directly with the DOL by the sponsor of the 103-12 IE no later than nine and a half months after the end of the 103-12 IE's year:

a.   Form 5500
b.   Schedule A for each insurance or annuity contract held in the 103-IE (see paragraph A.74)
c.   Schedule C, Part I, if any service provider was paid $5,000 or more, and Part II, if the accountant was terminated (see paragraph A.75)
d.   Schedule D, Part 2 (see paragraph A.76)
e.   Schedule H (see paragraph A.78)
f.   Schedule G (see paragraph A.77)
g.   A report of an IQPA regarding the preceding items and other books and records of the 103-12 IE that meets the requirements of 29 CFR 2520.103-1(b)(5)

See 29 CFR 2520.103-12 and paragraph A.61.

Limited-scope audit exemption

A.58   Under DOL regulations, any assets held by a bank or similar institution (for example, a trust company) or insurance company that is regulated and subject to periodic examination by a state or federal agency may be excluded from the annual audit provided the plan administrator exercises this option and the institution holding the assets certifies the required information. The limited-scope audit exemption does not exempt the plan from the requirement to have an audit.[22] All noninvestment activity of the plan, such as contributions, benefit payments, and plan administrative expenses, are subject to audit whether or not the assets of the plan have been certified as described previously. See paragraphs 8.167–.174 and 11.57–.71 for limited-scope audit procedures and reporting.

---

[21] The plan administrator cannot use this alternative method of reporting unless the report of the investment entity has been submitted to DOL in accordance with the requirements specified in Form 5500 instructions.

[22] This limitation on the scope of an auditor's examination applies to plans sponsored by a "regulated" bank or insurance carrier for its own employees, as well as to other plans.

A.59 The limited-scope audit exemption does not apply to assets held by a broker or dealer or an investment company. It also does not extend to benefit payment information [ref: DOL Reg. 29 CFR 2520.103-8; 2520.103-3; and 2520.103-4]. See paragraphs 8.167–.174 and 11.57–.71 for a discussion of the auditor's responsibilities when the scope of the audit is so restricted.

A.60 The Securities and Exchange Commission will not accept a limited-scope audit report in connection with a Form 11-K filing, even if the plan has elected to file financial statements that are prepared in accordance with the financial reporting requirements of ERISA. (See paragraphs 5.213–.218 for further discussion of SEC reporting requirements.)

103-12 IEs

A.61 If a plan's assets include assets of a 103-12 IE, the examination and report of an IQPA required by 29 CFR 2520.103-1 need not extend to such assets, if the entity reports directly to the DOL pursuant to 29 CFR 2520.103-12 and the instructions to Form 5500. Under 29 CFR 2520.103-12, the entity is required to include the report of an IQPA.

What to file (see exhibit A-3)

A.62 File Form 5500 annually for each plan required to file (see 29 CFR 2520.104a-5 and -6 and paragraphs A.30–.42, A.61, and A.83). Plans with 100 or more participants at the beginning of the plan year must file as a *large plan*. Plans with fewer than 100 participants at the beginning of the year must file as a *small plan*, using either Form 5500, 5500-SF, or 5500-EZ, as applicable.

A.63 *Exception to paragraph A.61.* If a plan has between 80 and 120 participants (inclusive) as of the beginning of the plan year, the plan may elect, instead of following paragraph A.62 to complete the current year's return/report in the same category (*large plan* or *small plan*) as was filed for the prior year. (See 29 CFR 2520.104a-5 and paragraph A.66.)

A.64 Amended reports should be filed as appropriate; however, they must include an original signature of the plan administrator.

A.65 A final report is required when all assets under a pension plan (including insurance or annuity contracts) have been distributed to the participants and beneficiaries or distributed to another plan or when all liabilities for which benefits may be paid under a welfare benefit plan have been satisfied and all assets, if the plan is not unfunded, have been distributed. A final report is filed on Form 5500.

Exemptions—audit

A.66 "Small" pension plans that file Form 5500 or 5500-SF will not be required to have an audit of their financial statements provided they meet the requirements of DOL Reg. 29 CFR 2520.104.46, as amended (see paragraph A.24). "Large" pension plans generally must engage an auditor (see paragraphs A.24 and A.62–.63 and 29 CFR 2520.104-41 and 2520.104-46).

A.67 Plan years of seven months or less, due to (1) initial year, (2) merger, or (3) change of plan year, can generally postpone (but not eliminate) the audit requirement (but not the requirement to file a Form 5500) until the following year. This rule also applies when a full plan year is followed by a short plan year of seven months or less. The audit report would therefore cover both the short year and the full plan year [ref: DOL Reg. 29 CFR 2520.104-50].

Exemptions—other filing requirements

A.68 Plans that are filing in a short plan year may defer the IQPA's report (see 29 CFR 2520.104-50).

A.69 The following is a list of variances that modify the general annual reporting requirements:

a. 29 CFR 2520.103-1(e) provides the regulatory authority for the reporting of financial information by plans participating in a master trust (see paragraph A.55).

b. 29 CFR 2520.103-3 and -4 provide exemptions for plans some or all the assets of which are held in a CCT of a bank or similar institution or a PSA of an insurance carrier from reporting information concerning the individual transactions of the CCTs and PSAs provided the conditions of the regulation are satisfied (see paragraph A.54).

c. 29 CFR 2520.103-9 permits the direct filing of financial information to the DOL by banks and insurance companies of information otherwise required to be submitted to IRS with Form 5500 when plans hold units of participation in CCTs or PSAs (see paragraph A.54).

d. 29 CFR 2520.104-20 provides a limited exemption for certain small welfare plans (see paragraphs A.36 and A.62).

e. 29 CFR 2520.104-21 provides a limited exemption for certain group insurance arrangements.

f. 29 CFR 2520.104-22 provides an exemption for apprenticeship and training plans (see paragraph A.37).

g. 29 CFR 2520.104-23 provides an alternative method of compliance for pension plans for certain selected employees (see paragraph A.38).

h. 29 CFR 2520.104-24 provides an exemption for welfare plans for certain selected employees (see paragraph A.38).

i. 29 CFR 2520.104-25 provides an exemption for day-care centers (see paragraph A.39).

j. 29 CFR 2520.104-26 provides a limited exemption for certain dues-financed welfare plans maintained by employee organizations (see paragraph A.40).

k. 29 CFR 2520.104-27 provides a limited exemption for certain dues-financed pension plans maintained by employee organizations.

l. 29 CFR 2520.104-41 prescribes simplified annual reporting requirements for plans with fewer than 100 participants (see paragraph A.63).

m. 29 CFR 2520.104-43 provides an exemption from annual reporting requirements for certain GIAs (see paragraph A.41).

n. 29 CFR 2520.104-44 provides a limited exemption and alternative method of compliance for the annual report of certain unfunded and insured plans (see paragraphs A.58–.60).[23]

---

[23] For purposes of 29 CFR 2520.104-44, a contract is considered to be "allocated" only if the insurance company or organization that issued the contract unconditionally guarantees, upon receipt of the required premium or consideration, to provide a retirement benefit of a specified amount, without adjustment for fluctuations in the market value of the underlying assets of the company or organization, to each participant, and each participant has a legal right to such benefits that is legally enforceable directly against the insurance company or organization.

---

o. 29 CFR 2520.104-46 provides a waiver of examination and report of an auditor for plans with fewer than 100 participants (see paragraph A.63).

p. 29 CFR 2520.104-47 provides a limited exemption and alternative method of compliance for filing of insurance company financial reports (see section 103[e]).

q. 29 CFR 2520.104-48 provides an alternative method of compliance for model simplified employee pensions (see paragraph A.42).

r. 29 CFR 2520.104-49 provides an alternative method of compliance for certain simplified employee pensions (see paragraph A.42).

A.70 *In-house asset manager (INHAM) class exemption.* Managers of many large pensions utilize the services of in-house asset managers, otherwise known as INHAMs. Oftentimes, these managers want to conduct transactions that are prohibited by ERISA. ERISA does provide, however, that the DOL has the authority to grant exemptions from the prohibited transaction restrictions if it can be demonstrated that a transaction is administratively feasible, in the interests of the plan and its participants and beneficiaries, and protective of the rights of the participants and beneficiaries of the plan. The DOL reviews applications for such exemptions and determines whether or not to grant relief. Individual exemptions relate to a particular plan or applicant; class exemptions are applicable to anyone engaging in the described transactions, provided the enumerated conditions are satisfied.

A.71 Related to INHAMs, the DOL issued a class exemption, Prohibited Transaction Exemption (PTE) 96-23, effective April 10, 1996, in which plans managed by in-house managers can engage in a variety of transactions with service providers if certain conditions are met. The special exemptions relate to the leasing of office or commercial space, leasing residential space to employees, and the use of public accommodations owned by plans. Only large employers whose plans have at least $250 million in assets, with $50 million under direct in-house management, can use the exemption, and it also requires that in-house managers be registered investment advisers and make all decisions concerning the affected transactions.

A.72 One of the provisions of the exemption requires that, an independent auditor, who has appropriate technical training or experience and proficiency with ERISA's fiduciary responsibility provisions and so represents in writing, must conduct an exemption audit on an annual basis. Upon completion of the audit, the auditor is required to issue a written report to the plan presenting its specific findings regarding the level of compliance with the policies and procedure adopted by the INHAM.

A.73 The exemption was published in the Federal Register on April 10, 1996, and may be found on the EBSA website at www.savingmatters.dol.gov/ebsa/programs/oed/archives/96-23.htm.

Schedules for Form 5500 series

A.74 Schedule A must be attached to Form 5500 if any benefits under the plan are provided by an insurance company, insurance service, or other similar organization (such as Blue Cross Blue Shield or a health maintenance organization) (see paragraphs A.55, A.57, and A.62).

A.75 Schedule C must be attached to Form 5500 (see paragraphs A.55, A.57, A.62, and A.85).

A.76 Schedule D must be attached to Form 5500 for DFE filings and for plans participating in a DFE.

A.77 Schedule G must be attached to Form 5500 to report certain supplemental information.

A.78 Schedule H generally must be attached to Form 5500 for employee benefit plans that covered 100 or more participants as of the beginning of the plan year and for DFE filings.

A.79 Schedule I generally must be attached to Form 5500 for employee benefit plans that covered less than 100 participants as of the beginning of the plan year. This is for plans that are not choosing to file using Form 5500-SF.

A.80 Schedule MB, *Multiemployer Defined Benefit Plan and Certain Money Purchase Plan Actuarial Information*, must be attached to Form 5500 for multiemployer defined benefit plans that are subject to the minimum funding standards.

A.81 Schedule R, *Retirement Plan Information*, generally must be attached to Form 5500 for both tax qualified and nonqualified pension benefit plans.

A.82 Schedule SB, *Single-Employer Defined Benefit Plan Actuarial Information*, must be attached to Form 5500 for single-employer defined benefit plans (including multiple-employer defined benefit plans) that are subject to the minimum funding standards.

A.83 Additional separate schedules must be attached to Form 5500 only in accordance with the instructions to the form and must always clearly reference the item number that requires this information (see exhibit A-1, "Examples of Form 5500 Schedules").

Termination of accountant or actuary

A.84 Terminations of certain service providers must be reported in Part II of Schedule C, which is attached to Form 5500. In addition, the plan administrator is required to provide terminated accountants and actuaries with a copy of the explanation for the termination as reported on Schedule C and a notice stating that the terminated party has the opportunity to comment directly to the DOL concerning the explanation (see Exhibit A-3).

Independence of IQPAs

A.85 ERISA section 103(a)(3)(A) requires that the accountant retained by an employee benefit plan be "independent" for purposes of examining plan financial information and rendering an opinion on the financial statements and schedules required to be contained in the annual report. Under this authority, the DOL will not recognize any person as an auditor who is in fact not independent with respect to the employee benefit plan upon which that accountant renders an opinion in the annual report.

The DOL has issued guidelines (29 CFR 2509.75-9) for determining when an auditor is independent for purposes of auditing and rendering an opinion on the annual report. For example, an accountant will not be considered independent with respect to a plan if

a. during the period of professional engagement to examine the financial statements being reported, at the date of the opinion, or during the period covered by the financial statements the accountant or his or her firm or a member thereof;

   i. had, or was committed to acquire, any direct financial interest or any material indirect financial interest in the plan or plan sponsor; or

   ii. was connected as a promoter, underwriter, investment adviser, voting trustee, director, officer, or employee of the plan or plan sponsor except that a firm will not be deemed not independent if a former officer or employee of the plan or plan sponsor is employed by the firm and such individual has completely disassociated himself or herself from the plan or plan sponsor and does not participate in auditing financial statements of the plan covering any period of his or her employment by the plan or plan sponsor.

b. An accountant or a member of an accounting firm maintains financial records for the employee benefit plan.

However, an auditor may permissibly engage in or have members of his or her firm engage in certain activities that will not have the effect of removing recognition of independence. For example, an accountant will not fail to be recognized as independent if

   i. at or during the period of his or her professional engagement the accountant or his or her firm is retained or engaged on a professional basis by the plan sponsor. However, the accountant must not violate the prohibitions in items (a) and (b) preceding.

   ii. the rendering of services by an actuary associated with the accountant or his or her firm should not impair the accountant's or the firm's independence. The auditor should ensure that the provision of these services complies with the prohibited transaction rules of ERISA section 406(a)(1)(c).

Penalties

A.86 ERISA and the IRC provide for the assessment or imposition of penalties for failures to comply with the reporting and disclosure requirements.

Annual reporting penalties

A.87 One or more of the following penalties may be imposed or assessed in the event of a failure or refusal to file reports in accordance with the statutory and regulatory requirements:

a. Up to $1,100 a day for each day a plan administrator fails or refuses to file a complete annual report (see ERISA section 502[c][2] and 29 CFR 2560.502c-2). Any failure of a plan's actuary to certify a plan's status in accordance with ERISA section 305(b)(3) is considered a failure to file a complete annual report.

Perfection Penalties for Deficient Filings

Presently the DOL assesses penalties of (1) $150 a day (up to $50,000) per annual report filing where the required auditor's report is missing or deficient, (2) $100 a day (up to $36,500) per annual report filing that contains deficient financial information (for example, missing required supplemental schedules), and (3) $10 a day (up to $3,650) for information required on Form 5500 Series reports (that is, failure to answer a question).

Nonfiler and Late Filer Penalties

Presently the DOL assesses nonfiler penalties of $300 per day, up to $30,000 per annual report, per year. Late filer penalties are assessed at $50 per day.

Egregious penalties may be assessed in addition to other penalty amounts.

b. $25 a day (up to $15,000) by the IRS for not filing returns for certain plans of deferred compensation, certain trusts and annuities, and bond purchase plans by the due dates(s) (see IRC section 6652[e]). This penalty also applies to returns required to be filed under IRC Section 6039D.
c. $1 a day (up to $5,000) by the IRS for each participant for whom a registration statement (Schedule SSA [Form 5500]) is required but not filed (see IRC section 6652[d][1]).
d. $1 a day (up to $1,000) by the IRS for not filing a notification of change of status of a plan (see IRC section 6652[d][2]).
e. $1,000 by the IRS for not filing an actuarial statement (see IRC section 6692).

These penalties may be waived or reduced if it is determined that there was reasonable cause for the failure to comply.

A.88 The following are other penalties:

a. Any individual who willfully violates any provision of Part 1 of Title I of ERISA should be fined not more than $5,000 or imprisoned not more than one year or both (see ERISA section 501).
b. A penalty up to $10,000, five years imprisonment, or both, for making any false statement or representation of fact, knowing it to be false, or for knowingly concealing or not disclosing any fact required by ERISA (see section 1027, Title 18, U.S.C., as amended by ERISA section 111).
c. Any employer maintaining a plan who fails to meet the notice requirement of section 101(d) with respect to any participant or beneficiary may in the court's discretion be liable to such participant or beneficiary in the amount of up to $100 a day from the date of such failure, and the court may in its discretion order such other relief as it deems proper (see ERISA section 502[c][3]).
d. Civil penalties may be assessed against parties in interest or disqualified persons who engage in prohibited transactions (see ERISA section 502[i]. An excise tax also exists for prohibited transactions under IRC section 4975).
e. ERISA section 502(l) requires a civil penalty to be assessed by the Secretary of Labor against a fiduciary who breaches his or her fiduciary duty or commits a violation of Part 4 of Title I or any other person who knowingly participates in such breach or violation. The civil penalty is 20 percent of the amount recovered pursuant to a settlement agreement with the Secretary or ordered to be paid by a court.[24]
f. A civil penalty of up to $100 a day may be assessed against a plan administrator for the failure or refusal to furnish notice to participants and beneficiaries of blackout period in accordance with section 101(i) of ERISA. Also, this civil penalty may be assessed for the failure or refusal to furnish the notice of the right to direct the proceeds from the divestment of employer securities in accordance with section 101(m) of ERISA. Each violation with respect to any single participant or beneficiary should be treated as a separate violation (see ERISA section 502[c][7]).

---

[24] An accountant who knows about a fiduciary breach or violation but chooses not to disclose it may knowingly participate in a breach or violation for purposes of ERISA section 502(l).

g. A civil penalty of not more than $1,000 per day may be assessed for failure or refusal to furnish (see ERISA section 502[c][4]) the following:
    i.   Notice of funding-based limits in accordance with section 101(j) of ERISA
    ii.   Actuarial, financial, or funding information in accordance with section 101(k) of ERISA
    iii. Notice of potential withdrawal liability in accordance with section 101(l) of ERISA
    iv.   Notice of rights and obligations under an automatic contribution arrangement in accordance with section 514(e)(3) of ERISA
    v.   A failure of refusal to furnish the item with respect to any person entitled to receive such item should be treated as a separate violation (see ERISA section 502[c][4])

h. A civil penalty of not more than $1,100 per day may be assessed against the plan sponsor of a multiemployer plan for each violation of the requirement under ERISA section 305 to adopt by deadline established in that section a funding improvement plan or rehabilitation plan with respect to a multiemployer plan which is in endangered or critical status. Also, in the case of a plan in endangered status which is not in seriously endangered status, this civil penalty may be assessed for the failure by the plan to meet the applicable benchmarks under ERISA section 305 by the end of the funding improvement period with respect to the plan.

Fiduciary responsibilities (ERISA Sections 401–414)

A.89   ERISA establishes standards for plan investments and transactions and imposes restrictions and responsibilities on plan fiduciaries.

A.90   A fiduciary's responsibilities include managing plan assets solely in the interest of participants and beneficiaries (with the care a prudent person would exercise) and diversifying investments to minimize the risk of large losses unless it is clearly not prudent to do so (see ERISA section 404). Plans are prohibited from acquiring or holding employer securities that are not qualifying employer securities (QES) or employer real property that is not qualifying employer real property (QERP). Furthermore, plans (other than certain individual account plans) may not acquire any QES or QERP if immediately after such acquisition the aggregate fair market value of QES and QERP held by the plan exceeds 10 percent of the assets of the plan (see ERISA section 407).

A.91   A plan fiduciary is prohibited from causing the plan to engage in certain transactions with a party in interest (see ERISA section 406).[25] The following transactions between a plan and a party in interest are generally prohibited (see ERISA section 406):

a. A sale, exchange, or lease of property, except to the extent allowed
b. A loan or other extension of credit
c. The furnishing of goods, services, or facilities, except as allowed under ERISA
d. A transfer of plan assets to a party in interest for the use or benefit of a party in interest
e. An acquisition of employer securities or real property, except to the extent allowed (see ERISA section 408[e])

---

[25] ERISA defines a *party in interest* generally as any fiduciary or employee of the plan, any person who provides services to the plan, an employer whose employees are covered by the plan, an employee association whose members are covered by the plan, a person who owns 50 percent or more of such an employer or employee association, or a relative of a person described in the foregoing (see ERISA section 3[14]).

However, conditional exemptions from the application of these provisions are provided by ERISA.

A.92 A fiduciary is also generally prohibited from using the plan assets for his or her own interest or account, acting in any plan transactions on behalf of a party whose interests are adverse to those of the plan or its participants, and receiving consideration for his or her own account from a party dealing with the plan in connection with a transaction involving the plan assets (see ERISA section 406[b]).

A.93 ERISA section 408 provides for exceptions to the rules on prohibited transactions. Section 408(a) gives authority to the Secretary of Labor to grant administrative exemptions from the prohibited transaction restrictions of ERISA sections 406 and 407. Section 408(b), (c), and (e) provide statutory exemptions from the prohibited transaction rules for various transactions, provided the conditions specified in the statutory exemptions are satisfied. For example, reasonable arrangements can be made with a party in interest to provide services if the one who selects and negotiates with the service provider on behalf of the plan is independent of the service provider. Advice of legal counsel should be obtained when investigating a possible prohibited transaction or a possible breach of fiduciary duty.

A.94 A fiduciary must make good any losses to the plan resulting from a breach of fiduciary duty and must return to the plan any profits he or she made through the use of plan assets (see ERISA section 409).

Plan termination insurance

A.95 The insurance provisions under Title IV of ERISA, as amended, apply to qualified, defined benefit pension plans, with certain statutory exceptions, and do not apply to defined contribution plans or welfare plans (see ERISA section 4021).

A.96 The PBGC's termination insurance program is funded in part through premiums paid to the PBGC. The designated payor must make annual premium payments to the PBGC (see ERISA section 4007). For this purpose, the designated payor for a single employer plan is the contributing sponsor or the plan administrator. The designated payor for a multiemployer plan is the plan administrator. For single employer plans, premiums are based on the number of participants in a plan and the amount by which the plan's benefits are underfunded (see ERISA section 4006). Premiums for multiemployer plans are based solely on the number of participants in the plan. In general, premiums may be paid by the contributing sponsor or by plan funds, whichever is permitted under the terms of the plan; however, premiums for a plan that is undergoing a distress termination or an involuntary termination must be paid by the contributing sponsor (see 29 CFR 2610.26). Each member of the contributing sponsor's controlled group, if any, is jointly and severally liable for the required premiums (see ERISA section 4007).

A.97 A plan administrator or contributing sponsor must notify the PBGC when a "reportable event" such as bankruptcy of the contributing sponsor or inability of the plan to pay benefits occurs (see ERISA sections 4041[c] and 4043; 29 CFR Part 2615). Each person who is a contributing sponsor of a single employer pension plan is responsible for quarterly contributions required to meet the minimum funding standards (see ERISA section 302[e]). If the contributing sponsor is a member of a controlled group, each person who is also a member of the controlled group is jointly and severally liable for the contributions (see ERISA section 302[c][11]). Failure to make the required contributions may result in a lien upon all property and property rights belonging to such persons, which lien may be enforced by the PBGC. ERISA provides for two types of voluntary single employer plan terminations for defined benefit pension plans: a standard termination and a distress termination (ERISA section 4041). A plan may be terminated voluntarily in a standard termination only if it can pay all benefit liabilities under the plan. A plan may be terminated in a distress termination only if the contributing sponsor and each member of the contributing sponsor's controlled group meet the necessary distress criteria (for example, undergoing liquidation). In either type of termination, an enrolled actuary's certification of the value of the plan's assets and benefits must be filed with the PBGC. When an underfunded single employer plan terminates in a distress termination, the contributing sponsor and each member of the contributing sponsor's controlled group are liable to the PBGC for the total amount of unfunded benefit liabilities and the total amount of unpaid minimum funding contributions and applicable interest (see ERISA section 4062). If an employer that contributes to a multiemployer plan withdraws from the plan in a complete or partial withdrawal, the employer is generally liable to the plan for an allocable share of the unfunded vested benefits of the plan (see ERISA section 4201).

Administration and enforcement (ERISA Sections 501–514)

A.98   Responsibility for administration of ERISA and enforcement of its provisions rests primarily with the IRS and the DOL. The agencies are empowered to bring suit in federal court in civil actions, criminal actions, or both.

A.99   Failure to meet ERISA's requirements can result in the imposition of substantial fines, excise taxes, and other penalties, including possible loss of tax-exempt status. Although ERISA states that the plan is subject to certain of the penalties, the penalties are likely to fall not on the plan but on the sponsoring employer because Congress, in formulating ERISA, sought to protect plan assets for participants and their beneficiaries, not to protect employers from liability (see paragraphs A.87–.88).

A.100   ERISA was intended to generally supersede state laws relating to employee benefit plans. Thus, plans subject to Title I of ERISA or Title IV of ERISA are generally not subject to state regulation. Preemption of state laws does not extend, however, to generally applicable criminal statutes or laws regulating insurance, banking, or securities.

A.101   Plans that are multiple employer welfare arrangements (MEWAs) may also be subject to state or local regulation even if the MEWA is also an employee benefit plan covered under Title I of ERISA. A MEWA is any employee welfare benefit plan or other arrangement that provides benefits to the employees of two or more employers but does not include arrangements maintained under or pursuant to one or more collective bargaining agreements, by a rural electric cooperative, or by two or more trades or businesses within the same control group (see ERISA section 3[40]). If the MEWA is a fully insured plan covered by Title I of ERISA, the state government may only provide standards requiring specified levels of reserves and specified levels of contributions adequate to be able to pay benefits in full when due. If the MEWA is a plan covered by Title I that is not fully insured, any law of a state regulating insurance may apply to the extent that it is not inconsistent with the provisions of Title I of ERISA. On February 11, 2000, the DOL published in the Federal Register (65 CFR 7152) an interim final rule requiring the administrator of a MEWA, or other entity, to file a form with the DOL for the purpose of determining whether the requirements of certain health care laws are being met. MEWAs and those entities claiming exemption from the rule's requirements were required to submit their first forms by May 1, 2000. Subsequent filings are due by the March 1 following any "year to be reported."

 Exhibit A-1 Examples of Form 5500 schedules required by the regulations [not permitted if filing by the statutory method]

Form 5500 requires that certain supplemental schedules be attached to the annual Form 5500 filing using Form 5500 series and not Form 5500-SF or 5500-EZ.

Information on all delinquent participant contributions should be reported on line 4a of either Schedule H or Schedule I of Form 5500, and should not be reported on line 4d of Schedule H or I or on Schedule G. Beginning for 2009 plan years, large plans with delinquent participant contributions should attach a schedule clearly labeled, "Schedule H, line 4a—Schedule of Delinquent Participant Contributions," using the following format.

Participant Contributions Transferred Late to Plan	Total That Constitute Nonexempt Prohibited Transactions			Total Fully Corrected Under Voluntary Fiduciary Correction Program (VFCP) and Prohibited Transaction Exemption 2002-51
Check Here If Late Participant Loan Repayments Are Included	Contributions Not Corrected	Contributions Corrected Outside VFCP	Contributions Pending Correction in VFCP	

Participant loan repayments paid to or withheld by an employer for purposes of transmittal to the plan that were not transmitted to the plan in a timely fashion must be reported either on line 4a in accordance with the reporting requirements that apply to delinquent participant contributions or on line 4d. See Advisory Opinion No. 2002-2A at https://www.dol.gov/agencies/ebsa/employers-and-advisers/guidance/field-assistance-bulletins for guidance regarding participant loan repayments.

Exhibit A-1 Examples of Form 5500 schedules required by the regulations [not permitted if filing by the statutory method] (continued)

Delinquent forwarding of participant loan repayments is eligible for correction under the Voluntary Fiduciary Correction Program and PTE 2002-51 on terms similar to those that apply to delinquent participant contributions.

For further guidance, refer to the instructions to the Form 5500 and the EBSA website frequently asked questions at https://www.dol.gov/agencies/ebsa/about-ebsa/our-activities/resource-center/faqs. Also, FAB 2003-2, Application of Participant Contribution Requirements in Multiemployer Defined Contribution Pension Plans, contains guidance regarding when participant contributions can be reasonably segregated from the general assets of participating employers in the context of a multiemployer defined contribution pension plan.

The following schedule is "Schedule H, line 4i—Schedule of Assets (Held at End of Year)." In column (a), place an asterisk (*) on the line of each identified person known to be a party in interest to the plan. The schedule must use the format shown as follows or a similar format and the same size paper as Form 5500 and be clearly labeled "Schedule H, line 4i—Schedule of Assets (Held at End of Year)."

(a)	(b) Identity of issue, borrower, lessor, or similar party	(c) Description of investment, including maturity date, rate of interest, collateral, and par or maturity value	(d) Cost[26]	(e) Current value[27]

Note 1: Participant loans may be aggregated and presented with a general description of terms and interest rates.

Note 2: In column (d), cost information may be omitted with respect to participant or beneficiary directed transactions under an individual account plan.

Note 3: Any assets held for investment purposes in the 401(h) account should be shown on Schedule H, line 4i—Schedule of Assets (Held at End of Year), and Schedule H, line 4j—Schedule of Reportable Transactions, for the pension plan.

---

[26] *Cost or cost of asset* refers to the original or acquisition cost of the asset. The DOL generally will accept any clearly defined and consistently applied method of determining historical cost that is based on the initial acquisition cost of the asset (for example, first in-first out or average cost). The use of revalued cost (the fair value of the asset at the beginning of the current plan year) for these schedules is not acceptable.

[27] *Current value* means fair market value where available. Otherwise, it means the fair value as determined in good faith under the terms of the plan by a trustee or a named fiduciary, assuming an orderly liquidation at the time of the determination.

Exhibit A-1 Examples of Form 5500 schedules required by the regulations [not permitted if filing by the statutory method] (continued)

The following schedule is "Schedule H, line 4i—Schedule of Assets (Acquired and Disposed of within Year)," (see 2520.103-11). This schedule must be clearly labeled, "Schedule H, line 4i—Schedule of Assets (Acquired and Disposed of within Year)," and must use the following format or similar format and the same size paper as Form 5500:

(a) Identity of issue, borrower, lessor, or similar party	(b) Description of investment, including maturity date, rate of interest, collateral, and par or maturity value	(c) Costs of acquisitions	(d) Proceeds of dispositions

Note: In column (c), cost information may be omitted with respect to participant or beneficiary directed transactions under an individual account plan.

The following schedule is "Schedule H, line 4j—Schedule of Reportable Transactions." This schedule must be clearly labeled, "Schedule H, line 4j—Schedule of Reportable Transactions," and must use the following format:

(a) Identity of party involved	(b) Description of asset (include interest rate and maturity in case of a loan)	(c) Purchase price	(d) Selling price	(e) Lease rental	(f) Expense incurred with transaction	(g) Cost of asset [26]	(h) Current value of asset on transaction date [27]	(i) Net gain or (loss)

Note 1: Participant or beneficiary directed transactions under an individual account plan should not be taken into account for purposes of preparing this schedule. The current value of all assets of the plan, including those resulting from participant direction, should be included in determining the 5 percent figure for all other transactions.

Note 2: Any assets held for investment purposes in the 401(h) account should be shown on Schedule H, line 4i—Schedule of Assets (Held at End of Year), and Schedule H, line 4j—Schedule of Reportable Transactions, for the pension plan.

Exhibit A-1 Examples of Form 5500 schedules required by the regulations [not permitted if filing by the statutory method] (continued)

The following schedule is the "Schedule of Loans or Fixed Income Obligations in Default or Classified as Uncollectible." **This schedule is required to be reported in Schedule G, Part I of Form 5500.** In column (*a*), place an asterisk (*) on the line of each identified person known to be a party in interest to the plan. Include all loans that were renegotiated during the plan year. Also, explain what steps have been taken or will be taken to collect overdue amounts for each loan listed. The following are the headings of Schedule G, Part I:

(*a*)	(*b*) Identity and address of obligor	(*c*) Original amount of loan	Amount received during reporting year		(*f*) Unpaid balance at end of year	(*g*) Detailed description of loan, including dates of making and maturity, interest rate, the type and value of collateral, any renegotiation of the loan and the terms of the renegotiation, and other material items	Amount overdue	
			(*d*) Principal	(*e*) Interest			(*h*) Principal	(*i*) Interest

The next schedule is the "Schedule of Leases in Default or Classified as Uncollectible." **This schedule is required to be reported in Schedule G, Part II of Form 5500.** In column (*a*), place an asterisk (*) on the line of each identified person known to be a party in interest to the plan. The following are the headings of Schedule G, Part II:

(*a*)	(*b*) Identity of lessor or lessee	(*c*) Relationship to plan, employer, employee organization, or other party in interest	(*d*) Terms and description (type of property, location, and date it was purchased; terms regarding rent, taxes, insurance, repairs, expenses, and renewal options; and date property was leased)	(*e*) Original cost	(*f*) Current value at time of lease	(*g*) Gross rental receipts during the plan year	(*h*) Expenses paid during the plan year	(*i*) Net Receipts	(*j*) Amount in arrears

Exhibit A-1 Examples of Form 5500 schedules required by the regulations [not permitted if filing by the statutory method] (continued)

The last schedule is the schedule of "Nonexempt Transactions." **This schedule is required to be reported in Schedule G, Part III of Form 5500**. The following are the headings of Schedule G, Part III:

(a) Identity of party involved	(b) Relationship to plan, employer, or other party in interest	(c) Description of transactions, including maturity date, rate of interest, collateral, and par or maturity value	(d) Purchase price	(e) Selling price	(f) Lease rental	(g) Expenses incurred in connection with transaction	(h) Cost of asset[26]	(i) Current value of asset[27]	(j) Net gain or (loss) on each transaction

Exhibit A-2 Employee benefits security admin., labor

Part 2520 subchapter C—Reporting and disclosure under the employee retirement income security Act of 1974

Part 2520—rules and regulations for reporting and disclosure	
Subpart A—general reporting and disclosure requirements	
Section	
2520.101-1	Duty of reporting and disclosure
Subpart B—Contents of plan descriptions and summary plan descriptions	
2520.102-1	Plan description
2520.102-2	Style and format of summary plan description
2520.102-3	Contents of summary plan description
2520.102-4	Option for different summary plan descriptions
2520.102-5	Limited exemption with respect to summary plan descriptions of welfare plans providing benefits through a qualified health maintenance organization
Subpart C—Annual report requirements	
2520.103-1	Contents of the annual report
2520.103-2	Contents of the annual report for a group insurance arrangement
2520.103-3	Exemption from certain annual reporting requirements for assets held in a common or collective trust

Exhibit A-2 Employee benefits security admin., labor (continued)

2520.103-4	Exemption from certain annual reporting requirements for assets held in an insurance company pooled separate account
2520.103-5	Transmittal and certification of information to plan administrator for annual reporting purposes
2520.103-6	Definition of reportable transaction for annual return or report
2520.103-7	Special accounting rules for plans filing the annual report for plan years beginning in 1975
2520.103-8	Limitation on scope of accountant's examination
2520.103-9	Direct filing for bank or insurance carrier trusts and accounts
2520.103-10	Annual report financial schedules
2520.103-11	Assets held for investment purposes
2520.103-12	Limited exemption and alternative method of compliance for annual reporting of investments in certain entities
Subpart D—provisions applicable to both reporting and disclosure requirements	
2520.104-1	General.
2520.104-2	Postponing effective date of annual reporting requirements and extending WPPDA reporting requirements
2520.104-3	Deferral of certain initial reporting and disclosure requirements
2520.104-4	Alternative method of compliance for certain successor pension plans
2520.104-5	Deferral of certain reporting and disclosure requirements relating to the summary plan description for welfare plans
2520.104-6	Deferral of certain reporting and disclosure requirements relating to the summary plan description for pension plans
2520.104-20	Limited exemption for certain small welfare plans
2520.104-21	Limited exemption for certain group insurance arrangements
2520.104-22	Exemption from reporting and disclosure requirements for apprenticeship and training plans
2520.104-23	Alternative method of compliance for pension plans for certain selected employees
2520.104-24	Exemption for welfare plans for certain selected employees
2520.104-25	Exemption from reporting and disclosure for day care centers
2520.104-26	Limited exemption for certain funded dues financed welfare plans maintained by employee organizations
2520.104-27	Alternative method of compliance for certain unfunded dues financed pension plans maintained by employee organizations
2520.104-28	Extension of time for filing and disclosure of the initial summary plan description
2520.104-41	Simplified annual reporting requirements for plans with fewer than 100 participants. 2520.104-42 Waiver of certain actuarial information in the annual report
2520.104-43	Exemption from annual reporting requirement for certain group insurance arrangements
2520.104-44	Limited exemption and alternative method of compliance for annual reporting by unfunded plans and by certain insured plans

2520.104-45	Temporary exemption from reporting insurance fees and commissions for insured plans with fewer than 100 participants
2520.104-46	Waiver of examination and report of an independent qualified public accountant for employee benefit plans with fewer than 100 participants
2520.104-47	Limited exemption and alternative method of compliance for filing of insurance company financial reports
2520.104-48	Alternative method of compliance for model simplified employee pensions IRS Form 5305-SEP
2520.104-49	Alternative method of compliance for certain simplified employee pensions
2520.104-50	Short plan years, deferral of accountant's examination and report

Subpart E—reporting requirements

2520.104a-1	Filing with the Secretary of Labor
2520.104a-2	Plan description reporting requirements
2520.104a-3	Summary plan description
2520.104a-4	Material modifications to the plan and changes in plan description information
2520.104a-5	Annual report filing requirements
2520.104a-6	Annual reporting for plans which are part of a group insurance arrangement
2520.104a-7	Summary of material modifications

Subpart F—disclosure requirements

2520.104b-1	Disclosure
2520.104b-2	Summary plan description
2520.104b-3	Summary of material modifications to the plan and changes in the information required to be included in the summary plan description
2520.104b-4	Alternative methods of compliance for furnishing the summary plan description and summaries of material modifications of a pension plan to a retired participant, a separated participant with vested benefits, and a beneficiary receiving benefits
2520.104b-5	ERISA Notice
2520.104b-10	Summary Annual Report
2520.104b-12	Summary Annual Report for 1975 Plan Year Optional method of distribution for certain multiemployer plans
2520.104b-30	Charges for documents
	Authority: Secs. 101, 102, 103, 104, 105, 109, 110, 111(b)(2), 111(c), and 505, Pub. L. 93-406, 88 Stat. 840-52 and 894 (29 U.S.C. 1021-25, 1029-31, and 1135); Secretary of Labor's Order No. 27-74, 13-76, 1-87, and Labor Management Services Administration Order No. 2-6

Exhibit A-3 Quick reference chart for filing Form 5500[28]

	Large pension plan	Small pension plan filing Form 5500 Series, Not Form 5500-SF or 5500-EZ	Large welfare plan	Small welfare plan filing Form 5500 series, not Form 5500-SF or 5500-EZ	DFE
Form 5500	Must complete	Must complete	Must complete	Must complete[29]	Must complete
Schedule A (Insurance Information)	Must complete if plan has insurance contracts	Must complete if plan has insurance contracts	Must complete if plan has insurance contracts	Must complete if plan has insurance contracts	Must complete if MTIA, 103-12 IE, or GIA has insurance contracts
Schedule C (Service Provider Information)	Must complete Part I if service provider was paid $5,000 or more, Part II if a service provider failed to provide information necessary for the completion of Part I, and Part III if an accountant or actuary was terminated	Not required	Must complete Part I if service provider was paid $5,000 or more, Part II if a service provider failed to provide information necessary for the completion of Part I, and Part III if an accountant or actuary was terminated	Not required	MTIAs, GIAs, and 103-12 IEs must complete Part I if service provider paid $5,000 or more, and Part II if a service provider failed to provide information necessary for the completion of Part I. GIAs and 103-12 IEs must complete Part III if accountant was terminated

---

[28] Unfunded, fully insured, and a combination unfunded or insured welfare plans covering fewer than 100 participants at the beginning of the plan year that meet the requirements of 29 CFR 2520.104-20 are exempt from filing an annual report. Such a plan with 100 or more participants must file an annual report, but it is exempt under [29] CFR 2520.104-44 from the accountant's report requirement and completing Schedule H, "Financial Information." However, such a plan must complete Schedule G, "Financial Transaction Schedules," Part III, to report any nonexempt transactions.

Exhibit A-3 Quick reference chart for filing Form 5500 (continued)

	Large pension plan	Small pension plan filing Form 5500 series, not Form 5500-SF or 5500-EZ	Large welfare plan	Small welfare plan filing Form 5500 series, not Form 5500-SF or 5500-EZ	DFE
Schedule D (DFE/Participating Plan Information)	Must complete Part I if plan participated in a CCT, PSA, MTIA, or 103-12 IE	Must complete Part I if plan participated in a CCT, PSA, MTIA, or 103-12 IE	Must complete Part I if plan participated in a CCT, PSA, MTIA, or 103-12 IE	Must complete Part I if plan participated in a CCT, PSA, MTIA, or 103-12 IE	All DFEs must complete Part II, and DFEs that invest in a CCT, PSA, or 103-12 IE must also complete Part I
Schedule G (Financial Transaction Schedules)	Must complete if Schedule H, lines 4b, 4c, or 4d are "Yes"[30]	Not required	Must complete if Schedule H, lines 4b, 4c, or 4d are "Yes"[29,30]	Not required	Must complete if Schedule H, lines 4b, 4c, or 4d for a GIA, MTIA, or 103-12 IE are "Yes"[30]
Schedule H (Financial Information)	Must complete[30]	Not required	Must complete[29,30]	Not required	All DFEs must complete Parts I, II, and III. MTIAs, 103-12 IEs, and GIAs must also complete Part IV.[30]
Schedule I (Financial Information)	Not required	Must complete	Not required	Must complete[29]	Not required
Schedule MB (Multiemployer Defined Benefit Plan and Certain Money Purchase Plan Actuarial Information)	Must complete if multiemployer defined benefit plan or money purchase plan subject to minimum funding standards[31]	Must complete if multiemployer defined benefit plan or money purchase plan subject to minimum funding standards[31]	Not required	Not required	Not required

---

[30] Schedules of assets and reportable (5 percent) transactions also must be filed with Form 5500 if Schedule H, line 4i or 4j, is "Yes," but use of printed form is not required.

[31] Certain money purchase defined contribution plans are required to complete lines 3, 9, and 10 of Schedule MB, "Multiemployer Defined Benefit Plan and Certain Money Purchase Plan Actuarial Information," in accordance with the instructions for line 5 of Schedule R, "Retirement Plan Information."

Exhibit A-3 Quick reference chart for filing Form 5500 (continued)

	Large pension plan	Small pension plan filing Form 5500 series, not Form 5500-SF or 5500-EZ	Large welfare plan	Small welfare plan filing Form 5500 series, not Form 5500-SF or 5500-EZ	DFE
Schedule R (Retirement Plan Information)	Must complete[32]	Must complete[32]	Not required	Not required	Not required
Schedule SB (Single-Employer Defined Benefit Plan Actuarial Information)	Must complete if single-employer or multiple-employer defined benefit plan, including an eligible combined plan, and subject to minimum funding standards	Must complete if single-employer or multiple-employer defined benefit plan, including an eligible combined plan, and subject to minimum funding standards	Not required	Not required	Not required
Accountant's Report	Must attach	Not required unless Schedule I, line 4k, is checked "No"	Must attach	Not required	Must attach for a GIA or 103-12 IE

---

[32] A pension plan is exempt from filing Schedule R if all of the following five conditions are met:

- The plan is not a multiemployer defined benefit plan.
- The plan is not a defined benefit plan or otherwise subject to the minimum funding standards of IRC section 412 or ERISA section 302.
- No in-kind distributions reportable on line 1 of Schedule R were distributed during the plan year.
- No benefits were distributed during the plan year which are reportable on Form 1099-R using an employer identification number other than that of the plan sponsor or plan administrator.
- In the case of a plan that is not a profit-sharing, employee stock-ownership, or stock bonus plan, no plan benefits were distributed during the plan year in the form of a single-sum distribution.

Exhibit A-4 Special rules

"Plan assets"—plan investments

DOL Regulation 29 CFR 2520.103-12 provides an alternative method of reporting for plans that invest in an entity (other than CCTs, PSAs, and master trusts), the underlying assets of which include "plan assets" (within the meaning of DOL Reg. 29 CFR 2510.3-101) of two or more plans that are not members of a "related group" of employee benefit plans. For reporting purposes, these investment entities (commonly referred to as 103-12 IEs) are required to provide certain information directly to DOL for the fiscal year of the entity ending with or within the plan year for which the plan's annual report is made. This information includes the report of an IQPA regarding the *statements* and *schedules* described in DOL Reg. 29 CFR 2520.103-12(b)(2)-(5), which meets the requirements of DOL Reg. 29 CFR 2520.103-1(b)(5).

Fringe benefit plans

Fringe benefit plans may also be welfare benefit plans required to file annual reports under Title I of ERISA.

Welfare benefit plans

Under ERISA, according to DOL Regulation 29 CFR 2510.3-1, a welfare plan provides medical, surgical, or hospital benefits, or benefits in event of sickness, accident, disability, death, or unemployment, or vacation benefits, apprenticeship or training programs, or day-care centers (distinct from dependent care assistance programs), scholarship funds, prepaid legal services and certain benefits under the Labor Management Relations Act of 1947. Plan sponsors have a great degree of discretion regarding the number of benefits provided through one welfare benefit plan.

Employee Benefit Plans Glossary

AAG – AICPA Audit and Accounting Guide, *Audits of Employee Benefit Plans*.

Accrued experience-rating adjustments – The refund at the end of the policy year of the excess of premiums paid over paid claims, reserves required by the insurance company, and the insurance company's retention (fee).

Accumulated eligibility credits – A liability of a plan arising from prior employee service for which employer contributions have been received.

Accumulated plan benefits – Benefits that are attributable under the provisions of an employee benefit plan to employees' service rendered to the benefit information date.

Act – The Employee Retirement Income Security Act of 1974.

Actuarial asset value – A value assigned by an actuary to the assets of a plan generally for use in conjunction with an actuarial cost method.

Actuarial cost method – A recognized actuarial technique used for establishing the amount and incidence of employer contributions or accounting charges for pension cost under a pension plan.

Actuarial value of accumulated plan benefits – The amount as of a benefit information date that results from applying actuarial assumptions to the accumulated plan benefits, with the actuarial assumptions being used to adjust those amounts to reflect the time value of money (through discounts for interest) and the probability of payment (by means of decrements such as for death, disability, withdrawal, or retirement) between the benefit information date and the expected date of payment.

AICPA – American Institute of Certified Public Accountants.

Allocated contract – A contract with an insurance company under which related payments to the insurance company are currently used to purchase immediate or deferred annuities for individual participants.

APB – AICPA Practice Bulletin.

APBO – Accumulated plan benefit obligations.

ASC – Accounting Standards Codification.

ASU – Accounting Standards Update.

Benefit information – The actuarial present value of accumulated plan benefits.

Benefit information date – The date as of which the actuarial present value of accumulated plan benefits is presented.

Benefit security – The plan's present and future ability to pay benefits when due.

Benefit-responsive investment contract – A contract between an insurance company, a bank, a financial institution, or any financially responsible entity and a plan that provides for a stated return on principal invested over a specified period and that permits withdrawals at contract value for benefit payments, loans, or transfers to other investment options offered to the participant by the plan. Participant withdrawals from the plan are required to be at contract value.

Benefits – Payments to which participants may be entitled under an employee benefit plan, including pension benefits, disability benefits, death benefits, health benefits, and benefits due on termination of employment.

Cash-or-deferred arrangement (section 401(k) plan) – A plan that may be incorporated into a profit-sharing or stock bonus plan (a few pre-ERISA money purchase pension plans also incorporate cash-or-deferred arrangements). Under such an arrangement, a participant is permitted to elect to receive amounts in cash or have them contributed to the plan as employer contributions on the participant's behalf.

CFR – Code of Federal Regulations.

COBRA – Consolidated Omnibus Budget Reconciliation Act.

CODA – Cash or deferred arrangement.

Common or commingled trust – A trust for the collective investment and reinvestment of assets contributed from employee benefit plans maintained by more than one employer or a controlled group of corporations that is maintained by a bank, trust company, or similar institution that is regulated, supervised, and subject to periodic examination by a state or federal agency.

Contract value – The value of an unallocated contract that is determined by the insurance company in accordance with the terms of the contract.

Contributions receivable – Amounts due as of the date of the financial statements, including legal or contractual obligations and, for a single employer plan, obligations resulting from a formal commitment.

Contributory plan – An employee benefit plan under which participants bear part of the cost.

Defined benefit pension plan – A pension plan that specifies a determinable pension benefit, usually based on factors such as age, years of service, and salary. Even though a plan may be funded pursuant to periodic agreements that specify a fixed rate of employer contributions (e.g., a collectively bargained multiemployer plan), such a plan may nevertheless be a defined benefit pension plan.

Defined contribution plan – A plan that provides an individual account for each participant and provides benefits that are based on (*a*) amounts contributed to the participant's account by the employer or employee, (*b*) investment experience, and (*c*) any forfeitures allocated to the account, less any administrative expenses charged to the plan.

Deposit administration contract (DA) – A type of contract under which contributions are not currently applied to the purchase of single-payment deferred annuities for individual participants. Payments to the insurance company that are intended to provide future benefits to present employees are credited to an account. For investment purposes, the monies in the account are commingled with other assets of the insurance company. The account is credited with interest at the rate specified in the contract; it is charged with the purchase price of annuities when participants retire and with any incidental benefits (death, disability, and withdrawal) disbursed directly from the account.

Directed trust – An arrangement in which the trustee acts as custodian of a plan's investments and is responsible for collecting investment income and handling trust asset transactions as directed by the party named as having discretion to make investment decisions, such as the plan administrator, the plan's investment committee, or the plan's investment advisor.

Discretionary trust – An arrangement in which the trustee has discretionary authority and control over investments and is authorized by the plan or its investment committee to make investment decisions.

DOL – Department of labor.

EBSA – Employee benefit security administration.

EIN – Employer identification number.

Employee – A person who has rendered or is presently rendering service.

Employee stock ownership plan (ESOP) – A stock bonus plan that borrows money from, or on the guarantee of, *a related party* (a *party in interest* as defined in section 3(14) of ERISA) for the purpose of acquiring securities issued by the plan sponsor and that invests primarily in such securities (a leveraged ESOP). The term "employee stock ownership plan" is also generally applied to (*a*) nonleveraged stock bonus plans that satisfy various requirements set forth in section 4975(e)(7) of the IRC and (*b*) profit-sharing plans (and certain pre-ERISA money purchase pension plans) that invest primarily in securities issued by the plan sponsor.

ERISA – The employee retirement income security Act of 1974.

ERISA plan – A plan that is subject to ERISA.

ESOT – Trust for an Employee Stock Ownership Plan.

Fair value – The amount that the plan could reasonably expect to receive for a plan investment in a current sale between a willing buyer and a willing seller.

FASB – Financial Accounting Standards Board.

Form 5500 – A joint-agency form developed by the IRS, DOL, and PBGC, which may be used to satisfy the annual reporting requirements of the IRC and Titles I and IV or ERISA.

Frozen plan – See **Wasting trust**.

Full-scope audit – An audit of the financial statements of an employee benefit plan in accordance with generally accepted auditing standards.

Funding agency – An organization or individual, such as a specific corporate or individual trustee or an insurance company, that provides facilities for the accumulation of assets to be used for paying benefits under a plan; an organization, such as a specific life insurance company, that provides facilities for the purchase of such benefits.

Funding policy – The program regarding the amounts and timing of contributions by the employer(s), participants, and any other sources (e.g., state subsidies or federal grants) to provide the benefits a plan specifies.

GAAP – Generally Accepted Accounting Principles.

GAAS – Generally Accepted Auditing Standards.

GASB – Governmental Accounting Standards Board.

General account – An undivided fund maintained by an insurance company that commingles plan assets with other assets of the insurance company for investment purposes. That is, funds held by an insurance company that are not maintained in a separate account are in its general account.

Guaranteed investment contract (GIC) – A contract between an insurance company and a plan that provides for a guaranteed return on principal invested over a specified time period.

HCE – Highly compensated employee.

HDHP – High-deductible health plans.

Health and welfare benefit plan – A plan that provides (*a*) medical, dental, visual, psychiatric, or long-term health care; severance benefits; life insurance; accidental death or dismemberment benefits; (*b*) unemployment, disability, vacation or holiday benefits; and (*c*) apprenticeships, tuition assistance, day-care, housing subsidies, or legal services benefits.

HIPPA – Health Insurance Portability and Accountability Act of 1996.

HRA – Health reimbursement account.

HSA – Health savings account.

IBNR – Claims incurred by eligible participants but not yet reported to the plan.

Immediate participation guarantee contract (IPG) – A type of contract under which contributions are not currently applied to the purchase of single-payment deferred annuities for individual participants. Payments to the insurance company that are intended to provide future benefits to present employees, plus its share of the insurance company's actual investment income, are credited to an account. The insurance company is obligated to make lifetime benefit payments to retired employees.

Individual separate account – A separate account in which only one plan participates. Also referred to as a separate-separate account.

Insured plan – A plan funded through an insurance contract.

Investment fund option – An investment alternative provided to a participant in a defined contribution plan. The alternatives are usually pooled fund vehicles, such as registered investment companies (meaning, mutual funds); commingled funds of banks, or insurance company pooled separate accounts providing varying kinds of investments, e.g., equity funds and fixed income funds. The participant may select from among the various available alternatives and periodically change that selection.

Investment unit – See **Unit of participation.**

IRA – Individual retirement account.

IRC – Internal Revenue Code.

IRS – Internal Revenue Service.

Keogh plan – Also called an HR 10 plan, any defined benefit or defined contribution plan that covers one or more self-employed individuals.

KSOP – ESOP that also has a 401(k) feature.

Limited-scope audit – An audit in which ERISA allows the plan administrator to instruct the auditor not to perform any auditing procedures with respect to information prepared and certified by a bank or similar institution, or by an insurance carrier that is regulated, supervised, and subject to periodic examination by a state or federal agency.

Master trust – A combined trust account made up of assets of some or all of the employee benefit plans of a company that sponsors more than one plan or a group of corporations under common control. Each plan has an undivided interest in the assets of the trust, and ownership is represented by a record of proportionate dollar interest or by units of participation.

Money purchase pension plan – A defined contribution plan under which employer contributions are based on a fixed formula that is not related to profit and that is designated as a pension plan by the plan sponsor.

Multiemployer plan – A plan in which more than one employer is required to contribute that is maintained pursuant to one or more collective bargaining agreements.

Multiple-employer plan – A plan that involves more than one employer and includes only plans whose contributions from individual employers are available to pay benefits to all participants.

Named fiduciary – The individual responsible for the operation and administration of a plan including the identification of a plan administrator, usually an officer or other employee of the plan sponsor who reports to the plan sponsor's board of directors or management.

Net asset information – Information regarding the net assets available for benefits.

Net assets available for benefits – The difference between a plan's assets and its liabilities. For purposes of this definition, a plan's liabilities do not include participants' accumulated plan benefits.

Noncontributory plan – An employee benefit plan under which participants do not make contributions.

Nonvested benefit information – The actuarial present value of nonvested accumulated plan benefits.

Participant – Any employee or former employee, or any member or former member of a trade or other employee association, or the beneficiaries of those individuals, for whom there are accumulated plan benefits.

Participant directed investment programs – A plan provides for participant-directed investment programs if it allows participants to choose among various investment alternatives. The available alternatives are usually pooled fund vehicles, such as registered investment companies or commingled funds of banks that provide varying kinds of investments – e.g., equity funds and fixed income funds. The participant may select among the various available alternatives and periodically change that selection.

Participating contract – An allocated contract that provides for plan participation in the investment performance and experience (e.g., mortality experience) of the insurance company.

Participation right – A plan's right under a participating contract to receive future dividends from the insurance company.

Party in interest – A fiduciary or employee of the plan, any person who provides services to the plan, an employer whose employees are covered by the plan, an employee association whose members are covered by the plan, a person who owns 50% or more of such an employer or employee association, or relatives of such person just listed.

PBGC – The Pension Benefit Guaranty Corporation.

PCAOB – Public Company Accounting Oversight Board.

Pension benefits – Periodic (usually monthly) payments made to a person who has retired from employment.

Pension fund – The assets of a pension plan held by a funding agency.

Pension plan – See **Defined benefit pension plan**.

Plan administrator – The person or group of persons responsible for the content and issuance of a plan's financial statements in much the same way that management is responsible for the content and issuance of a business enterprise's financial statements.

Pooled separate account – A separate account in which several plans participate.

Prior service costs – See **Supplemental actuarial value**.

Profit-sharing plan – A defined contribution plan that is not a pension plan (as defined in the IRC) or a stock bonus plan. Employer contributions may be discretionary or may be based on a fixed formula related to profits, compensation, or other factors. Before 1987, contributions had to be made from the plan sponsor's current or accumulated profits. This requirement is no longer in effect. A profit-sharing plan must be designated as such in the plan document.

Prohibited transaction – A transaction between a plan and a party in interest that is prohibited under section 406(a) of ERISA.

Reporting date – The date of which information regarding the net assets available for benefits is presented.

Retired life fund – That portion of the funds under an immediate participation guarantee contract that is designated as supporting benefit payments to current retirees.

SAS – Statement of Auditing Standards.

SEC – Securities and Exchanges Commission.

Self-directed plan – A defined contribution plan in which the participant authorizes specific investment transactions, such as purchases and sales of specific common stocks or bonds. A self-directed plan does not provide predetermined investment fund options.

Self-funded plan – A plan funded through accumulated contributions and investment income.

Separate account – A special account established by an insurance company solely for the purpose of investing the assets of one or more plans. Funds in a separate account are not commingled with other assets or the insurance company for investment purposes.

Service – Periods of employment taken into consideration under an employee benefit plan.

Single employer plan – A plan sponsored by one employer.

SOP – Statement of Position.

Split-funded plan – A plan funded through a combination of accumulated contributions and investment income and insurance contracts.

Sponsor – In the case of a pension plan established or maintained by a single employer, the employer; in the case of a plan established or maintained by an employee organization, the employee organization; in the case of a plan established or maintained jointly by two or more employers or by one or more employers and one or more employee organizations, the association, committee, joint board of trustees, or other group of representatives of the parties who have established or who maintain the pension plan.

Stock bonus plan – A defined contribution plan under which distributions are normally made in stock of the employer, unless the distributee elects otherwise.

Supplemental actuarial value – The amount assigned under the actuarial cost method in use for years before a given date.

Target benefit plan – A form of money purchase pension plan under which the employer's annual contribution on behalf of each participation is the actuarially determined amount required to fund a target benefit established by a plan formula. The target benefit is usually based on compensation and length of service. For some target benefit plans, the substance of the plan may be to provide a defined benefit.

Tax credit employee stock ownership plan – A profit-sharing or stock bonus plan established before 1987 that satisfies the requirements of section 409 of the IRC. The sponsor of such a plan is allowed a tax credit, rather than a deduction, for its contributions. Before 1982 these plans were commonly known as TRASOPs (for Tax Reduction Act Stock Ownership Plan), and the maximum allowable credit was based on the plan sponsor's investments that qualified for the investment tax credit. In 1982, TRASOPs were succeeded by PAYSOPs, under which the credit was based on the plan sponsor's payroll.

Third-party administrator (TPA) – A party unrelated to the plan who contracts to be responsible for plan administration.

Thrift plan – A profit-sharing or stock bonus plan under which participants make after-tax employee contributions that are usually matched, in whole or in part, by employer contributions.

Unallocated contract – A contract with an insurance company under which related payments to the insurance company are accumulated in an unallocated fund to be used to meet benefit payments when employees retire, either directly or through the purchase of annuities. Funds in an unallocated contract may also be withdrawn and otherwise invested.

Unfunded plan – A plan whereby benefits are paid directly from the general assets of the employer or the employee organization that sponsors the plan.

Unit of participation – An undivided interest in the underlying assets of a trust.

Vested benefit information – The actuarial present value of vested accumulated plan benefits.

Vested benefits – Benefits that are not contingent on an employee's future service.

Wasting trust – A plan under which participants no longer accrue benefits but that will remain in existence as long as necessary to pay already-accrued benefits.

Accounting and Auditing Glossary

Account – Formal record that represents, in words, money or other unit of measurement, certain resources, claims to such resources, transactions or other events that result in changes to those resources and claims.

Account payable – Amount owed to a creditor for delivered goods or completed services.

Account receivable – Claim against a debtor for an uncollected amount, generally from a completed transaction of sales or services rendered.

Accountants' report – Formal document that communicates an independent accountant's (1) expression of limited assurance on financial statements as a result of performing inquiry and analytic procedures (Review Report); (2) results of procedures performed (type of Attestation Report); (3) non-expression of opinion or any form of assurance on a presentation in the form of financial statements information that is the representation of management (Compilation Report); or (4) an opinion on an assertion made by management in accordance with the Statements on Standards for Attestation Engagements (Attestation Report). An accountant's report does not result from the performance of an audit.

Accounting – Recording and reporting of financial transactions, including the origination of the transaction, its recognition, processing, and summarization in the financial statements.

Accounting change – Change in (1) an accounting principle; (2) an accounting estimate; or (3) the reporting entity. The correction of an error in previously issued financial statements is not an accounting change.

Accrual basis – Method of accounting that recognizes revenue when earned, rather than when collected. Expenses are recognized when incurred rather than when paid.

Accrued expense – An expense incurred during an accounting period for which payment is not due until a later accounting period. This results from the purchase of services which at the time of accounting have only been partly performed, are not yet billable, or have not been paid for.

Accumulated depreciation – Total depreciation pertaining to an asset or group of assets from the time the assets were placed in service until the date of the financial statement or tax return. This total is the contra account to the related asset account.

Additional paid in capital – Amounts paid for stock in excess of its par value or stated value. Also, other amounts paid by stockholders and charged to equity accounts other than capital stock.

Adjusting entries – Accounting entries made at the end of an accounting period to allocate items between accounting periods.

Amortization – The process of reducing a recognized liability systematically by recognizing revenues or by reducing a recognized asset systematically by recognizing expenses or costs. In accounting for postretirement benefits, amortization also means the systematic recognition in net periodic postretirement benefit cost over several periods of amounts previously recognized in other comprehensive income, that is, gains or losses, prior service cost or credits, and any transition obligation or asset.

Analytical procedures – Substantive tests of financial information which examine relationships among data as a means of obtaining evidence. Such procedures include (1) comparison of financial information with information of comparable prior periods; (2) comparison of financial information with anticipated results (e.g., forecasts); (3) study of relationships between elements of financial information that should conform to predictable patterns based on the entity's experience; and (4) comparison of financial information with industry norms.

Annual report – The annual report to shareholders is the principal document used by most public companies to disclose corporate information to their shareholders. It is usually a state-of-the-company report, including an opening letter from the Chief Executive Officer, financial data, results of continuing operations, market segment information, new product plans, subsidiary activities, and research and development activities on future programs. The Form 10-K, which must be filed with the SEC, typically contains more detailed information about the company's financial condition than the annual report.

Assertion – Explicit or implicit representations by an entity's management that are embodied in financial statement components and for which the auditor obtains and evaluates evidential matter when forming his/her opinion on the entity's financial statements.

Audit risk – The risk that the auditor may unknowingly fail to modify appropriately his/her opinion on financial statements that are materially misstated.

Audit sampling – Application of an audit procedure to less than 100% of the items within an account balance or class of transactions for the purpose of evaluating some characteristic of the balance or class.

Auditors' report – Written communication issued by an independent certified public accountant (CPA) describing the character of his/her work and the degree of responsibility taken. An auditor's report includes a statement that the audit was conducted in accordance with generally accepted auditing standards (GAAS), which require that the auditor plan and perform the audit to obtain reasonable assurance about whether the financial statements are free of material misstatement, as well as a statement that the auditor believes the audit provides a reasonable basis for his/her opinion.

Bad debt – All or portion of an account, loan, or note receivable considered to be uncollectible.

Balance sheet – Basic financial statement, usually accompanied by appropriate disclosures that describe the basis of accounting used in its preparation and presentation of a specified date the entity's assets, liabilities, and the equity of its owners. Also known as a statement of financial condition.

Bond – One type of long-term promissory note, frequently issued to the public as a security regulated under federal securities laws or state blue sky laws. Bonds can either be registered in the owner's name or are issued as bearer instruments.

Book value – Amount, net or contra account balances, that an asset or liability shows on the balance sheet of a company. Also known as carrying value.

Business combinations – Combining of two entities. Under the purchase method of accounting, one entity is deemed to acquire another and there is a new basis of accounting for the assets and liabilities of the acquired company.

Business segment – Any division of an organization authorized to operate, within prescribed or otherwise established limitations, under substantial control by its own management.

Capital stock – Ownership shares of a corporation authorized by its articles of incorporation. The money value assigned to a corporation's issued shares. The balance sheet account with the aggregate amount of the par value or stated value of all stock issued by a corporation.

Capitalized cost – Expenditure identified with goods or services acquired and measured by the amount of cash paid or the market value of other property, capital stock, or services surrendered. Expenditures that are written off during two or more accounting periods.

Carrying value – Amount, net or contra account balances, that an asset or liability shows on the balance sheet of a company. Also known as book value.

Cash basis – A special purpose framework in which revenues and expenditures are recorded when they are received and paid.

Cash equivalents – Short-term (generally less than three months), highly liquid investments that are convertible to known amounts of cash.

Cash flows – Net of cash receipts and cash disbursements relating to a particular activity during a specified accounting period.

Casualty loss – Sudden property loss caused by theft, accident, or natural causes.

Change in engagement – A request, before the completion of the audit (review), to change the engagement to a review or compilation (compilation) of financial statements.

Class actions – A federal securities class action is a court action filed on behalf of a group of shareholders under Rule 23 of the Federal Rules of Civil Procedure. Instead of each shareholder bringing an individual lawsuit, one or more shareholders bring a class action for the entire class of shareholders.

Common stock – Capital stock having no preferences generally in terms of dividends, voting rights, or distributions.

Companies, going public – Companies become public entities for different reasons, but usually to raise additional capital. The SEC has prepared a guide for companies – Q&A: Small Business and the SEC – that provides a basic understanding about the various ways companies can become public and what securities laws apply. The SEC also has a list of some of the registration and reporting forms and related regulations that pertain to small and large companies.

Comparative financial statement – Financial statement presentation in which the current amounts and the corresponding amounts for previous periods or dates also are shown.

Compilation – Presentation in the form of financial statements information that is the representation of management (owners) without the accountant's assurance as to conformity with generally accepted accounting principles (GAAP).

Comprehensive income – Change in equity of a business entity during a period from transactions and other events and circumstances from nonowner sources. The period includes all changes in equity except those resulting from investments by owners and distributions to owners.

Confirmation – Auditor's receipt of a written or oral response from an independent third party verifying the accuracy of information requested.

Consolidated financial statements – Combined financial statements of a parent company and one or more of its subsidiaries as one economic unit.

Consolidation – The presentation of a single set of amounts for an entire reporting entity. Consolidation requires elimination of intra-entity transactions and balances.

Contingent liability – Potential liability arising from a past transaction or a subsequent event.

Continuing accountant – An accountant who has been engaged to audit, review, or compile and report on the financial statements of the current period and one or more consecutive periods immediately prior to the current period.

Control risk – Measure of risk that errors exceeding a tolerable amount will not be prevented or detected by an entity's internal controls.

Controls tests – Tests directed toward the design or operation of an internal control structure policy or procedure to assess its effectiveness in preventing or detecting material misstatements in a financial report.

Current asset – Asset that one can reasonably expect to convert into cash, sell, or consume in operations within a single operating cycle, or within a year if more than one cycle is completed each year.

Current liability – Obligation whose liquidation is expected to require the use of existing resources classified as current assets, or the creation of other current liabilities.

Current value – (1) Value of an asset at the present time as compared with the asset's historical cost. (2) In finance, the amount determined by discounting the future revenue stream of an asset using compound interest principles.

Debt – General name for money, notes, bonds, goods, or services which represent amounts owed.

Definite criteria – A special purpose framework using a definite set of criteria having substantial support that is applied to all material items appearing in financial statements, such as the price-level basis of accounting.

Depreciation – Expense allowance made for wear and tear on an asset over its estimated useful life.

Derivatives – Derivatives are financial instruments whose performance is derived, at least in part, from the performance of an underlying asset, security or index. For example, a stock option is a derivative because its value changes in relation to the price movement of the underlying stock.

Detection risk – Risk that the auditor will not detect a material misstatement.

Disclosure – Process of divulging accounting information so that the content of financial statements is understood.

Discount – Reduction from the full amount of a price or debt.

Dividends – Distribution of earnings to owners of a corporation in cash, other assets of the corporation, or the corporation's capital stock.

Earnings per share (EPS) – The amount of earnings attributable to each share of common stock. For convenience, the term is used to refer to either earnings or loss per share.

Employee stock options plans – An employee stock ownership plan is an employee benefit plan that is described by the Employee Retirement Income Security Act of 1974 and the Internal Revenue Code of 1986 as a stock bonus plan, or combination stock bonus and money purchase pension plan, designed to invest primarily in employer stock. Also called an employee share ownership plan. Employee Stock Options Plans should not be confused with the term "ESOPs," or Employee Stock Ownership Plans, which are retirement plans.

Employee stock ownership plans (ESOPs) – An employee stock ownership plan (ESOP) is a retirement plan in which the company contributes its stock to the plan for the benefit of the company's employees. With an ESOP, you never buy or hold the stock directly. This type of plan should not be confused with employee stock options plans, which are not retirement plans. Instead, employee stock options plans give the employee the right to buy their company's stock at a set price within a certain period of time.

Equity – Residual interest in the assets of an entity that remains after deducting its liabilities. Also, the amount of a business' total assets, less total liabilities. Also, the third section of a balance sheet, the other two being assets and liabilities.

Equity security – Any security representing an ownership interest in an entity (for example, common, preferred, or other capital stock) or the right to acquire (for example, warrants, rights, and call options) or dispose of (for example, put options) an ownership interest in an entity at fixed or determinable prices. However, the term does not include convertible debt or preferred stock that by its terms either must be redeemed by the issuing entity or is redeemable at the option of the investor.

Error – Act that departs from what should be done; imprudent deviation, unintentional mistake or omission.

Executive compensation: Where to find in SEC reports – The federal securities laws require clear, concise and understandable disclosure about compensation paid to CEOs and certain other high-ranking executive officers of public companies. You can locate information about executive pay in (1) the company's annual proxy statement; (2) the company's annual report on Form 10-K; and (3) registration statements filed by the company to register securities for sale to the public.

Expenditures – Expenditures to which capitalization rates are to be applied are capitalized expenditures (net of progress payment collections) for the qualifying asset that have required the payment of cash, the transfer of other assets, or the incurring of a liability on which interest is recognized (in contrast to liabilities, such as trade payables, accruals, and retainages on which interest is not recognized).

Extraordinary items – Events and transactions distinguished by their unusual nature and by the infrequency of their occurrence. Extraordinary items are reported separately, less applicable income taxes, in the entity's statement of income or operations.

Fair disclosure, regulation FD – On August 15, 2000, the SEC adopted Regulation FD to address the selective disclosure of information by companies and other issuers. Regulation FD provides that when an issuer discloses material nonpublic information to certain individuals or entities – generally, securities market professionals, such as stock analysts, or holders of the issuer's securities who may well trade on the basis of the information – the issuer must make public disclosure of that information. In this way, the new rule aims to promote the full and fair disclosure.

Fair market value – Price at which property would change hands between a buyer and a seller without any compulsion to buy or sell.

Federal securities laws – The laws that govern the securities industry, include the Securities Act of 1933; Securities Exchange Act of 1934; Investment Company Act of 1940; Investment Advisers Act of 1940; and Public Utility Holding Company Act of 1935.

Financial statements – Presentation of financial data including balance sheets, income statements and statements of cash flow, or any supporting statement that is intended to communicate an entity's financial position at a point in time and its results of operations for a period then ended.

First in, first out (FIFO) – Accounting method of valuing inventory under which the costs of the first goods acquired are the first costs charged to expense. Commonly known as FIFO.

Fiscal year – Period of 12 consecutive months chosen by an entity as its accounting period which may or may not be a calendar year.

Fixed asset – Any tangible asset with a life of more than one year used in an entity's operations.

Foreign currency translation – Restating foreign currency in equivalent dollars; unrealized gains or losses are postponed and carried in Stockholder's Equity until the foreign operation is substantially liquidated.

Form 10-K – This is the report that most publicly traded companies file with the SEC on an annual basis. It provides a comprehensive overview of the company's business and financial condition. Some companies choose to send their Form 10-K to their shareholders instead of sending a separate annual report. Currently, Form 10-K must be filed with the SEC within 90 days after the end of the company's fiscal year.

Form 10-Q – The Form 10-Q is a report filed quarterly by most reporting companies. It includes unaudited financial statements and provides a continuing view of the company's financial position during the year. The report must be filed for each of the first three fiscal quarters of the company's fiscal year and is currently due within 45 days of the close of the quarter. In addition to Form 10-Q, companies provide annual reports to their shareholders and file Form 10-K on an annual basis with the SEC.

Form 8-K – This is the "current report" used to report material events or corporate changes that have previously not been reported by the company in a quarterly report (Form 10-Q) or annual report (Form 10-K).

Forms 3, 4, 5 – Corporate insiders-meaning a company's officers and directors, and any beneficial owners of more than 10% of a class of the company's equity securities registered under Section 12 of the Securities Exchange Act of 1934 – must file with the SEC a statement of ownership regarding those securities. The initial filing is on Form 3. Changes in ownership are reported on Form 4. Insiders must file a Form 5 to report any transactions that should have been reported earlier on a Form 4 or were eligible for deferred reporting.

Fraud – Willful misrepresentation by one person of a fact inflicting damage on another person.

Gain – Excess of revenues received over costs relating to a specific transaction.

General ledger – Collection of all assets, liability, owners' equity, revenue, and expense accounts.

Generally accepted accounting principles (GAAP) – Conventions, rules, and procedures necessary to define accepted accounting practice at a particular time. The highest level of such principles is set by the Financial Accounting Standards Board (FASB).

Generally accepted auditing standards (GAAS) – Standards set by the American Institute of Certified Public Accountants (AICPA) which concern the auditor's professional qualities and judgment in the performance of his/her audit and in the actual report.

Going concern – Assumption that a business can remain in operation long enough for all of its current plans to be carried out.

Going private – A company "goes private" when it reduces the number of its shareholders to fewer than 300 and is no longer required to file reports with the SEC.

Goodwill – An asset representing the future economic benefits arising from other assets acquired in a business combination or an acquisition by a not for profit entity that are not individually identified and separately recognized.

Gross income – A tax term meaning all income from whatever source derived, except as otherwise provided in the income tax code.

Guaranty – Legal arrangement involving a promise by one person to perform the obligations of a second person to a third person, in the event the second person fails to perform.

Hedges – Protect an entity against the risk of adverse price or interest-rate movements on its assets, liabilities, or anticipated transactions. A hedge is used to avoid or reduce risks by creating a relationship by which losses on positions are counterbalanced by gains on separate positions in another market.

Historical cost – The generally accepted method of accounting used in the primary financial statements that is based on measures of historical prices without restatement into units, each of which has the same general purchasing power.

Income – Inflow of revenue during a period of time.

Income statement – Summary of the effect of revenues and expenses over a period of time.

Income tax basis – A special purpose framework that the reporting entity uses or expects to use to file its income tax return for the period covered by the financial statements.

Initial public offerings (IPO) – IPO stands for initial public offering and occurs when a company first sells its shares to the public.

Initial public offerings, lockup agreements – Lockup agreements prohibit company insiders – including employees, their friends and family, and venture capitalists – from selling their shares for a set period of time. In other words, the shares are "locked up." Before a company goes public, the company and its underwriter typically enter into a lockup agreement to ensure that shares owned by these insiders do not enter the public market too soon after the offering.

Insider trading – "Insider trading" actually includes both legal and illegal conduct. The legal version is when corporate insiders – officers, directors, and employees – buy and sell stock in their own companies. Illegal insider trading refers generally to buying or selling a security, in breach of a fiduciary duty or other relationship of trust and confidence, while in possession of material, nonpublic information about the security. Insider trading violations may also include "tipping" such information, securities trading by the person "tipped," and securities trading by those who misappropriate such information.

Intangible asset – Asset having no physical existence such as trademarks and patents.

Interest – Payment for the use or forbearance of money.

Interim financial statements – Financial statements that report the operations of an entity for less than one year.

Internal control – Process designed to provide reasonable assurance regarding achievement of various management objectives such as the reliability of financial reports.

Inventory – Tangible property held for sale, or materials used in a production process to make a product.

Investment – Expenditure used to purchase goods or services that could produce a return to the investor.

Journal – Any book containing original entries of daily financial transactions.

Last in, first out (LIFO) – Accounting method of valuing inventory under which the costs of the last goods acquired are the first costs charged to expense. Commonly known as LIFO.

Lease – Conveyance of land, buildings, equipment, or other assets from one person (Lessor) to another (Lessee) for a specific period of time for monetary or other consideration, usually in the form of rent.

Leasehold – Property interest a lessee owns in the leased property.

Ledger – Any book of accounts containing the summaries of debit and credit entries.

Lessee – Person or entity that has the right to use property under the terms of a lease.

Lessor – Owner of property, the temporary use of which is transferred to another (lessee) under the terms of a lease.

Liability – Debts or obligations owed by one entity (Debtor) to another entity (Creditor) payable in money, goods, or services.

Listing and delisting requirements – Before a company can begin trading on an exchange or the Nasdaq Stock Market, it must meet certain initial requirements or "listing standards." The exchanges and the Nasdaq Stock Market set their own standards for listing and continuing to trade. The SEC does not set listing standards. The initial listing requirements mandate that a company meet specified minimum thresholds for the number of publicly traded shares, total market value, stock price, and number of shareholders. After a company starts trading, it must continue to meet different standards set by the exchanges or the Nasdaq Stock Market. Otherwise, the company can be delisted. These continuing standards usually are less stringent than the initial listing requirements.

Long-term debt – Debt with a maturity of more than one year from the current date.

Loss – Excess of expenditures over revenue for a period or activity. Also, for tax purposes, an excess of basis over the amount realized in a transaction.

Lower of cost or market – Valuing assets for financial reporting purposes. Ordinarily, "cost" is the purchase price of the asset and "market" refers to its current replacement cost. Generally accepted accounting principles (GAAP) requires that certain assets (e.g., inventories) be carried at the lower of cost or market.

Management discussion and analysis (MD&A) – SEC requirement in financial reporting for an explanation by management of significant changes in operations, assets, and liquidity.

Manipulation – Manipulation is intentional conduct designed to deceive investors by controlling or artificially affecting the market for a security. Manipulation can involve a number of techniques to affect the supply of, or demand for, a stock. They include spreading false or misleading information about a company; improperly limiting the number of publicly-available shares; or rigging quotes, prices, or trades to create a false or deceptive picture of the demand for a security.

Marketable securities – Stocks and other negotiable instruments which can be easily bought and sold on either listed exchanges or over-the-counter markets.

Mark-to-market – Method of valuing assets that results in adjustment of an asset's carrying amount to its market value.

Matching principle – The concept that all costs and expenses incurred in generating revenues must be recognized in the same reporting period as the related revenues.

Materiality – Magnitude of an omission or misstatements of accounting information that, in the light of surrounding circumstances, makes it probable that the judgment of a reasonable person relying on the information would change or be influenced.

Mergers – Mergers are business transactions involving the combination of two or more companies into a single entity. Most state laws require that mergers be approved by at least a majority of the company's shareholders if the merger will have a significant impact on the company.

Modified cash basis – A special purpose framework that begins with the cash basis method (see **Cash basis**) and applies modifications having substantial support, such as recording depreciation on fixed assets or accruing income taxes.

Nasdaq – Nasdaq stands for the National Association of Securities Dealers Automated Quotation System. Unlike the New York Stock Exchange where trades take place on an exchange, Nasdaq is an electronic stock market that uses a computerized system to provide brokers and dealers with price quotes. The National Association of Securities Dealers, Inc. owns and operates The Nasdaq Stock Market.

Net assets – Excess of the value of securities owned, cash, receivables, and other assets over the liabilities of the company.

Net income – Excess or deficit of total revenues and gains compared with total expenses and losses for an accounting period.

Net sales – Sales at gross invoice amounts less any adjustments for returns, allowances, or discounts taken.

Net worth – Similar to equity, the excess of assets over liabilities.

Nonpublic entity – Any entity other than (a) one whose securities trade in a public market either on a stock exchange (domestic or foreign) or in the over-the-counter market, including securities quoted only locally or regionally; (b) one that makes a filing with a regulatory agency in preparation for the sale of any class of its securities in a public market; or (c) a subsidiary, corporate joint venture, or other entity controlled by an entity covered by (a) or (b).

No-par stock – Stock authorized to be issued but for which no par value is set in the articles of incorporation. A stated value is set by the board of directors on the issuance of this type of stock.

No-par value – Stock or bond that does not have a specific value indicated.

Notional – Value assigned to assets or liabilities that is not based on cost or market (e.g., the value of a service not yet rendered).

Objectivity – Emphasizing or expressing the nature of reality as it is apart from personal reflection or feelings; independence of mind.

Paid in capital – Portion of the stockholders' equity which was paid in by the stockholders, as opposed to capital arising from profitable operations.

Par value – Amount per share set in the articles of incorporation of a corporation to be entered in the capital stocks account where it is left permanently and signifies a cushion of equity capital for the protection of creditors.

Parent company – Company that has a controlling interest in the common stock of another.

Predecessor accountant – An accountant who (a) has reported on the most recent compiled or reviewed financial statements or was engaged to perform but did not complete a compilation or review of the financial statements, and (b) has resigned, declined to stand for reappointment, or been notified that his or her services have been or may be terminated.

Preferred stock – Type of capital stock that carries certain preferences over common stock, such as a prior claim on dividends and assets.

Premium – (1) Excess amount paid for a bond over its face amount. (2) In insurance, the cost of specified coverage for a designated period of time.

Prepaid expense – Cost incurred to acquire economically useful goods or services that are expected to be consumed in the revenue-earning process within the operating cycle.

Prescribed form – Any standard preprinted form designed or adopted by the body to which it is to be submitted, for example, forms used by industry trade associations, credit agencies, banks, and governmental and regulatory bodies other than those concerned with the sale or trading of securities. A form designed or adopted by the entity whose financial statements are to be compiled is not considered to be a prescribed form.

Present value – Current value of a given future cash flow stream, discounted at a given rate.

Principal – Face amount of a security, exclusive of any premium or interest. The basis for interest computations.

Proxy statement – The SEC requires that shareholders of a company whose securities are registered under Section 12 of the Securities Exchange Act of 1934 receive a proxy statement prior to a shareholder meeting, whether an annual or special meeting. The information contained in the statement must be filed with the SEC before soliciting a shareholder vote on the election of directors and the approval of other corporate action. Solicitations, whether by management or shareholders, must disclose all important facts about the issues on which shareholders are asked to vote.

Purchase method of accounting – Accounting for a merger by adding the acquired company's assets at the price paid for them to the acquiring company's assets.

Quiet period – The term "quiet period," also referred to as the "waiting period," is not defined under the federal securities laws. The quiet period extends from the time a company files a registration statement with the SEC until SEC staff declares the registration statement "effective." During this period, the federal securities laws limit what information a company and related parties can release to the public. Rule 134 of the Securities Act of 1933 discusses these limitations.

Ratio analysis – Comparison of actual or projected data for a particular company to other data for that company or industry in order to analyze trends or relationships.

Real property – Land and improvements, including buildings and personal property that is permanently attached to the land or customarily transferred with the land.

Receivables – Amounts of money due from customers or other debtors.

Reconciliation – Comparison of two numbers to demonstrate the basis for the difference between them.

Registration under the securities act of 1933 – Often referred to as the "truth in securities" law, the Securities Act of 1933 has two basic objectives: (1) To require that investors receive financial and other significant information concerning securities being offered for public sale; and (2) To prohibit deceit, misrepresentations, and other fraud in the sale of securities. The SEC accomplishes these goals primarily by requiring that companies disclose important financial information through the registration of securities. This information enables investors, not the government, to make informed judgments about whether to purchase a company's securities.

Regulation D offerings – Under the Securities Act of 1933, any offer to sell securities must either be registered with the SEC or meet an exemption. Regulation D (or Reg D) provides three exemptions from the registration requirements, allowing some smaller companies to offer and sell their securities without having to register the securities with the SEC.

Regulatory basis – A special purpose framework that the reporting entity uses to comply with the requirements or financial reporting provisions of a governmental regulatory agency to whose jurisdiction the entity is subject. An example is a basis of accounting insurance companies use pursuant to the rules of a state insurance commission.

Reissued report – A report issued subsequent to the date of the original report that bears the same date as the original report. A reissued report may need to be revised for the effects of specific events; in these circumstances, the report should be dual-dated with the original date and a separate date that applies to the effects of such events.

Related party transaction – Business or other transaction between persons who do not have an arm's-length relationship (e.g., a relationship with independent, competing interests). The most common is between family members or controlled entities. For tax purposes, these types of transactions are generally subject to a greater level of scrutiny.

Research and development (R&D) – Research is a planned activity aimed at discovery of new knowledge with the hope of developing new or improved products and services. Development is the translation of research findings into a plan or design of new or improved products and services.

Retained earnings – Accumulated undistributed earnings of a company retained for future needs or for future distribution to its owners.

Revenue recognition – Method of determining whether or not income has met the conditions of being earned and realized or is realizable.

Revenues – Sales of products, merchandise, and services; and earnings from interest, dividend, rents.

Review – Accounting service that provides some assurance as to the reliability of financial information. In a review, a certified public accountant (CPA) does not conduct an examination under generally accepted auditing standards (GAAS). Instead, the accountant performs inquiry and analytical procedures that provide the accountant with a reasonable basis for expressing limited assurance that there are no material modifications that should be made to the statements for them to be in conformity with GAAP or, if applicable, with a special purpose framework.

Risk management – Process of identifying and monitoring business risks in a manner that offers a risk/return relationship that is acceptable to an entity's operating philosophy.

Security – Any kind of transferable certificate of ownership including equity securities and debt securities.

Short-term – Current; ordinarily due within one year.

SSARS – Statements on Standards for Accounting And Review Services issued by the AICPA Accounting and Review Services Committee (ARSC).

Start-up costs – (1) Costs, excluding acquisition costs, incurred to bring a new unit into production. (2) Costs incurred to begin a business.

Statement of cash flows – A statement of cash flows is one of the basic financial statements that is required as part of a complete set of financial statements prepared in conformity with generally accepted accounting principles. It categorizes net cash provided or used during a period as operating, investing and financing activities, and reconciles beginning and ending cash and cash equivalents.

Statement of financial condition – Basic financial statement, usually accompanied by appropriate disclosures that describe the basis of accounting used in its preparation and presentation as of a specified date, the entity's assets, liabilities, and the equity of its owners. Also known as *balance sheet*.

Statutory basis – See **Regulatory basis**.

Straight-line depreciation – Accounting method that reflects an equal amount of wear and tear during each period of an asset's useful life. For instance, the annual straight-line depreciation of a $10,000 asset expected to last ten years is $1,000.

Strike price – Price of a financial instrument at which conversion or exercise occurs.

Submission of financial statements – Presenting to a client or third party's financial statements that the accountant has prepared either manually or through the use of computer software.

Subsequent event – Material event that occurs after the end of the accounting period and before the publication of an entity's financial statements. Such events are disclosed in the notes to the financial statements.

Successor accountant – An accountant who has been invited to make a proposal for an engagement to compile or review financial statements and is considering accepting the engagement or an accountant who has accepted such an engagement.

Tangible asset – Assets having a physical existence, such as cash, land, buildings, machinery, or claims on property, investments or goods in process.

Tax – Charge levied by a governmental unit on income, consumption, wealth, or other basis.

Third party – All parties except for members of management who are knowledgeable about the nature of the procedures applied and the basis of accounting and assumptions used in the preparation of the financial statements.

Trade date – Date when a security transaction is entered into, to be settled on at a later date. Transactions involving financial instruments are generally accounted for on the trade date.

Treasury bill – Short-term obligation that bears no interest and is sold at a discount.

Treasury bond – Long-term obligation that matures more than five years from issuance and bears interest.

Treasury note – Intermediate-term obligation that matures one to five years from issuance and bears interest.

Treasury stock – Stock reacquired by the issuing company. It may be held indefinitely, retired, issued upon exercise of stock options, or resold.

Trial balance – A trial balance consists of a listing of all of the general ledger accounts and their corresponding debit or credit balances. Also, in a trial balance, no attempt is made to establish a mathematical relationship among the assets, liabilities, equity, revenues, and expenses except that total debits equal total credits.

Unearned income – Payments received for services which have not yet been performed.

Updated report – A report issued by a continuing accountant that takes into consideration information that he/she becomes aware of during his/her current engagement and that reexpresses his/her previous conclusions or, depending on the circumstances, expresses different conclusions on the financial statements of a prior period as of the date of his/her current report.

Valuation allowance – Method of lowering or raising an object's current value by adjusting its acquisition cost to reflect its market value by use of a contra account.

Variance – Deviation or difference between an estimated value and the actual value.

Work in progress – Inventory account consisting of partially completed goods awaiting completion and transfer to finished inventory.

Working capital – Excess of current assets over current liabilities.

Working papers – (1) Records kept by the auditor of the procedures applied, the tests performed, the information obtained, and the pertinent conclusions reached in the course of the audit. (2) Any records developed by a certified public accountant (CPA) during an audit.

Yield – Return on an investment an investor receives from dividends or interest expressed as a percentage of the cost of the security.

Index

A

Absence 2-19, 2-34,
    3-16, 3-18, 6-11, 6-29
Accounting Estimates 2-20, 2-27,
    2-33, 3-7, 3-11, 4-9, 6-47, 6-48
Accrued Liabilities 4-31
Audit Risk Factors 2-15

B

Benefit Claims Payable 7-24

C

Cash Balances 4-29
Commitments 2-19, 2-23,
    6-2, 6-10, 6-11, 6-12, 6-13, 7-24, 7-26
Common/Commingled Trust Funds 4-13, 5-8
Contingencies 2-30, 6-2,
    6-10, 6-11, 6-12, 6-13, 7-24
Contributions from Employers 1-4, 1-6, 5-9
Control Risk...2-8, 2-18,
    3-10, 3-12, 3-14, 3-17, 4-18

D

Derivatives 1-16, 2-19,
    4-9, 4-21, 4-22, 7-25
Disclosures...1-16, 2-15,
    2-34, 3-7, 3-11, 4-3, 4-4, 4-8, 4-10, 4-16, 4-19,
    4-24, 4-27, 6-8, 6-9, 6-11, 6-33, 6-36, 6-39, 6-47,
    6-48, 7-1, 7-3, 7-5, 7-11, 7-14, 7-16, 7-24, 7-25,
    7-26, 7-27
Discretionary... 1-3, 1-6,
    3-11, 4-11, 4-12, 5-9, 5-10
Discrimination...3-11, 4-31,
    6-2, 6-6, 6-7, 6-9
Documentation...1-17, 2-13,
    2-26, 3-9, 3-16, 3-17, 3-19, 4-10, 4-21, 4-22,
    4-27, 4-31, 5-4, 5-18, 5-20, 5-22, 6-45, 6-49, 7-4

E

Excess Contributions Refundable............ 4-31, 6-9

F

Form 11-K..1-10, 1-17,
    2-4, 3-2, 6-12, 6-44, 6-46, 7-7, 7-16, 7-17, 7-20
Form 5500..1-5, 1-10,
    1-11, 1-13, 1-14, 1-19, 2-4, 2-11, 2-18, 4-2, 4-7,
    4-9, 4-11, 4-17, 4-20, 4-24, 4-27, 4-28, 5-5, 5-14,
    6-1, 6-8, 6-12, 6-21, 6-22, 6-23, 6-24, 6-25, 6-26,
    6-28, 6-29, 6-30, 6-31, 6-32, 6-35, 6-37, 7-4, 7-7,
    7-14, 7-24, 7-25
Fraud 2-8, 2-11,
    2-15, 2-21, 2-22, 3-1, 3-2, 3-18, 6-8, 6-48
Fraudulent Financial Reporting 2-22, 2-23,
    2-24, 2-25, 2-28

G

Going Concern...2-7, 2-34,
    7-10, 7-27

I

Initial Audit... 2-3, 2-4, 6-41
Internal Control Structure.......................1-16, 2-12,
    2-21, 2-29, 2-32, 3-1, 3-7, 3-9, 3-10, 3-11, 4-14,
    6-9
Internet Recordkeeping System.............2-32, 3-16
Investments 1-3, 1-4,
    1-5, 1-6, 1-8, 1-19, 1-20, 2-3, 2-4, 2-5, 2-10, 2-12,
    2-18, 2-20, 2-21, 2-26, 2-27, 2-28, 2-29, 3-4, 3-5,
    3-6, 3-13, 4-1, 4-2, 4-4, 4-5, 4-6, 4-7, 4-8, 4-9,
    4-10, 4-11, 4-12, 4-13, 4-14, 4-15, 4-16, 4-17,
    4-18, 4-19, 4-20, 4-21, 4-22, 4-23, 4-24, 4-25,
    4-27, 4-28, 4-31, 5-1, 5-2, 5-3, 5-4, 5-5, 5-6, 5-8,
    5-13, 6-2, 6-3, 6-5, 6-13, 6-24, 6-25, 6-26, 6-28,
    6-31, 7-14, 7-16, 7-21, 7-24, 7-25, 7-26, 7-27

L

Limited-Scope Audit 1-19, 1-20, 2-3, 2-5, 3-4, 3-5, 3-6, 3-13, 4-24, 4-25, 5-7, 6-28, 6-30, 7-16, 7-21, 7-24

Limited-Scope Report............ 4-24, 7-21

Loans 1-4, 1-6, 1-8, 1-9, 1-10, 1-19, 2-12, 2-21, 2-26, 2-32, 3-4, 3-9, 3-11, 3-16, 4-2, 4-9, 4-16, 4-23, 4-24, 4-27, 4-28, 5-13, 5-19, 5-20, 6-10, 6-25, 6-26, 6-38, 7-26

M

Master Trusts 4-11, 4-13, 4-20

Misappropriation of Assets...........2-22, 2-25, 2-26, 2-27

Modified Reports................ 7-10, 7-12

N

Non-Exempt Transactions................1-8, 1-10, 6-25, 7-12

Non-GAAP.................................... 7-14

O

Omission........................ 2-23, 6-29, 6-30

Other Assets...............................2-25, 4-7, 4-30

Other Qualified Opinions....................... 7-14

P

Participant Eligibility 2-8, 2-10, 5-15, 5-17

Participant Loans 1-19, 4-23, 4-24, 4-27, 4-28, 5-13, 5-20, 6-25, 6-26, 7-26

Party-in-Interest Transactions...............1-16, 2-11, 2-12, 2-23, 2-30, 2-31, 6-1, 6-10, 6-36, 6-37

Plan Mergers...........................2-10, 6-35, 7-24, 7-27

Plan Tax Status 6-2

Plan Termination..................... 4-31, 6-32

Preliminary Analytical Review 2-14

R

Reconciliation 2-27, 5-13, 7-24, 7-25

Registered Investment Companies 4-6, 4-13, 5-5

Related-Party Transactions 2-23, 7-24

Reportable Conditions 6-8

Representations from Plan Management..................2-19, 6-14

Risks and Uncertainties 7-24, 7-27

S

Sarbanes-Oxley Act 1-17, 2-1, 2-4, 6-44, 7-7

Significant Accounting Policies......................6-47, 7-14, 7-24

Standard Report...........................7-7

Statement of Changes in Net Assets Available for Benefits................ 4-9, 5-1, 5-2, 5-3, 5-5, 5-8, 5-11, 6-42, 7-3, 7-4, 7-7, 7-16, 7-22

Subsequent Events..................6-12, 6-13, 6-33, 7-24

Supplemental Information 1-12, 2-26

Supplemental Schedules.........................1-8, 1-10, 1-20, 2-3, 2-4, 2-31, 4-9, 4-24, 6-1, 6-8, 6-21, 6-25, 6-26, 6-28, 6-29, 7-5, 7-7, 7-12, 7-21, 7-22

T

Terminating Plans..............................6-32

Third-Party Service Organizations 1-19, 2-3, 2-12, 2-29, 3-11

U

Unit Value Disclosures 7-24

V

Valuation...............................2-4, 2-22, 3-10, 4-5, 4-9, 4-10, 4-17, 4-19, 4-21, 6-32, 7-24, 7-26

Voice Response....................2-32, 3-16, 5-14, 5-17

W

Withdrawals.......................1-4, 1-19, 2-12, 2-27, 2-29, 2-32, 3-4, 3-11, 4-2, 4-13, 4-16, 4-24, 5-10, 5-13, 5-19, 5-20, 6-7

AUDITS OF 401(K) PLANS

BY DELOITTE & TOUCHE, LLP

Solutions

The AICPA publishes *CPA Letter Daily*, a free e-newsletter published each weekday. The newsletter, which covers the 10-12 most important stories in business, finance, and accounting, as well as AICPA information, was created to deliver news to CPAs and others who work with the accounting profession. Besides summarizing media articles, commentaries, and research results, the e-newsletter links to television broadcasts and videos and features reader polls. *CPA Letter Daily*'s editors scan hundreds of publications and websites, selecting the most relevant and important news so you don't have to. The newsletter arrives in your inbox early in the morning. To sign up, visit smartbrief.com/CPA.

Do you need high-quality technical assistance? The AICPA Auditing and Accounting Technical Hotline provides non-authoritative guidance on accounting, auditing, attestation, and compilation and review standards. The hotline can be reached at 877.242.7212.

Solutions

Chapter 1

Knowledge check solutions

1.

    a. Incorrect. The named fiduciary is responsible for the general operation and administration of the plan in addition to identifying the plan administrator.

    b. Incorrect. The fiduciary has responsibility to make sure that the plan is operating in accordance with the terms of the plan document, trust instrument, if any, and all applicable government rules and regulations.

    c. Incorrect. The ultimate responsibility for the oversight of the plan including day-to-day administration rests with the fiduciary even if the fiduciary engages various entities to assist it.

    d. Correct. The trustee or custodian is responsible for certifying plan investments, and not the fiduciary.

2.

    a. Incorrect. A plan with 121 or more participants at the beginning of the plan year does require an audit.

    b. Correct. A plan (1) with fewer than 100 participants at the beginning of the plan year, and (2) that files as a small plan does not require an audit.

    c. Incorrect. A plan (1) with fewer than 100 participants at the beginning of the plan year, and (2) that files as a large plan does require an audit.

    d. Incorrect. A plan with 121 or more participants at the beginning of the plan year does require an audit.

3.

- a. Incorrect. The 77 vested employees are counted as participants in the plan; however, others must be included as well.
- b. Incorrect. The 77 vested employees and the 12 nonvested employees earning service are counted as participants in the plan; however, others must be counted as well.
- c. Incorrect. The 77 vested employees and the 12 nonvested employees earning service are counted as participants in the plan, but the 14 nonvested employees are not counted because they are not eligible as they do not meet the age and service requirements established by the plan.
- d. Correct. The 77 vested employees, the 12 nonvested employees earning service and the 22 nonvested employees who are eligible for the plan are all counted as participants. The 22 nonvested employees are still counted, even though they chose not to participate in the plan. Because they are eligible, they must be counted as participants in the plan.
- e. Incorrect. The vested 77 employees, the 12 nonvested employees earning service and the 22 nonvested employees who are eligible for the plan are all counted as participants; however, the 14 nonvested employees are not included in participant counts as they are not eligible for the plan due to age and service requirements.

4.

- a. Incorrect. Five years is not the required time period to maintain working papers that support an audit of an employee benefit plan. The DOL requires a longer period of time.
- b. Correct. Six years is the period required by the DOL to maintain working papers that support an audit of an employee benefit plan.
- c. Incorrect. The Sarbanes-Oxley Act of 2002 has a seven-year requirement for plans that file with the SEC on Form 11-K.
- d. Incorrect. Working papers are not required to be maintained indefinitely to support an audit of an employee benefit plan. The DOL provides regulations related to how long working papers that support audits of employee benefit plans must be maintained for.

5.

- a. Correct. The entity is qualified and the certification contains the proper wording.
- b. Incorrect. This certification only indicates the information was accurate and does not contain the information on completeness.
- c. Incorrect. A recordkeeper maintains the day-to-day records of operation of the plan and is not an entity that is qualified to certify for ERISA limited-scope purposes.
- d. Incorrect. A brokerage company is not an entity that is qualified to certify for ERISA limited-scope purposes.

6.

a. Correct. The auditor may limit only the testing of the investments certified by the bank, which is regulated, supervised, and subject to periodic examination by a state or federal agency.

b. Incorrect. The investments held by the broker-dealer must be tested under full scope procedures.

c. Incorrect. The auditor may limit only the testing of the investments certified by entities that are regulated, supervised, and subject to periodic examination by a state or federal agency.

d. Incorrect. The auditor should perform full-scope testing on the 5 percent of investments held by the broker-dealer.

7.

a. Incorrect. An unqualified report may be issued only when full-scope audit procedures are performed.

b. Correct. An ERISA limited-scope audit report, which will be a disclaimer, must be issued when an ERISA limited-scope audit is performed and no errors or irregularities are noted.

c. Incorrect. A disclaimer opinion will be issued; however, the disclaimer is due to limited testing, not omitted information.

d. Incorrect. An adverse opinion is not required when limited-scope procedures are performed.

8.

a. Incorrect. Participant account activity, including investment allocation, should be tested for all individual account plans.

b. Incorrect. Employee and employer contributions should be tested for all plans.

c. Incorrect. Material expense activity and related accruals should be audited for all plans.

d. Correct. Only investments and investment activity are not tested for an ERISA limited-scope audit because the regulated entity certifies that the investment information is accurate and complete.

Chapter 2

Knowledge check solutions

1.
   a. Incorrect. The timing of the audit is required to be communicated to those charged with governance.
   b. Incorrect. An overview of planned audit scope is required to be communicated to those charged with governance.
   c. Correct. The auditor does not have a responsibility to communicate a detailed listing of planned audit procedures to be performed during the audit.
   d. Incorrect. The auditor's assessment of risk and identification of significant risks are required to be communicated to those charged with governance.

2.
   a. Incorrect. Marketable securities are valued at readily available market prices and therefore would not increase the level of risk associated with an employee benefit plan audit.
   b. Correct. The merger of a plan into the plan during the year may not be fairly presented in the financial statements and not appropriately disclosed.
   c. Incorrect. The existence of an audit committee with financial oversight responsibilities for the plan will actually decrease the level of audit risk associated with an employee benefit plan audit.
   d. Incorrect. Use of a third-party bank as a trustee or custodian for safekeeping of the investments does not increase audit risk.

3.
   a. Incorrect. An auditor does use professional judgment to determine the actual level of testing to be performed on the basis of the risk of error associated with a particular account. Higher risk may result in more testing, the nature and extent of which requires the use of professional judgment.
   b. Incorrect. An auditor does use professional judgment to determine the actual level of testing to be performed on the basis of the decision to rely or not rely on controls. Reliance on controls may result in less substantive testing. The nature and extent of controls and substantive testing requires the use of professional judgment.
   c. Incorrect. An auditor does use professional judgment to determine the actual level of testing to be performed on the basis of the expected effectiveness of the audit tests to be performed.
   d. Correct. An auditor does not use input from the audit committee of the plan to determine the actual level of testing to be performed. The audit committee has responsibility for oversight of the financial reporting process.

4.

    a. Correct. Preliminary analytical review procedures should be performed at the beginning of the audit, not near the completion of the audit.

    b. Incorrect. Preliminary analytical review procedures should generally be performed on account balances aggregated at the financial statement level.

    c. Incorrect. Preliminary analytical review procedures are generally performed to identify fluctuations that have occurred that may indicate a specific risk associated with that account.

    d. Incorrect. Preliminary analytical review procedures serve to highlight transactions that have occurred since the prior-year audit.

5.

    a. Incorrect. When the plan sponsor's industry is experiencing significant downturns, the auditor should be concerned for fraudulent financial reporting. Significant downturns can place pressure on management to report fraudulently in an attempt to present more optimal results.

    b. Incorrect. When a significant portion of the plan investments are invested in stock of the employer, the auditor should be concerned for fraudulent financial reporting. Significant investment in stock of the employer may indicate an attempt to present financial stability.

    c. Incorrect. When significant or unusual parties-in-interest transactions not in the ordinary course of plan operations are occurring, the auditor should be concerned for fraudulent financial reporting. Significant or unusual parties-in-interest transactions may indicate that such parties are colluding to commit fraud.

    d. Correct. An outside bank or insurance company serving as trustee or custodian of the plan (or both) actually lessens the risk for fraudulent financial reporting as there is greater segregation of duties.

6.

    a. Incorrect. An employee of the plan sponsor is considered to be a party in interest of the plan.

    b. Incorrect. An independent auditor is a service provider for the plan and is therefore considered to be a party in interest of the plan.

    c. Incorrect. A union whose members are covered by the plan is considered to be a party in interest of the plan.

    d. Correct. The father of an employee of a bank, where the bank is the trustee of the plan assets, is not considered to be a party in interest of the plan.

Chapter 3

Knowledge check solutions

1.
   a. Incorrect. *Control environment* sets the tone of an organization influencing the control consciousness of its people—it is the foundation for all other components of internal control, providing discipline and structure.
   b. Incorrect. *Risk assessment* is the entity's identification and analysis of relevant risks to the achievement of its objectives and forms a basis for determining how such risks should be managed.
   c. Incorrect. *Information and communication systems* are the identification, capture, and exchange of information in a form and time frame that enable people to carry out their responsibilities.
   d. Incorrect. *Control activities* are the policies and procedures that help make sure that management directives are carried out.
   e. Correct. *Scope of the audit* does not represent a component of internal control. The five components of internal control include control environment; the entity's risk assessment process; the information system, including the related business processes relevant to financial reporting and communication; control activities relevant to the audit; and monitoring of controls.

2.
   a. Correct. The auditor is not required to document internal controls as they relate to investments when the plan administrator has engaged the auditor to perform an ERISA limited-scope audit because investment and investment income balances are certified by a qualifying institution.
   b. Incorrect. If the plan administrator has engaged the auditor to perform an ERISA limited-scope audit with respect to investments, the auditor is still required to document internal controls as they relate to plan contributions covering remittance and allocation to the appropriate investments for the participants' individual accounts.
   c. Incorrect. If the plan administrator has engaged the auditor to perform an ERISA limited-scope audit with respect to investments, the auditor is still required to document internal controls as they relate to financial reporting, effectiveness and efficiency of operations, and compliance of applicable laws and regulations for the plan.
   d. Incorrect. If the plan administrator has engaged the auditor to perform an ERISA limited-scope audit with respect to investments, the auditor is still required to document internal controls as they relate to areas such as plan benefit payments, transfers, loans, rollover, and forfeitures.

3.

    a. Incorrect. Tests of controls that you may perform include inquiries of plan management and personnel involved with plan administration.

    b. Incorrect. Tests of controls that you may perform include examination of supporting records and documents; for example, examination of reconciliation from trustee statements to records from recordkeeper, and review of SOC reports.

    c. Incorrect. Tests of controls that you may perform include the observation of the processing of transactions; however, this is not commonly applied. Also consider the extent of services provided by third parties.

    d. Correct. Confirmation of investments held is with the trustee (not the recordkeeper) and is part of substantive testing, not really a test of controls. Consider the applicability of controls at the recordkeeper to the audit of the plan.

4.

    a. Incorrect. A SOC 1® report specifically excludes user controls at the plan sponsor.

    b. Incorrect. A type 1 SOC 1® report does not test the operating effectiveness of controls and therefore does not provide a basis for the auditor to reduce testing. Even if operating effectiveness was tested, some level of substantive testing would be required as control reliance does not eliminate testing.

    c. Incorrect. A type 1 SOC 1® report does not test the operating effectiveness of controls and therefore does not provide an opinion on such. A type 2 SOC 1® report covers tests of operating effectiveness of controls.

    d. Correct. A SOC 1® report provides a description of controls in place at the service provider so that the auditor may have an understanding of controls at the service provider but may not rely on those controls for the purpose of reducing testing.

5.

    a. Incorrect. Whether the SOC 1® report covers the entity the plan is using is an appropriate consideration. In some cases, the larger service organizations commonly engage their auditors to issue multiple service auditor reports to cover different parts of their operations.

    b. Incorrect. Whether the SOC 1® report is a type 1 or type 2 report is an appropriate consideration. Type 2 may result in reduced planned substantive procedures

    c. Incorrect. Whether there are any exceptions to any controls is an appropriate consideration for reassessing risks and planning substantive testing.

    d. Correct. The service provider's report can be obtained directly from the plan sponsor and does not have to be obtained directly from the service provider.

6.

a. Incorrect. While it is best practice to discuss deficiencies with management when they are identified, it is not a requirement that written communications of significant deficiencies and material weaknesses be made within 60 days of identifying the deficiency.

b. Incorrect. While the auditor may communicate significant deficiencies and material weaknesses and when deficiencies are assessed as such, it is not a requirement that written communications of significant deficiencies and material weaknesses be made within 60 days of assessment of the deficiencies.

c. Incorrect. The auditor may not even begin the audit until much later than 60 days after the plan year-end.

d. Correct. The written communication, while best made by the report date, should be issued no later than 60 days following the report release date.

Chapter 4

Knowledge check solutions

1.

a. Incorrect. A master trust does not have to include all the employee benefit plans offered by one employer.

b. Correct. A master trust may combine some or all of the employee benefit plans offered by one employer. It is used when the assets of more than one related plan are pooled together for investment purposes.

c. Incorrect. A master trust does not combine all of the employee benefit plans offered by two or more unrelated employers. A master trust may involve two or more employers, but it must be a group of corporations under common control.

d. Incorrect. A master trust does not combine some or all of the employee benefit plans offered by two or more unrelated employers. A master trust may involve two or more employers, but it must be a group of corporations under common control.

2.

a. Incorrect. A pooled separate account can be one in which only one plan participates.

b. Incorrect. A pooled separate account can be one in which two or more unrelated plans participate.

c. Correct. A pooled separate account's assets are not combined with the general assets of the sponsoring insurance company. The assets must be separately identified from those of the sponsoring insurance company.

d. Incorrect. A pooled separate account should be recorded on the plan's financial statements as an investment because it is an unallocated contract.

3.

   a. Incorrect. A description of events and circumstances that would allow issuers to terminate the contract at an amount different from contract value is a required disclosure of FASB ASC 962-325.

   b. Correct. Expenses charged to the contract are not a disclosure requirement of FASB ASC 962-325.

   c. Incorrect. The total contract value for each type of investment contract is a required disclosure of FASB ASC 962-325.

   d. Incorrect. A description of events that limits the ability of the plan to transact at contract value is a required disclosure of FASB ASC 962-325.

4.

   a. Incorrect. Participants may have a self-directed account in which they may direct purchases of individual stock and bonds, investments in real estate, limited partnerships, or other investment vehicles. Limited partnerships are not readily marketable securities.

   b. Incorrect. Some 401(k) plans may invest in securities that do not have a ready market price (specialized or unique investment such as junk bonds, options, limited partnerships, real estate mortgage investment conduits, private equity funds, hedge fund, and derivative products). Hedge funds are not readily marketable securities.

   c. Incorrect. Reverse repurchase agreements are not readily marketable securities.

   d. Correct. A pooled separate account, maintained by an insurance company, is a pooled account established by an insurance company for the purpose of investing assets of one or more employee benefit plans of one or more sponsors. In a pooled separate account, like a common collective trust or mutual fund, units of participation or shares are used to distinguish one plan's share of assets from the other. Pooled separate accounts are readily marketable securities.

5.

   a. Incorrect. Although a qualifying certifying institution may certify participant loans, you are still required to test participant loans as part of participant account testing.

   b. Incorrect. You are still required to perform audit procedures to test accounts—such as contributions, benefits, and other expenses.

   c. Incorrect. The plan administrator may make an election to limit the scope of the audit as it relates to investments and related investment income if plan assets are held by a qualifying bank, trust company, or insurance company that is state or federally chartered and subject to regulation and periodic examination by a state or federal agency. You are still required to perform an audit of the plan under an ERISA limited scope audit.

   d. Correct. An ERISA limited-scope audit permits you to rely on a qualified trustee's certification for investments and related income. However, you are still responsible for ensuring the financial statements match what is certified, and to the extent that investments are not certified by a qualified trustee, you are required to test those investment balances and related investment income that are not certified by a qualified trustee.

6.

a. Incorrect. Participant loans are not investments of the 401(k) plan for financial statement purposes but are considered investments in Form 5500.

b. Correct. Many 401(k) plans offer participants the ability to borrow against the vested portion of their individual accounts. Participant loans are receivables of the 401(k) plan.

c. Incorrect. Participant loans do earn interest for the plan in accordance with the plan document. The interest rate must also be reasonable when compared to the prevailing market for interest rates.

d. Incorrect. When the loan is made, the amount is deducted from the participant's account and then repaid to the participant's account, generally through payroll deductions based on the repayment schedule for the loan.

7.

a. Incorrect. A plan may have liabilities for amounts owed for securities purchased by the plan but not yet remitted or expenses for administrative fees that may still be payable at plan year-end. Accrued expenses should be recorded as a liability.

b. Correct. GAAP for benefit plans require that benefits payable not be recorded as a liability. As all assets are available for the payment of benefits, it is not appropriate to segregate out only a portion as a liability. Benefits payable are disclosed in the notes to the financial statements.

c. Incorrect. A liability for investment settlement payable should be recorded.

d. Incorrect. Material refunds to participants (for example, excess contributions that need to be refunded to plan participants because of plan's failure under the required antidiscrimination tests) should be recorded as a liability on the statement of net assets available for benefits.

Chapter 5

Knowledge check solutions

1.

a. Incorrect. The auditor should separate the investments into similar groupings (for example, fixed income, equity, bonds, mutual funds, temporary, and so on) before determining the rate of return.

b. Incorrect. The auditor should compare the average rate of return to an independent source (for example, WSJ).

c. Incorrect. The auditor should consider using the average balance of investments held during the plan year.

d. Correct. Testing the investment expenses for a sample selection to determine that the amounts are properly assessed is a test of detail and not a substantive analytical procedure.

2.

    a. Incorrect. The auditor should recalculate the employer contribution as part of the audit procedures to test employer contributions whether or not board approval is required.

    b. Correct. The auditor should verify that the calculation used to make the employer match is in accordance with the plan document.

    c. Incorrect. There is no requirement that the employer contribution may not exceed the employee's contribution, though this would be a rare occurrence.

    d. Incorrect. The employer contribution should be allocated to investments in accordance with the plan document. For 401(k) plans, employer contributions are generally allocated based on employee contribution investment allocations.

3.

    a. Incorrect. The plan document sets forth minimum and maximum contribution limits.

    b. Incorrect. Employee contributions are not subject to forfeiture because they are vested immediately. Only employer contributions may be forfeited if an employee has not met the maximum vesting requirement.

    c. Correct. This answer is the one that is incorrect. Employee contributions may be invested in plan sponsor stock if that is an investment option of the plan.

    d. Incorrect. Employee contributions should be deposited to the trustee as soon as practicable.

4.

    a. Incorrect. The auditor should determine that the benefit payment is made in accordance with plan provisions.

    b. Incorrect. The auditor should determine if a forfeiture results from any portion of the employer contribution.

    c. Correct. Employee contributions are never subject to forfeiture as this is the employee's money that was deducted from his or her pay.

    d. Incorrect. The auditor should verify that the participant has terminated employment and is eligible to receive a benefit payment.

5.

    a. Incorrect. The auditor should consider whether procedures exist to investigate long outstanding benefit checks.

    b. Incorrect. The auditor should confirm benefit payments directly with the participant.

    c. Incorrect. The auditor should verify that a lump sum or installment distribution was made to the terminated or retired participant.

    d. Correct. A participant is not required to have reached at least age 65 to qualify for benefit payments. Many plans allow for benefit payments in other forms and such is described in the plan document.

Chapter 6

Knowledge check solutions

1.

   a. Incorrect. The plan should comply on an annual basis with certain operating tests such as tests of coverage, anti-discrimination, and maximum benefit limitations to retain a qualified status.

   b. Incorrect. The existence of a letter does not necessarily guarantee that the plan continues to be qualified.

   c. Correct. The plan should operate in accordance with the plan document and comply on an annual basis with certain operating tests such as tests of anti-discrimination. The plan may not continue to qualify even if a favorable determination letter from the IRS exists.

   d. Incorrect. While the auditors include a representation in the representation letter related to the plan's tax status, this is not something that enables the plan to maintain its qualified status.

2.

   a. Incorrect. An auditor would consider whether the plan has taxes recorded for unrelated business taxable income (UBTI). A tax-exempt entity may incur taxes if they have UBTI, such as investment income from certain investments in partnerships; real estate investment trusts; or options to buy or sell securities, such as short sales or repurchase agreements.

   b. Incorrect. If the plan has lost its tax-exempt status, then considering whether the plan has appropriately recorded any income tax liability and expense for any realized investment income earned by the plan and has disclosed that matter in accordance with generally accepted accounting principles is appropriate.

   c. Incorrect. Considering whether a receivable from the plan sponsor should be recorded on the plan's financial statements if the plan has any income tax exposure is appropriate.

   d. Correct. Obtaining a determination letter indicates that the plan document, if applied correctly, results in a qualified plan; however, the auditor should consider whether the plan operated in accordance with the plan document in order for it to maintain its qualified tax status.

3.

    a. Incorrect. Also important are existence of a determination letter for the plan, and whether or not the plan administrator has consulted an ERISA specialist regarding a payment made from the plan to the plan sponsor.

    b. Incorrect. Also important are whether or not the plan administrator has consulted an ERISA specialist regarding a payment made from the plan to the plan sponsor, and consideration of whether refunds for the plan year were required as a result of the discrimination testing.

    c. Incorrect. Also important are consideration of whether refunds for the plan year were required as a result of the discrimination testing, and existence of a determination letter for the plan.

    d. Correct. When considering the plan's tax status, consideration of whether refunds for the plan year were required as a result of the discrimination testing, existence of a determination letter for the plan, and whether or not the plan administrator has consulted an ERISA specialist regarding a payment made from the plan to the plan sponsor are all important. The employer making a discretionary contribution to the plan, if in accordance with the plan document, does not affect the tax status of the plan.

4.

    a. Incorrect. A plan may not pass the required anti-discrimination tests for a given plan year. Normally, a plan fails these tests as a result of excess contributions to the plan by highly compensated employees who participate in the plan. The plan administrator can take corrective action by refunding the required amount of money to those employees, so that the plan will then pass the anti-discrimination test. Note the plan is not automatically disqualified.

    b. Correct. Failure to pass anti-discrimination tests does not automatically disqualify the plan and result in the plan no longer being tax exempt. The plan may take corrective action by refunding the required amount of money to the highly compensated employees, so that the plan will then pass the anti-discrimination tests. Another alternative is to make a contribution to non-highly compensated employees to enable the plan to pass the anti-discrimination tests.

    c. Incorrect. A plan may not pass the required anti-discrimination tests for a given plan year. Normally, a plan fails these tests as a result of excess contributions to the plan by highly compensated employees who participate in the plan. The plan administrator can take corrective action by refunding the required amount of money to those employees, so that the plan will then pass the anti-discrimination test. Note that regulations require the plan administrators that corrective action as soon as reasonably possible to avoid additional fines and penalties.

    d. Incorrect. A plan may not pass the required anti-discrimination tests for a given plan year. Normally, a plan fails these tests as a result of excess contributions to the plan by highly compensated employees who participate in the plan. The plan administrator can take corrective action by refunding the required amount of money to those employees, so that the plan will then pass the anti-discrimination test.

5.

    a. Correct. Even when plan management informs the auditor that legal counsel was not consulted during the plan year, the auditor should obtain a representation from plan management regarding the absence of legal matters affecting the plan.

    b. Incorrect. Even when plan management informs the auditor that legal counsel was not consulted during the plan year, the auditor should obtain a representation from plan management regarding the absence of legal matters affecting the plan.

    c. Incorrect. There is no requirement to disclose in the plan's notes to the financial statements.

    d. Incorrect. There is no requirement to inform the DOL.

6.

    a. Correct. If a significant period of time has lapsed between the last day of fieldwork and the report issuance date or the date the report was available to be issued, subsequent events procedures should be performed through the issuance date of the report on the plan's financial statements, even though these procedures were already performed through the last day of fieldwork.

    b. Incorrect. Even though subsequent procedures were already performed through the last day of fieldwork, if a significant period of time has lapsed between the last day of fieldwork and the report issuance date, subsequent events procedures should be performed through the issuance date of the report or the date the report was available to be issued on the plan's financial statements.

    c. Incorrect. Subsequent events procedures should be performed through the issuance date of the report on the plan's financial statements or the date the report was available to be issued, if a significant period of time has lapsed between the last day of fieldwork and the report issuance date, not through the last day of fieldwork.

    d. Incorrect. Subsequent events procedures should be performed through the issuance date of the report on the plan's financial statements or the date the report was available to be issued, even though such procedures were already performed through the last day of fieldwork if a significant period of time has lapsed between the last day of fieldwork and the report issuance date.

7.

    a. Incorrect. You should obtain written representations from plan officials, which should include the plan administrator, who is responsible for the plan's investment and management functions. In addition to the plan administrator's signature, you may also consider obtaining the signatures of the following officials based on specific circumstances: chief financial officer, the chief human resources officer, or a member of the board of trustees.

    b. Correct. The representation letter should cover all financial statements and periods included in your report.

    c. Incorrect. The representation letter should be typed on the plan sponsor's letterhead and dated as of the independent auditor's report date.

    d. Incorrect. The representation letter should be tailored to meet specific circumstances of the engagement.

8.

    a. Incorrect. The auditor does not have responsibility, unless otherwise engaged, to verify that all areas of the Form 5500 are complete and to make sure the Form 5500 is completed accurately and filed timely.

    b. Correct. Before issuing the audit report, the auditor should determine whether the amounts presented in the financial statements agree to those reported on the Form 5500. If there are any differences in the amounts included in the audited financial statements from those reported on the Form 5500 (other than differences in grouping the investments and classification of participant loans), then those differences must be disclosed in the footnotes to the financial statements.

    c. Incorrect. The auditor does not have responsibility, unless otherwise engaged, to prepare the Form 5500 on behalf of the plan.

    d. Incorrect. The auditor does have certain responsibilities in relation to the plan's Form 5500.

9.

   a. Incorrect. If a decision is made to terminate a plan after the end of the plan year, only note disclosure of the planned termination is required. However, if the decision is made to terminate a plan before the end of the plan year, the plan's financial statements must also be presented on the liquidation basis of accounting.

   b. Correct. If a decision is made to terminate a plan before the end of the plan year, this is a Type I subsequent event. Note disclosure of the planned termination is required and the plan's financial statements should be presented on the liquidation basis of accounting.

   c. Incorrect. If the decision is made to terminate a plan before the end of the plan year, and a note disclosure in the financial statements is required along with presenting the plan's financial statements on a liquidation basis of accounting.

   d. Incorrect. If the decision is made to terminate a plan before the end of the plan year, the plan's financial statements must be presented on the liquidation basis of accounting and a note disclosure in the financial statements is required.

10.

   a. Incorrect. When a plan is going to merge with another employee benefit plan, the plan's final Form 5500 is due to be filed 7 months after the effective date of the plan merger if the effective date of the merger is the same date that the asset transfer occurred. An extension of 2 ½ months is available beyond the 7-month period.

   b. Incorrect. The final Form 5500 is due 7 months following the date of the final asset transfer with an extension available by request of the plan administrator.

   c. Correct. The final Form 5500 is due 7 months following the date of the final asset transfer (as of the end of the month of that transfer) with a 2 ½-month extension available.

   d. Incorrect. When a plan merges with another employee benefit plan, the plan's final Form 5500 is due 7 months following date of the final asset transfer.

11.

   a. Correct. An employer contribution to the plan made in accordance with the plan document does not constitute a prohibited transaction.

   b. Incorrect. A sale, exchange, or lease of property between the plan and a party in interest does constitute a prohibited transaction.

   c. Incorrect. A loan or other extension of credit (this includes untimely deposits to the trust of employee salary deferral deposits) between the plan and a party in interest does constitute a prohibited transaction.

   d. Incorrect. The furnishing of goods, services, or facilities between the plan and a party-in-interest does constitute a prohibited transaction.

   e. Incorrect. A transfer of plan assets to a party in interest for the use or benefit of a party in interest does constitute a prohibited transaction.

12.

    a. Incorrect. Section 404 does not apply to 11-Ks.

    b. Incorrect. Section 302 does not apply to 11-Ks.

    c. Correct. Partner rotation is required for all public entities including those which file 11-Ks.

    d. Incorrect. Reporting a material weakness to plan management and the audit committee is required, but reporting this on the 11-K to the SEC is not required.

Chapter 7

Knowledge check solutions

1.

    a. Incorrect. The financial statements and auditor's report are affected by the decision to terminate the plan when liquidation is deemed to be imminent.

    b. Incorrect. An emphasis-of-matter paragraph in the unqualified auditor's report is required.

    c. Correct. The notes to the financial statements should disclose that the plan is terminating and liquidation is imminent.

    d. Incorrect. The financial statements should be prepared using the liquidation basis of accounting.

2.

    a. Correct. A qualified opinion or adverse opinion may be issued when a material nonexempt party in interest transaction has not been disclosed in the appropriate supplemental schedule and is also considered to be a related party transaction which is not properly disclosed in the notes to the financial statements.

    b. Incorrect. A disclaimer of opinion is not issued in this situation. In this situation and for situations that do result in a disclaimer of opinion, the Form 5500 filing will generally be rejected by the DOL.

    c. Incorrect. An unqualified opinion with an other-matter paragraph will not be issued in this situation. An example of a situation in which an other-matter paragraph in accordance with AU-C section 706, is issued, is when the plan presents the supplemental schedules with the financial statements.

    d. Incorrect. An unqualified opinion with an emphasis-of-matter paragraph will not be issued in this situation. An example of a situation in which an unqualified opinion with an emphasis-of-matter paragraph may be issued includes when a 401(k) plan has been terminated or a decision has been made to terminate the plan and liquidation is deemed to be imminent.

3.

    a. Incorrect. The auditor's report on special purpose financial statements should include an emphasis-of-matter paragraph, under an appropriate heading, that indicates that the financial statements are prepared in accordance with the applicable special purpose framework.

    b. Correct. In accordance with AU-C section 800, the auditor's report on special-purpose financial statements should include an emphasis-of-matter paragraph, under an appropriate heading, that (a) indicates that the financial statements are prepared in accordance with the applicable special purpose framework, (b) refers to the note in the financial statements that describes that framework, and (c) states that the special purpose framework is a basis of accounting other than GAAP.

    c. Incorrect. The scope is not limited if the modified cash basis is used. The auditor issues an unqualified report with an emphasis-of-matter paragraph in accordance with AU-C section 800.

    d. Incorrect. While the modified cash basis of accounting is allowed, an emphasis of matter paragraph is still required in accordance with AU-C section 800.

4.

    a. Correct. Only one year statement of changes in net assets available for benefits is required to be presented in the plan's Form 11-K filing if the plan has elected to file the Form 11-K under the election of following ERISA.

    b. Incorrect. Two years of statements of net assets available for benefits are required to be presented in the plan's Form 11-K filing if the plan has elected to file the Form 11-K under the election of following ERISA.

    c. Incorrect. Three years of statements net assets available for benefits or changes in net assets available for benefits are not required to be presented in the plan's Form 11-K filing if the plan has elected to file the Form 11-K under the election of following ERISA.

    d. Incorrect. The instructions to the Form 11-K indicate presentation requirements for plans subject to the provisions of ERISA.

5.

    a. Incorrect. One or more audit opinion(s) is (are) required for plans that file a Form 11-K.

    b. Incorrect. The PCAOB does not allow references to other standards in the opinion for public entities and the DOL requires references to generally accepted auditing standards.

    c. Correct. The PCAOB requires that audit opinions for public entities refer only to the PCAOB standards and the DOL requires that the opinion refer to generally accepted auditing standards. Therefore, the auditor should issue two opinions.

    d. Incorrect. Less than three opinions is required for plans that file a Form 11-K.

6.

    a. Incorrect. Regardless of materiality, disclosure of prohibited transactions is required for a 401(k) plan, assuming they exist for the plan.

    b. Incorrect. Tax status of the plan including disclosure of information concerning whether a tax ruling or determination letter has been obtained is required for a 401(k) plan.

    c. Correct. Plan mergers and terminations that have occurred during the year are required for a 401(k) plan. Pending merger related to the plan sponsor is not required to be disclosed in the plan's financial statements.

    d. Incorrect. Plan sponsor uncertainty for a sponsor with a going concern uncertainty is required for 401(k) plans, assuming it is applicable.

7.

    a. Incorrect. Disclosure of information in the financial statements about the net assets and significant components of changes in net assets relating to the nonparticipant-directed investment program is a required disclosure regardless of audit scope.

    b. Incorrect. Disclosure of information in the financial statements about the net assets and significant components of changes in net assets relating to the nonparticipant-directed investment program is a required disclosure regardless of audit scope.

    c. Correct. Disclosure of information in the financial statements about the net assets and significant components of changes in net assets relating to the nonparticipant-directed investment program can be shown on the face of the financial statements. Note that if such disclosures are included in the face of the financial statement, no additional disclosures are required.

    d. Incorrect. Disclosure of information in the financial statements about the net assets and significant components of changes in net assets relating to the nonparticipant-directed investment program can be shown on the face of the financial statements. Note that if such disclosures are included in the face of the financial statement, no additional disclosures are required.

8.

    a. Incorrect. Litigation is a risk or uncertainty that must be disclosed.

    b. Incorrect. Going concern issue at the plan sponsor is a risk or uncertainty that must be disclosed.

    c. Incorrect. Filing of bankruptcy by the plan sponsor is a risk or uncertainty that must be disclosed.

    d. Correct. Answers a, b, and c are all required to be disclosed, as they provide information about the plan sponsor's going concern which could result in termination of the plan in future. Plan sponsor's plans to purchase another company that has a 401(k) plan is not required to be disclosed as the plans may be confidential and not affect the future of the plan.

The AICPA publishes *CPA Letter Daily*, a free e-newsletter published each weekday. The newsletter, which covers the 10-12 most important stories in business, finance, and accounting, as well as AICPA information, was created to deliver news to CPAs and others who work with the accounting profession. Besides summarizing media articles, commentaries, and research results, the e-newsletter links to television broadcasts and videos and features reader polls. *CPA Letter Daily*'s editors scan hundreds of publications and websites, selecting the most relevant and important news so you don't have to. The newsletter arrives in your inbox early in the morning. To sign up, visit smartbrief.com/CPA.

Do you need high-quality technical assistance? The AICPA Auditing and Accounting Technical Hotline provides non-authoritative guidance on accounting, auditing, attestation, and compilation and review standards. The hotline can be reached at 877.242.7212.

Learn More

Continuing Professional Education

Thank you for selecting the Association of International Certified Professional Accountants as your continuing professional education provider. We have a diverse offering of CPE courses to help you expand your skillset and develop your competencies. Choose from hundreds of different titles spanning the major subject matter areas relevant to CPAs and CGMAs, including:

- Governmental and not-for-profit accounting, auditing, and updates
- Internal control and fraud
- Audits of employee benefit plans and 401(k) plans
- Individual and corporate tax updates
- A vast array of courses in other areas of accounting and auditing, controllership, management, consulting, taxation, and more!

Get your CPE when and where you want

- Self-study training options that includes on-demand, webcasts, and text formats with superior quality and a broad portfolio of topics, including bundled products like –
  - ➤ CPExpress Online Learning™ for immediate access to hundreds of one and two-credit hour online courses for just-in-time learning at a price that is right
  - ➤ Annual Webcast Pass offering live Q&A with experts and unlimited access to the scheduled lineup, all at an incredible discount.
- Staff training programs for audit, tax and preparation, compilation, and review
- Certificate programs offering comprehensive curriculums developed by practicing experts to build fundamental core competencies in specialized topics
- National conferences presented by recognized experts
- Affordable courses on-site at your organization – visit **aicpalearning.org/on-site** for more information.
- Seminars sponsored by your state society and led by top instructors. For a complete list, visit **aicpalearning.org/publicseminar**.

Take control of your career development

The Association's Competency and Learning website at **https://competency.aicpa.org** brings together a variety of learning resources and a self-assessment tool, enabling tracking and reporting of progress toward learning goals.

Visit www.AICPAStore.com to browse our CPE selections.

Governmental audits have never been more challenging.

Are you with a CPA firm or state auditor office? If so, join the Governmental Audit Quality Center and get the support, information and tools you need. Save time. Maximize audit quality. Enhance your practice.

The GAQC is committed to helping firms and state audit organizations (SAOs) achieve the highest quality standards as they perform financial statement audits of government, single audits, HUD audits, or other types of compliance audits. If you are not yet a member, consider joining the GAQC to maximize your audit quality and practice success!

Join online today at gaqc.aicpa.org/memberships and start on the path to even greater audit success. Membership starts at just $210 (for firms or SAOs with fewer than 10 CPAs).

Benefits at a glance
The GAQC offers:

- **Email alerts** with audit and regulatory updates

- A dedicated **website (aicpa.org/GAQC)** where you can network with other members

- Access to Resource Centers on Single Audits (both under the Uniform Guidance for Federal Awards and OMB Circular A-133), *Government Auditing Standards*, HUD topics, GASB Matters, and much more

- Audit Practice Tools and Aids (e.g., GASB's new pension standards, internal control documentation tools, schedule of expenditures of federal awards practice aids, Yellow Book independence documentation practice aid, etc.)

- Savings on **professional liability insurance**

- A **website listing** as a firm or SAO committed to quality, which makes your information available to the public and/or potential purchasers of audit services

- Exclusive **webcasts** on timely topics relevant to governmental financial statement audits and compliance audits (optional CPE is available for a small fee, and events are archived online)

Topics the GAQC webcasts cover include:

- Sampling in a Single Audit Environment

- Uniform Guidance: Challenging Compliance Areas

- Developing and Reporting Audit Findings

- Commonly Asked Uniform Guidance and Yellow Book Questions

- Single Audit Fundamentals — A Four Part Series

- HUD Update: For-Profit Entities Subject to HUD Consolidated Audit Guide

- The Continued Complexities of Auditing Governmental Pension Plans and Participating Employers

- Avoiding Common Errors in Not-for-Profit Financial Reporting

To learn more about the Governmental Audit Quality Center, its membership requirements or to apply for membership, visit aicpa.org/GAQC, email us at gaqc@aicpa.org or call us at 202.434.9207.

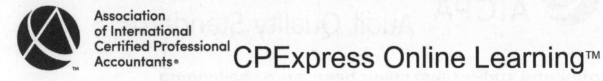